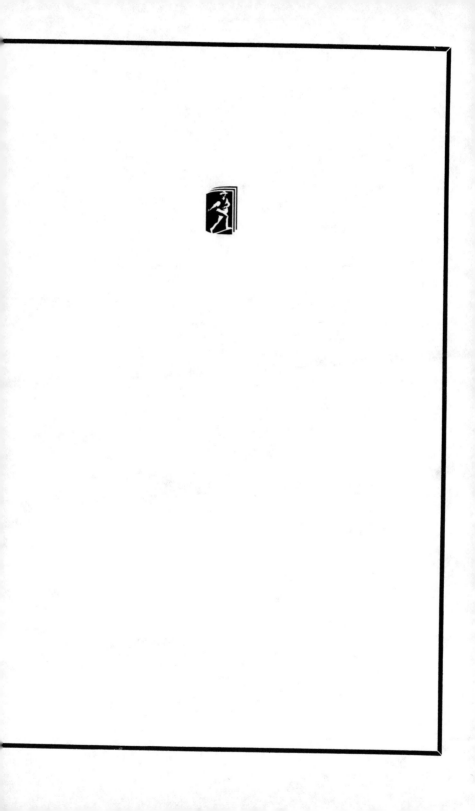

The
GROUCHO
Letters

Letters from and to Groucho Marx

Simon & Schuster Paperbacks
New York   London   Toronto   Sydney

ACKNOWLEDGMENTS

Copyright © 1965 by Fred Allen

Reprinted by permission of William Morris Agency, LLC on behalf of the Author.

We wish also to thank the following of Groucho's friends and correspondents, of their heirs and assigns, for permission to publish their letters to Groucho in this volume: Goodman Ace, Irwin Allen, Brooks Atkinson, Irving Berlin, John Mason Brown, Eddie Cantor, Elaine Dundy, T. S. Eliot, Bergen Evans, Alex Gottlieb, Nunnally Johnson, Walter Kerr, Norman Krasna, Harry Kurnitz, Jerry Lewis, Leonard Lyons, *McCall's* magazine, Marjorie Nedford, Mrs. Arthur Murray, S. J. Perelman, Harry Ruby, M. Lincoln Schuster, Sylvia Sheekman, Frank Sullivan, David Susskind, Booth Tarkington, James Thurber, Joseph T. Welch, and E. B. White.

Simon & Schuster Paperbacks
1230 Avenue of the Americas
New York, NY 10020

First Simon & Schuster trade paperback edition August 2007

SIMON & SCHUSTER and colophon are registered trademarks of Simon & Schuster, Inc.

For information about special discounts for bulk purchases, please contact Simon & Schuster Special Sales at 1-800-456-6798 or business@simonandschuster.com

Manufactured in the United States of America

10 9 8 7 6 5 4 3 2 1

Library of Congress Cataloging-in-Publication Data

ISBN-13:978-1-4165-3603-1
ISBN-10:   1-4165-3603-5

Contents

CONTENTS

(6)

Introduction

When the publishers first suggested that his letters be put into a book, Groucho, a diffident man—well, *fairly* diffident—beat about no bushes. He wired back:

YOUR LETTER RECEIVED AND PROMPTLY BURNED. I PREFER NOT TO HAVE STRANGERS PRYING INTO MY MAIL. WOULD DISCUSS THIS IN DETAIL BUT MY SECRETARY HAS A DATE IN FIVE MINUTES—WITH ME.

Then, after a sporadic correspondence tapered off into silence, the publishers went about their business, and Groucho went about his, which at the time consisted of bicycle trips to the A&P, weekly appearances on television, letterwriting, becoming a legend, and having his feet scratched—a diversion enjoyed by all of the Marx Brothers. What the significance of this is, I cannot tell you. I know only that, as a hobby, Groucho devotes most of his time to reading, and accosting strangers—especially if the strangers happen to be girls. If they *are* girls, they don't usually remain strangers long. (On entering a theater, his conversation with the usher is likely to start with the question: "What is it tonight—sad or high-kicking?" Or, if in a mood to parody the small-time comedians, he might say to a waiter—or waitress—"Have you got frog legs?" And no matter what the reply, Groucho will look painfully disappointed and say, "That's the wrong answer. *You* were supposed to say, 'No; it's rheumatism that makes me walk this way.'")

Although the comedian's reluctance to publishing his letters was genuine, it was by no means fanatical. It was overcome by two things: (1) The suggestion that the book include, also, letters written *to* as well as *by* him. (This was persuasive indeed since his correspondents, whom I'll get to in a moment, are among the English-speaking world's wittiest men. And (2) there was that official communication from Washington.

It asked Groucho to donate his personal papers to the Library of Congress where they would be permanently stored—for the edification, no doubt, of future scholars who might be engaged in a study of the comic viewpoint. Surely, they would want to know something about the mind of a man who, on giving up his membership in a Hollywood club, wrote to its president: "Please accept my resignation. I don't care to belong to any club that will have me as a member."

There, in a few satirical words, is one of the most astute and revealing observations about the self-hating, socially ambitious human animal.

As P.S. 84's most prominent drop-out, Groucho was of course impressed by the Library of Congress's request for his papers. After all, he had spent less time in academic classrooms than in the classroom act called "Fun in Hi Skule." Although not yet out of his teens, Groucho was his brothers' teacher; and while obviously no great shakes at spelling, he did manage to bring a fresh approach to the subject of geography.

When he asked Harpo the shape of the world, Harpo (he had not yet turned exclusively to pantomime), said candidly, that he didn't know. Whereupon Groucho gave him a hint.

"What," he asked, "is the shape of my cuff buttons?"

"Square," from Harpo.

"I mean the cuff buttons I wear on Sunday—not every day. Now! What is the shape of the world?"

"Round on Sunday, square on weekdays," replied Harpo who, shortly after, took his vow of professional silence.

Groucho can honestly say with Falstaff that he is not only

witty himself but "the cause of wit in other men." Most of the letters written *to* him are richly seasoned with the comic spirit. That most of them are from professional writers is not surprising, since most of Groucho's friends are professional writers.

If there is very little correspondence between the brothers it's because they were not apart often, or for any considerable length of time. Besides, Groucho is the one member of the family with a passion for letters.

Chico's writing was pretty much limited to the signing of checks, payable to card players who, he was convinced, were less skillful at games than himself. To prove that this was so, Chico spent most of his happy, carefree life—and money.

As for dear, eternally boyish Harpo, his friends, like Groucho's, were mostly writers. And yet Harpo liked to pretend, for comic effect, that he was completely illiterate. Shortly after our first meeting (I had been brought to Hollywood to help prepare a Marx Brothers' movie script), Harpo asked me to tell him how to make a "J." I can recall another meeting when I found him impishly answering a letter he had received, exactly five years before, from S. N. Behrman, the playwright.

It is sometimes said that Brother Groucho is a comical fellow because he will say boldly, and of course quickly, what the rest of us might think but are too timid to say. This is less than half true. What really distinguishes his comic impudence is not boldness but wit. Of course the darts sometimes miss their mark but—need I tell you?—Babe Ruth struck out more than once.

As an example of Groucho's amusing insolence, I remember a remark he made at a large, formal dinner given for his television sponsor. As a tribute to the boss's twenty-five years with the corporation, his employees had bought him an expensive gift, which Groucho was asked to present. He did.

Rising to his feet, he turned to his sponsor and, indicating the beautifully wrapped parcel, said:

"Charlie, as a token of their devotion, the men working for you have bought you this gift. What it is, I'm not sure, but if I were you, I wouldn't open the package until it's been submerged in a tub of water."

His wit can also be *gently* withering. Do you remember a magazine called Confidential? Until it was put out of business by lawsuits (or was it the Postal Department?), it specialized in slimy scandals about movie people. I suppose that some of their stories were true, or partly true. More often they were neither. But that didn't make them any less feared by the stars who, when a new issue came out, skimmed through their copies with trembling hands to see if any of the current dirt had been tossed in their direction.

When the magazine printed a page, comparatively tepid, about Groucho, accusing him of liking girls (a fact that he has certainly not denied), he was annoyed but said nothing.

However, a month or two later, when Confidential implied that his quiz show was crooked, that was going too far. Turning resolutely to his typewriter, Groucho dashed off the following warning:

> Confidential Magazine
>
> Gentlemen:
>
> If you continue to publish slanderous pieces about me, I shall feel compelled to cancel my subscription.
>
> > Sincerely,
> >
> > Groucho Marx

There is a funny man.

ARTHUR SHEEKMAN

Movie
Business

TO CHICO MARX

Dear Chico,

My Favorite Picture Producer was at our house for dinner the other night and each year he eats progressively louder. The sucking of chicken bones and corn on the cob (a terrible mistake, I now realize) could be heard for miles around. Many people thought it was an air raid and began drawing the blackout curtains and dousing the lights.

We then proceeded, at his insistent behest, to the loges of the Pantages Theater where he snored through two of the longest pictures since the beginning of the talkies.

Tune in again next week for another thrilling chapter of the little fat man with the sucking cavities.

In the meantime, always examine the dice.

Groucho

RUNNING BATTLE WITH WARNER BROTHERS

When the Marx Brothers were about to make a movie called "A Night in Casablanca," there were threats of legal action from the Warner Brothers, who, five years before, had made a picture called, simply, "Casablanca" (with Humphrey Bogart and Ingrid Bergman as stars). Whereupon Groucho, speaking for his brothers and himself, immediately dispatched the following letters:

Dear Warner Brothers:

Apparently there is more than one way of conquering a city and holding it as your own. For example, up to the time that we contemplated making this picture, I had no idea that the city of Casablanca belonged exclusively to Warner Brothers. However, it was only a few days after our announcement appeared that we received your long, ominous legal document warning us not to use the name Casablanca.

It seems that in 1471, Ferdinand Balboa Warner, your great-great-grandfather, while looking for a shortcut to the city of Burbank, had stumbled on the shores of Africa and, raising his alpenstock (which he later turned in for a hundred shares of the common), named it Casablanca.

I just don't understand your attitude. Even if you plan on re-releasing your picture, I am sure that the average movie fan could learn in time to distinguish between Ingrid Bergman and Harpo. I don't know whether I could, but I certainly would like to try.

You claim you own Casablanca and that no one else can use that name without your permission. What about "Warner Brothers"? Do you own that, too? You probably have the right to use the name Warner, but what about Brothers? Professionally, we were brothers long before you were. We were touring the sticks as The Marx Brothers when Vitaphone was still a gleam in the inventor's eye, and even before us there had been other brothers—the Smith Brothers; the Brothers Karamazov; Dan Brothers, an outfielder with Detroit; and "Brother, Can You Spare a Dime?" (This was originally

"Brothers, Can You Spare a Dime?" but this was spreading a dime pretty thin, so they threw out one brother gave all the money to the other one and whittled it down to, "Brother, Can You Spare a Dime?")

Now Jack, how about you? Do you maintain that yours is an original name? Well, it's not. It was used long before you were born. Offhand, I can think of two Jacks—there was Jack of "Jack and the Beanstalk," and Jack the Ripper, who cut quite a figure in his day.

As for you, Harry, you probably sign your checks, sure in the belief that you are the first Harry of all time and that all other Harrys are imposters. I can think of two Harrys that preceded you. There was Lighthouse Harry of Revolutionary fame and a Harry Appelbaum who lived on the corner of 93rd Street and Lexington Avenue. Unfortunately, Appelbaum wasn't too well known. The last I heard of him, he was selling neckties at Weber and Heilbroner.

Now about the Burbank studio. I believe this is what you brothers call your place. Old man Burbank is gone. Perhaps you remember him. He was a great man in a garden. His wife often said Luther had ten green thumbs. What a witty woman she must have been! Burbank was the wizard who crossed all those fruits and vegetables until he had the poor plants in such a confused and jittery condition that they could never decide whether to enter the dining room on the meat platter or the dessert dish.

This is pure conjecture, of course, but who knows—perhaps Burbank's survivors aren't too happy with the fact that a plant that grinds out pictures on a quota settled in their town, appropriated Burbank's name and uses it as a front for their films. It is even possible that the Burbank family is prouder of the potato produced by the old man than they are of the fact that from your studio emerged "Casablanca" or even "Gold Diggers of 1931."

This all seems to add up to a pretty bitter tirade, but I assure you it's not meant to. I love Warners. Some of my best friends are Warner Brothers. It is even possible that I am doing you an injustice and that you, yourselves, know nothing at all about this dog-in-the-Wanger attitude. It wouldn't surprise me at all to discover that the heads of your legal department are unaware of this absurd dispute, for I am acquainted with many of them and they are fine fellows with curly black hair, double-breasted suits and a love of their fellow man that out-Saroyans Saroyan.

I have a hunch that this attempt to prevent us from using the title is the brainchild of some ferret-faced shyster, serving a brief apprenticeship in your legal department. I know the type well—hot out of law school, hungry for success and too ambitious to follow the natural laws of promotion. This bar sinister probably needled your attorneys, most of whom are fine fellows with curly black hair, double-breasted suits, etc., into attempting to enjoin us. Well, he won't get away with it! We'll fight him to the highest court! No pasty-faced legal adventurer is going to cause bad blood between the Warners and the Marxes. We are all brothers under the skin and we'll remain friends till the last reel of "A Night in Casablanca" goes tumbling over the spool.

Sincerely,
Groucho Marx

For some curious reason, this letter seemed to puzzle the Warner Brothers legal department. They wrote—in all seriousness—and asked if the Marxes could give them some idea of what their story was about. They felt that something might be worked out. So Groucho replied:

Dear Warners:

There isn't much I can tell you about the story. In it I play a Doctor of Divinity who ministers to the natives and, as a sideline, hawks can openers and pea jackets to the savages along the Gold Coast of Africa.

When I first meet Chico, he is working in a saloon, selling sponges to barflies who are unable to carry their liquor. Harpo is an Arabian caddie who lives in a small Grecian urn on the outskirts of the city.

As the picture opens, Porridge, a mealy-mouthed native girl, is sharpening some arrows for the hunt. Paul Hangover, our hero, is constantly lighting two cigarettes simultaneously. He apparently is unaware of the cigarette shortage.

There are many scenes of splendor and fierce antagonisms, and Color, an Abyssinian messenger boy, runs Riot. Riot, in case you have never been there, is a small night club on the edge of town.

There's a lot more I could tell you, but I don't want to spoil it for you. All this has been okayed by the Hays Office, Good Housekeeping and the survivors of the Haymarket Riots; and if the times are ripe, this picture can be the opening gun in a new worldwide disaster.

Cordially,
Groucho Marx

Instead of mollifying them, this note seemed to puzzle the attorneys even more; they wrote back and said they still didn't understand the story line and they would appreciate it if Mr. Marx would explain the plot in more detail. So Groucho obliged with the following:

Dear Brothers:

Since I last wrote you, I regret to say there have been some changes in the plot of our new picture, "A Night in Casablanca." In the new version I play Bordello, the sweetheart of Humphrey Bogart. Harpo and Chico are itinerant rug peddlers who are weary of laying rugs and enter a monastery

just for a lark. This is a good joke on them, as there hasn't
been a lark in the place for fifteen years.

Across from this monastery, hard by a jetty, is a water-
front hotel, chockfull of apple-cheeked damsels, most of whom
have been barred by the Hays Office for soliciting. In the fifth
reel, Gladstone makes a speech that sets the House of Com-
mons in a uproar and the King promptly asks for his resignation. Harpo marries a hotel detective; Chico operates an
ostrich farm. Humphrey Bogart's girl, Bordello, spends her
last years in a Bacall house.

This, as you can see, is a very skimpy outline. The only
thing that can save us from extinction is a continuation of the
film shortage.

> Fondly,
> Groucho Marx

*After that, the Marxes heard no more from the Warner
Brothers' legal department.*

TO SAM ZOLOTOW
OF THE NEW YORK TIMES
DRAMA DEPARTMENT

December 5, 1945

Dear Sam,

My plans are still in embryo. In case you've never been
there, this is a small town on the outskirts of wishful thinking.
At the moment, I'm deep in the heart of "Casablanca" and it's
thrilling work. I arise at seven every morning, kick the alarm
clock in the groin and speed to the studio. I always get a nine
o'clock call, which means I shoot promptly at three in the

afternoon. There's no use protesting—this is the way the movie business is geared and I suspect that's the chief reason why so much bilge appears in your neighborhood theater.

Yours,
Groucho

January 23, 1946

Dear Sam Zolotow,

Today for the first time since the last of September, I emerged from my molehill at General Service Studio and saw daylight. For the past nine weeks I've been leading a life that closely parallels that of one of the minor performers in Swain's Rat and Cat Act.

In case you are too young to remember this offering, it consisted of six rats, dressed as jockeys, perched on six cats, dressed as horses, galloping furiously around a miniature race track. It was an extraordinary act.

Of course, I get more salary then Swain paid his actors; as a matter of fact, they didn't get any salary. Swain paid them off in cheese. Each rat got two pounds of mouse-trap cheese a week. With the country facing a three-hundred-billion-dollar deficit, this perhaps doesn't seem like much, but you must remember, this was all net. These rats didn't have an agent— they knew their own kind and booked themselves independently. They didn't even have to shop for their cheese—they just sat in their dressing room and waited for Swain to throw their salary over the transom.

If "A Night in Casablanca" turns out disastrously, and there is no reason it shouldn't, I am going to look up Swain and ask him if he would be interested in reviving his act with me playing one of the jockeys.

Yours,
Groucho

TO ARTHUR SHEEKMAN

June 24, 1939

Dear Sheek,

I'm still thinking of the exit you made at the depot. Suitcases and parcels still litter the floor of the Union Station, awaiting your return. In all my years of one night stands and ad-lib train hopping, I have never seen any scene like the one I witnessed that night!

Our picture "A Day at the Circus" is progressing rather rapidly considering that it's our picture and we'll almost finish on schedule. I believe it will be much better than I thought. This isn't saying a hell of a lot, but, really, I think the scenes are going to be pretty funny, although I must admit, in establishing an alibi, that I have seen very little of the rushes.

I'm getting too old for rushes—the projection rooms, or at least the ones they give us, are either a long climb or in an air-conditioned cellar, and I've decided to wait until the picture plays the Marquis before seeing it. At least if I don't like it, I might win the Chevrolet. There's some talk of the Ritz Theater raffling off a Buick and if they do, I might not see the picture at all.

Our radio program is gaining in popularity and in its Crosley. Although we are bowing out after July 9th, there's more than a strong likelihood that we'll reappear in the fall in a slightly revamped edition of the present show—probably on a week night and whittled down to thirty minutes.

Love to you and the beautiful lady—I forget her name—you know, the one who always sings "St. James' Infirmary."

Yours,
Groucho

October 27, 1939

Dear Sheek and Mrs. Sheek,

I finally cured my cold at White Sulphur Springs but picked up another one as soon as I got home so I may have to go back to White Sulphur Springs again and do the whole thing over. Because of my cold, I haven't been to see your daughter—it seemed much wiser to keep away from her until I'm in the full bloom of health, which will probably be around November 28 or 29. However, I phoned the school and was told that she was doing very well and liked it there.

The boys at the studio have lined up another turkey for us and there's a strong likelihood that we'll be shooting in about three or four weeks. I'm not looking forward to it but I guess it's just as well to get it over with. I saw the present one the other day and didn't care much for it. I realize I'm not much of a judge but I'm kind of sick of the whole thing and, on leaving the theater, vowed that I'd never see it again. I don't feel this way about all of our pictures: "A Night at the Opera," for example, I always enjoyed looking at and, to a lesser degree, "A Day at the Races," but the rest sicken me and I'll stay clear of them in the future.

Yours,
Groucho

June 12, 1940

Dear Sheek,

I'm not able to sleep any more. You probably ask, "Why can't he sleep? He has money, beauty, talent, vigor and many teeth"—but the possession of all of these riches has nothing to do with it. I see Bund members dropping down my chimney, Commies under my bed, Fifth Columnists in my closets, a bearded dwarf, called Surtax, doing a gavotte on my desk with a little lady known as Confiscation. I'm setting aside a small sum for poison which I'm secreting in a little sack under my mattress.

We hope to start our picture July 1, by which time, I'm sure, we will have forgotten all the dialogue so carefully rehearsed on the road. I just came back from Lake Arrowhead where I spent my time getting confused in a sailboat.

Yours,
Groucho

July 1, 1940

Dear Sheek,

I received the letters and check. This time, I'll keep the check and deposit the letters—I'm taking no chances! That last sentence, I hope you noticed, was the type of joke where you just take two objects and twist them around. This makes a very funny routine and leaves you with no joke at all, which is just as well.

Did you see that little piece I wrote for Reader's Digest? It's not much of a piece but it's a good ad except that I can't remember what I'm trying to advertise. I have given up the idea of an Ediphone for on investigating, I discovered that after drooling into one of those machines, it's necessary to have the record shaved. I have enough trouble shaving myself, even with an electric razor, and if, in addition to that, I'm going to have to shave an unfriendly and strange piece of steel, I'll just abandon my literary career and collect beer bottles—with beer in them! (God, what a comedian—how does he think of that stuff?)

"Go West" is being constantly postponed. I read the script and I don't blame them. If they were smart, they'd pay us off and get three other fellows or take all that money and open up a big, gaudy cat house. Perhaps a drive-in with girls between the layers of bread. For dressing, they could use mayonnaise! (Will nothing stop that fellow?)

I'll probably vote for Willkie—I'm dead set against a third term. I think this fellow is intelligent, courageous, and although I didn't hear him, I understand he gave an excellent performance on "Information, Please." In order for Roosevelt to get my vote, he'd have to go on "Information, Please" and top Levant.

Well, I could go on like this for days but I know you're a busy man, playing with that toilet plunger, and I don't want to keep you from your work.

Remember, Brockway Hotel, Lake Tahoe—second table to the left in the dining room—July 3 to 10—hurry, hurry, hurry!

Love to your two women, Sylvia and Gloria.

Yours,
Groucho

TO HIS SON ARTHUR

Summer, 1940

Dear Arthur,

. . . "Go West" has again been postponed. I don't know why the studio doesn't come right out and say they are afraid to make it. All I get from them is a weekly announcement to come to the wardrobe department and be fitted for a pair of early American pants. The writers have been taking some big hacks at the story, and from what I hear, once we begin we should be able to shoot the whole thing in three days, and get the Academy Award. Irv Brecher [one of the authors] says this picture will be known as the longest short ever made. Well, it doesn't bother me. My attitude is, take the money and to hell with it. I had my hair darkened to match my grease-paint mustache, but it has been so long since the scheduled starting date that the dye has faded and now I will have to have it done all over again. So you see my theatrical career has dwindled to being fitted once a week for a pair of early American pants and having my hair dyed every three weeks. This is a fine comedown for a man who used to be the Toast of Broadway . . .

Love,
Padre

TO ARTHUR SHEEKMAN

September 5, 1940

Dear Sheek,

I'm working terribly hard and I don't like it. I really don't mind the work; it's just that when I work, I sleep badly; and it's insomnia rather than labor that makes me feel lousy.

Last night I had dinner with Chaplin at Dave Chasen's and he was in high humor—unusual for him. He told me, among other things, that he's not Jewish but wishes he were. He said he was part Scotch, English and Gypsy, but I think that he isn't quite sure what he is. He's very happy about his movie ["The Great Dictator"]. He ran it yesterday for the Breen office—it runs over 13,000 feet and there wasn't a foot cut out of it. He thinks it will be a big hit. He's very odd. In some ways, he has no sense of humor at all and then again it's wonderful. He told me he hated the English but that he hoped they would win the war. He also hates Noel Coward and even refuses to see his playlets, which are now running at El Capitan.

At the finish of the meal, the most astonishing thing happened: he grabbed the check (for six; it came to around $30) and refused to let me have it. I was quite relieved, but luckily I'm sunburned and I don't think the white or my nervousness was discernible through the tan. He has a reputation for stinginess but I have always found him generous—not only with his money but with his praise. He thinks I'm wonderful and said that he envies my glibness and wishes he could talk as swiftly on the screen as I do. Well, enough of Chaplin and me!

Last week I saw "Ladies in Retirement," an English murder mystery, and it was great. I've never seen finer individual characterizations on the stage, but whether Hollywood doesn't like murder plays or whether the trip to the Biltmore is too long, I don't know, but the show didn't do very well. El Capitan, on the other hand, has done magnificently with the Coward one-acts—the proceeds are given to British War Relief and the actors all donate their services. The casts are practically a roster of the English acting colony here.

Arthur [Groucho's son] went to the finals in the Santa Monica Tennis Tournament and then lost to Carl Earn, a tennis player with the weirdest assortment of strokes ever seen. To begin with, he's a left-hander and slashes and cuts and overspins his opponent dizzy. Arthur lost the first set, 6-0; then 8-6; then 6-4. I think that in another year Arthur will probably be better than this guy. When he teamed up with Earn, they won the doubles. Arthur was quite disappointed in not being able to compete in the Nationals at Forest Hills but hopes to dump a few national-ranking players at the Southwest in two weeks. The Southwest will be the same old Southwest—Paul Lucas will be there with his beret; Gilbert Roland will get eliminated in the first round of the men's doubles and singles; all the glamour gals will be sporting their

winter furs in the hottest week of the year and I will wind up
the tournament with acute indigestion from frankfurter
lunches and paternal nervousness.

Yours,
Groucho

October 10, 1940

Dear Sheek,

We're about through with "Go West." I haven't seen
it hooked up but I imagine it's pretty good. It could have been
much better, I'm sure, had it been a larger subject; however,
there's no use going all through that again. I'm shaping my am-
bitions in other directions and discussing a radio show that I
might do with Irving Brecher. It's a kind of Aldrich Family
except that we hope to make it a little funnier. By that I don't
mean joke, joke, joke but a kind of human interest story with
a slightly wacky father, who, of course, would be me.

We are going to make a record of it as soon as it's written.
We even have two or three suckers who claim they can hardly
wait until they hear it. This statement, as you know, could
lead to all kinds of funny answers but I'll just leave them to
you. I'm pretty sick of having the answers. My idea of an
ideal program would be a show where I would have all the
questions and some other bastard would have to figure out the
funny answers. Of course, I wouldn't like the salary a man
gets for asking the questions but why go on—there's no one
going to offer me anything as attractive as that. In addition to
the radio show, I have a deal on with Krasna to write a play.

I may motor east with my son Arthur if the radio deal
brodies, to see your "Mr. Big" and to eat sturgeon at Green-
grass's with one of the friendly natives—say, Max Gordon.
Lincoln was my favorite president until Gordon produced

him in collaboration with Goetz, but now I'm all for Martin Van Buren. I'll take good care not to mention his name to Gordon for that would only mean that sometime next year Henry Fonda would be playing Martin Van Buren at the Radio City Music Hall to the lowest gross in the history of the movies.

I'm very happy about the World Series. I won two dollars from Miriam [Groucho's older daughter], or, in other words, two weeks' allowance. Miriam's allowance is becoming my chief source of income and when she grows up and flies away from the home, as they say, I don't know what I'll do for spending money.

Love to your family from my family and your Broadway and mine.

Groucho

June 23, 1941

Dear Sheek,

Here I am on Stage 18 waiting to shoot some retakes. I had some dialogue with three models that wasn't particularly funny at the last preview so they brought in a little man to write some jokes to replace it—the result will be that these jokes will be six times as unfunny when they reach the screen. I am champing at the bit—it's 11:45, and at one Art plays Frank Parker in the quarterfinals of the 55th Annual Los Angeles Tournament. Parker will probably beat him but it'll be an interesting match and I'm eager to get there. However, with the customary dilatory tactics of the cinema, it looks like I'll have to forget about seeing Art sweat in the noonday sun.

As I told you, we previewed the picture twice—the first time, it went fairly well; then they took out 900 feet, previewed it again and it flopped. They are now straightening out the story (this they do with every picture after a preview)—they imagine the audience hasn't laughed because the plot wasn't understood. The fact of the matter is, the audience hasn't laughed because they didn't understand the jokes! However, this is my farewell, and regardless of what the future holds in store for me, I'm happy to escape from this kind of picture, for the character I'm playing I now find wholly repulsive.

Well, enough of me. When does your show open and where or don't you know yet? The Bucks County Playhouse wired and asked me if I would play "Sherlock Holmes" (the William Gillette version) for a week this summer. I read it and thought that it didn't have enough amusing moments to be comic and I felt it wouldn't be safe for me to play it straight so I turned it down. Besides this, I have a couple of radio irons in the fire. Acting in the movies no longer interests me and unless I were to get something that I was crazy about, I don't think I'll be seen again in any of the local studios.

Yours,
Groucho

July 25, 1941

Dear Sheek,

We have been ejected from MGM and are now conducting what little business we have in a barnlike building cater-cornered from the Bank of America. It's very convenient, especially for Chico, who now has only to cross the street to stop payment on the checks he's written the night before.

We are allowed only eighty telephone calls a month here and that is really quite a hardship! In the old days, I used to call up Rachel* and she'd call me fifteen or twenty times a day. We always had the same conversation—I would say, "This is

* The Marx Brothers' secretary.

Doctor Hackenbush. What's new, Rachel?" and she would say, "Nothing." Then we'd both hang up. Now, if I want to find out if there's anything new in my office, I have to make a personal visit or write her a note. The personal visit is the most satisfactory way of finding out that she has nothing to tell me except that parking space is at a premium around this ramshackle building. Sometimes I have to walk half a mile from my parked car to the office and by the time I get there, I've forgotten what I wanted to ask her.

I went to the Pastor-Turkey Thompson fracas last night—tickets by Ryskind, propaganda by Senator Wheeler. I've never seen such ineffectual fighters in all my years of fight-going. It was a beautiful night—all the stars were out, including Cary Grant, and in the ring two incompetent stevedores were clutching, mauling and groaning through ten long, interminable rounds. The supporting card had eight incompetent amateurs going through the motions. It's the first fight I've seen in a year and it will be a long time before I go again.

I'm going on the USO show—that's the U.S. Defense Bond program, which is broadcast every Wednesday night at 9 P.M. over CBS. This will be August 20 and I'll probably arrive in New York around the tenth. I plan on staying three weeks in and around New York watching Arthur get quickly eliminated at the Nationals and Forest Hills and then I'll scurry back to California to my old routine.

Love to Gloria and the kid and let me hear from you.

Yours,
Groucho

February 12, 1942

Dear Sheek,

I'm leading an undisciplined and squirish sort of life—tweeds, briar pipe and all that kind of Ronald Colman—but any day now I expect a forty-pound shell to come hurtling through my roof and announce the arrival of the Mikado. In a way, it would be a blessing. The indifference, the blasé attitude and the smugness that seems to pervade this whole coast can only by cured by shell shock. Plus this, I have invested a fortune in blackout curtains, candles, lump sugar, rubber tires, kerosene lamps and pemmican and I'd like to get my money's worth out of them.

And what servant trouble we're having! The local slaveys have all become privy (ah there, Mencken) to the fact that the defense industries offer much bigger salaries, better food and certainly better social contacts than they could possibly get lumbering around my kitchen and the result is that I now have what is known as the servant-of-the-week. If it keeps up, I'll either join the Army or subsist entirely on canned foods for the duration. I had no idea that this war would dare disturb my private life and I may have to write a letter to the London Times.

Had an offer from Berlin (Irving, not Hitler) to star in a Music Box Revue but that would mean the black mustache again and I'm ducking it as long as it is economically feasible. I'm hopeful that I'll get a good radio job in the fall and am gambling to the extent that I won't take any other kind of offer that might get in its way. I won't write you any war news as I imagine they still have newspapers in New York.

Young Vanderbilt was playing singles at the Tennis Club yesterday and he doesn't hit the ball any better than a fellow without money.

With love to you all,

Yours,
Groucho

September 17, 1942

Dear Sheek,

Max Gordon wrote me that your play looks very funny in rehearsal but then so does Gordon.

I had an offer from the New Opera Company to appear in an Offenbach play called "La Vie Parisienne" and the book was just about as good as the title. It had a very novel idea in it—it was all about a rich American who goes to Paris. Well, you wouldn't want anything better than that, would you? Oh, yes, he also gets mixed up with a French girl. The second act is a race between a number of horses and, although I'm supposed to lose, my horse wins and the girl turns out to be extremely wealthy in her own right and not really an adventuress at all. It's a little hazy, but in the last act I believe the girl marries the horse and she becomes the most popular brood mare in Antibes. I don't think I'll do this play unless they give me the horse's part.

Well, these are my plans and for the balance of this week you can reach me at Gilmore Stadium between Harry Ruby and first base. If you find time, read "Cross Creek" by Marjorie Rawlings.

My love to your two women and let me hear from you.

Yours,

Groucho

P.S. As you know, I'm campaigning for Will Rogers Jr. I went to a meeting the other night—prepared to make my customary speech—way over on the other side of West Adams, and when I got there one lone worn-heel politician was pacing up and down. The joint was hermetically closed up and I assumed that it was sold out. I grilled this lone sentry out front and he told me that the meeting had been called off as the motion picture theater around the corner was having a special bank night, and therefore, no one would show up. I never thought the time would come when I would be outdrawn by a box of crockery.

Love to you all.

December 16, 1942

Dear Sheek,

I am leading a quiet, sinless life. A good deal of my time is spent in the balcony or shelf of the Marquis Theater. The pictures there are indescribably putrid. I think there's a special brand of pictures ground out at the studios that only play the Marquis. These pictures usually have Don Ameche or Jeanette MacDonald playing leads. Still and all, as Lardner would say, it's a very cozy little place. It's always empty and it only takes about a quart of gas to motor there. The place has been all done over—new carpets, fixtures—they even have a new manager. I sit all alone in the balcony, alternately smoking and sleeping. No matter how warm the night, I take my overcoat with me—doubled up, it makes an excellent pillow. On cold nights, it makes a warm blanket. It's a violation of the fire ordinance to smoke at the Marquis, but inasmuch as I am usually the sole occupant of the balcony, this law is never enforced. As a matter of fact, the other night the manager, grateful for my attention, dusted off my car while I was upstairs sleeping through a Jeanette MacDonald opus. I'm not learning much about the picture business, frequenting the Marquis, but you ought to see my car.

My love to your two women and yourself. Let me hear from you.

Yours,
Groucho

January 26, 1943

Dear Sheek,

I don't hear from you any more. I imagine you're dead. If you fail to answer this, I'll send a wreath to 48th Street. My son Arthur is home and reports that you treated him royally.

At the moment, I'm doing nothing but ogling dames, bike-riding, eating and any other innocent pursuit that presents itself. I have a couple of radio things brewing but the heat under them is very low and God knows what will become of me. At this point, the chorus of 110 voices sings the whole choral arrangement of Beethoven's 9th. My social life is negligible. I play anagrams, pool, pinochle and listen to music. I smoke constantly and I have a mole on my left shoulder. Would like to meet a sociable widow, around 55, object wet nursing.

The Kaufman-Hart "Sherlock Holmes" thing is out. We all came to the same conclusion that it could be funny, but by the end of the second act—having no solid story, only satire—it could get awfully monotonous. George suggested a revue but that will be a last resort. I'm not much interested in high kicking on the New York stage or any other place.

You must feel much better about "Mr. Big" now that the season is drawing to a close. So far the critics have blunderbussed Kaufman, Ferber, Connelly, Ryskind, MacArthur, Kraft, Hammerstein, Romberg, Krasna and almost anyone else that you care to mention—so you see you're in very good company. As a matter of fact, much better company than if you had a hit, for in that case you'd be with only Dorothy Fields, Chodorov and Fields and Benny Fields.

I have an appointment this afternoon to have my toenails painted and a permanent and I just must beg off.

Love to you and your two girl friends.

Yours,
Groucho

(33)

TO EARL WILSON

October 18, 1949

Dear Earl:

I found your reference to the picture "Copacabana" in shockingly bad taste. One doesn't speak disparagingly of the dead. The fact of the matter is, I did very well on "Copacabana." It gave me an opportunity to rise every morning at 6 o'clock, glue on a fake mustache, eat an extraordinarily bad lunch in the studio restaurant and get home in time to miss dinner. Plus all this, it gave me a chance to look at my producer fourteen hours a day. No other picture can make that statement.

Regards,
Groucho

TO HOWARD HUGHES

January 23, 1951

Dear Mr. Hughes:

Between retooling for the war effort and dueling with Wald and Krasna, I presume you are a fairly busy man. However, I wonder if you could spare a few moment to release a picture that was made some years ago involving Jane Russell, Frank Sinatra and your correspondent. The name of the picture, if memory serves, is "It's Only Money." I never did see it but I have been told that at its various previews it was received with considerable enthusiasm.

I am not a young man any more, Mr. Hughes, and before I shuffle off this mortal coil if you could see your way clear to pry open your strong box and send this minor masterpiece whizzing through the film exchanges of America, you would not only have earned my undying gratitude but that of the United Nations, the popcorn dealers of America and three RKO stockholders who at the moment are trying to escape from the Mellon bank of Pittsburgh.

Sincerely,
Groucho Marx

FROM IRWIN ALLEN*

November 13, 1953

Dear Groucho:

I'm very worried but it's too late to ask for your advice; for tomorrow the King and Queen of Greece will be in Hollywood and (may God help them) they'll have lunch at the RKO studio.

Having yourself been fed in the RKO commissary, you will, I think, suspect a communist plot. After consuming the chef's Special, which is practically anything that's inedible, it's eight to five their Majesties will leave Hollywood, with bellyaches, convinced they've been poisoned. How this will affect our hitherto satisfactory relations with Greece, I hesitate even to guess.

You are no doubt wondering why I don't stand in the commissary doorway and whisper, as the King and Queen come in:

"Your highnesses! For God's sake, order cornflakes! They come in sealed packages and can be eaten even in *this* studio!"

I don't think it would work. In the first place, the local gendarmes might regard me as a crackpot. If they dragged me

* Screen and television producer.

off to the bastille, it would be very inconvenient, since next Friday night I am previewing a picture that looks pretty good.

In the second place, although generally regarded as a man of the world, I've never had too much luck with the *upper* upper classes. I remember, a little sadly, a girl I had who'd been Queen for a Day. Once, when I was returning from location, she not only failed to meet me at the airport (as planned); she failed to meet me in my own Cadillac, which she had been driving throughout the week I was away.

I have since turned in my old Cadillac on a new one. Likewise the girl.

Love,
Irwin

TO BEN KALMENSON

July 15, 1955

Dear Mr. Kalmenson:

You hardly know me but I have heard about you for years and you are generally considered one of the shrewdest and ablest men in the film industry.

The reason I am writing this is that my wife's sister is married to Howard Hawks. She is coming to spend a month with me in September and if you could give me an approximate idea of the gross of "Land of Pharaohs" [directed by Mr. Hawks] it would help me to create the proper social climate.

For example, if the picture should make a net profit of say, $2,000,000, she would have the large guest room. Included in this is a tub and shower, private commode, and steaks from Elgee's Meat Market.

If the picture, on the other hand, loses money, there is

(36)

a room over the garage that we have been using for storing moleskins and betel nuts (we always keep a supply of betel nuts on hand in case any natives drop in from Universal Studios). There are no toilet or bathing facilities in this room and the only exit is through a trap door.

She will be fed, of course. No one starves in my home. Obviously there won't by any steaks from Elgee's, but she will get sufficient nourishment to keep body and soul together. A sample meal, for example, would be mildewed haggis, lamb fries and a steaming cup of chicory.

I would appreciate an early answer to this for I will need time to grease the trap door.

Thanking you in advance, I remain,

Respectfully yours,
Groucho Marx

Private Life

TO IRVING HOFFMAN

1946

Dear Irving:

Between strokes of good fortune, I have been toying with the idea of making you my impending child's godfather. However, before doing this officially, I would like to see a notarized statement of your overall assets. I don't intend to repeat the unhappy experience that befell my parents late in the 19th century.

At that time there was an Uncle Julius in our family. He was five feet one in his socks, holes and all. He had a brown spade beard, thick glasses and a head topped off with a bald spot about the size of a buckwheat cake. My mother somehow got the notion that Uncle Julius was wealthy and she told my father, who never did quite understand my mother, that it would be a brilliant piece of strategic flattery were they to make Uncle Julius my godfather.

Well, as happens to all men, I was finally born and before I could say "Jack Robinson," I was named Julius. At the moment this historic event was taking place, Uncle Julius was in the back room of a cigar store on Third Avenue, dealing them off the bottom. When word reached him that he had been made my godfather, he dropped everything, including two aces he had up his sleeve for an emergency, and quickly rushed over to our flat.

In a speech so moist with emotion that he was blinded by his own eyeglasses, he said that he was overwhelmed by this sentimental gesture on our part and hinted that my future—a rosy one—was irrevocably linked with his. At the conclusion of his speech, still unable to see through his misty lenses, he kissed my father, handed my mother a cigar and ran back to the pinochle game.

Two weeks later he moved in, paper suitcase and all. As time went by, my mother became suspicious and one day, in discussing him with my father, she not only discovered that Uncle Julius seemed to be without funds, but what was even worse, that he owed my father $34.

Since he was only five feet one, my father volunteered to throw him out but my mother advised caution. She said that she had read of many cases where rich men, after living miserly lives, died leaving tremendous fortunes to their heirs.

Uncle Julius remained with us until I got married. By this time, he had the best room in the house and owed my father $84. Shortly after my wedding, my mother finally admitted that Uncle Julius had been a hideous mistake and ordered my father to give him the bum's rush. But Uncle Julius had grown an inch over the years while my father had shrunk proportionately, so he finally convinced my mother that violence was not the solution to the problem.

Soon after this Uncle Julius solved everything by kicking off, leaving me his sole heir. His estate, when probated, consisted of a nine ball that he had stolen from the poolroom, a box of liver pills and a celluloid dickey.

I suppose I should be more sentimental about the whole

thing, but it was a severe shock to all of us, and, if I can help it, it's not going to happen again.

Well, Irving, that's the story. If you are interested, let me hear from you as soon as possible and, remember, a financial statement as of today will expedite things considerably.

Regards,
Groucho

TO HIS SON, ARTHUR

Summer of 1940

Dear Art:

For a tennis bum, you're certainly leading a luxurious life and I only hope you can keep it up. I see by the papers that it rained in St. Louis yesterday, so that gave you time to eat six meals at the hotel instead of the customary five.

We just came back from Lake Arrowhead. It's a wonderful spot and we had a fine time sailing on the lake. With the wind on my back, I was Sir Thomas Lipton, Sir Francis Drake and Captain Kidd. However, when I tried to tack against it and sail into home plate, I botched it up completely and finally had to suffer the humiliation of being towed back to port by a small boy in an outboard motor. This made Miriam very happy, for during the entire voyage she kept telling me that I didn't know how to manipulate a sailboat and predicted that it was only a question of time before I'd be towed back to shore. Despite my inadequacies as commander, I would spend a good part of my declining years on the bounding waves. That's really the life. You need no golf ball, no caddy, no racket or busted gut. All you need is a stout heart, a strong back, plenty of wind and a cast-iron stomach. Avast, mates! Yo-ho and a bottle of rum! Tonight I'll listen to "Pinafore" on the record player.

We expect to start shooting around July first, so for the next eight weeks you can reach me on the back lot at MGM. Please bring ice packs and menthol and a portable air conditioner.

I'm brushing up on all the current movies. I saw "Strange Cargo" and was having a pretty good time until the head usher at the Marquis tapped me on the shoulder and sharply told me that no smoking was allowed.

He walked away and I began smoking again. Again he tapped me on the shoulder. This time he didn't walk away—he just stood there, arms folded, and glared at the back of my head. Then my cigar went out: and then I went out. Sometime, I wish you'd let me know what happened to the nature girl in the last four reels.

Last night, I saw "Waterloo Bridge" at the Westwood Theater. It's quite a bit different from the old version. MGM, being a more leisurely studio, didn't make the girl a streetwalker until the fourth reel. In the original version, they opened up in the first reel with the little lady hustling on Waterloo Bridge. It was better that way—I could get home earlier.

I can't write any more at this time as I have to take dancing lessons for the next three days. Our friends, the Arthur Murrays, have bestowed the lessons upon us, which, you may be sure, is the only reason I am submitting to them.

Love,

Padre

P.S. Saturday night, the Beverly Hills Tennis and Bad Food club is throwing a barn dance and it's going to be a sensation. How surprised we'll all be when we gather there that evening to see all the new faces that we had left only an hour before on the tennis court.

The food won't be served until midnight, so I've arranged

with your mother to pay for the privilege of eating stale delicatessen food and listening to Dave's wife, who used to be a
showgirl, sing a medley of airs from "The Chocolate Soldier."
If this keeps up, I may take to drinking in a serious way. I've
often wondered why people drink. It's gradually beginning to
dawn on me.

Summer, 1940

Dear Arthur,

Well, the affair was a big success. They had ninety people,
a good band and open-air dancing around the pool. The cater-
ing was delegated to Levitoff, the demon pastrami prince, and
the crowd ate like vultures and drank the same way. If it
hadn't been for the police, the party would still be going on,
but at the fatal hour of two, the cops arrived, brandished their
clubs, and announced that the band would either cease firing
or continue playing at the local jail.

The disturbing feature of the party was its success. Because of that the girls are beginning to discuss the next one,
whether to have white tie and tails or have everybody come as
coal miners. At any rate, the club cleared a nice profit at the
bar. Many of the members, loyal to the core, decided to try to
drink the club out of its deficit, and with the help of a few
guests, who were generous enough to sacrifice their kidneys,
a healthy profit was cleared.

I notice that you disappeared rather abruptly from the
Baltimore Tournament and it must have been the day you
played Elwood Cooke. I've come to the conclusion that it's
not so hot being the father of a tennis player. Hundreds of
people to whom I wouldn't talk normally, rush up to me and
immediately begin a long, involved conversation, explaining
why you either won or lost in the last tournament. As you
know, I'm deeply interested in your athletic progress, but not

to the degree that I want to discuss it twelve hours a day. Now, whenever anyone asks me how you're doing at whatever tournament you happen to be in, I say, "Don't you know? He's quit the game and taken up squash. This baffles them. A lot of people have only heard of squash as a low grade vegetable and they can't understand why anyone should want to stand in a cheap restaurant and throw vegetables.

I picked up the paper Tuesday morning, nervously turned to the sports section and read that you had been eliminated by Gilbert Hunt. A few moments later I discovered that you had been eliminated by Gilbert Mumps. We received your wire at eight Thursday morning and read that you were in a hotel at Seabright, swollen up with mumps, and I imagine pretty well disgusted with the whole tennis tour. Well, that's life. As you journey through it, you will encounter all sorts of these nasty little upsets, and you will either learn to adjust yourself to them or gradually go nuts.

According to the wire, you are resting well and are being taken care of by a nurse. I hope she is beautiful and that she has red hair. I don't know why, but whenever I dream of a nurse she always has red hair. Red hair makes a man want to recover his health quickly, so that he can get on his feet and the nurse off hers.

Love,
Padre

Summer, 1940

Dear Arthur:

Glad to hear from you and to know that you are recovering. I am also pleased to learn that you have a rich dame who wants to put you up while you are recuperating. How does she have her money? Is it in jewels or securities, or just plain gold? Some night, when you are grappling with her in the moonlight, you might find out. Do it discreetly, for God's sake. Don't come out bluntly and say, "How much dough have you got?" That wouldn't be the Marxian way. Use finesse. Well, I will leave the whole thing to you.

Love,

Padre

Summer of 1941

Dear Arthur:

Gummo tells me that the Tommy Riggs show, which I spurned, now has a Crosley rating of seventeen. This will give you an idea of how little I know about audiences and what they want. I guess I missed the boat with that one. I am sure, however, that other radio shows will come along.

I am going to take good care of my health and when the next radio comic dies, I will go to the funeral, disguised as a pall bearer, and strike up an acquaintanceship with the sponsor who, I am sure, will have to attend the funeral, if only for appearance. Before you know it, I will be on the air, killing the audiences with my rapier wit and personality.

I feel pretty smart today. I just finished reading your Reader's Digest for July, and I know now why the Boston and Maine Railroad has had a comeback, why Japan is tiring of the war in the East, and the proper way to bring up a child. The magazine also contains a condensation of Budd Schulberg's book "What Makes Sammy Run" and a very amusing portrait by Stephen Leacock of an uncle of his. So now you don't have to read the Digest for this month. In my next letter I will tell you all about the Digest for next month.

I was hopeful of getting a letter from you today, but instead I got a letter from Standard Statistics showing me how

(47)

I can clean up a fortune in the market if only I follow their sure-fire tips; a letter from an art dealer in Glendale offering me a solid-silver serving set for six thousand dollars, and a bill from Hokum the Plumber. One more batch of mail like today's and I will rip out the mailbox.

As a result, I don't know whether you are playing in a tennis tournament in Cincinnati, or working in a brewery. The local papers carry no news of any tournament in the sleepy little village on the Ohio. I am going to stop guessing and this is the last mail you get from the good, gray ghost until I hear from you, either by post, telegraph or Alexander Bell.

Love,
Padre

Summer of 1941

Dear Arthur:

I can't understand why you don't get any mail from me. Perhaps it's because I haven't been writing. However, now that you've broken your silence, I will do the same, despite the fact that you probably wouldn't have written if you hadn't needed money. Well, that's one of the nice things about holding the purse strings. Eventually, children come around to seeing things your way.

Since I had to stay in town to work with Krasna and couldn't get away for a vacation, your mother and her sister left today for a tour of the outlying hot spots. She was vague as to their ultimate destination, but I have a hunch that they will wind up at Las Vegas playing the machines.

Miriam and I are alone. Tonight the Arthur Murrays are coming to dinner and tomorrow night, the Krasnas. Bertha is leaving for a vacation tomorrow, and her sister is coming into the kitchen to wreck my stomach for the next two weeks.

Gummo is at Catalina under the delusion that he is going to catch a marlin or a swordfish. He's taken his wife and Bobby, and I can just see that scene in the boat, with the hook from Bobby's line landing in the rear end of Gummo's pants—a typical Marxian fishing expedition. He should have talked to me first.

Love,
Padre

Fall of 1943

Dear Arthur:

I received a letter from you this morning with your usual complaint that you get practically no mail. I don't understand this as I write to you at least three times a week. Either you are drunk or I am, or maybe my letters are so unimpressive that you don't even remember receiving them.

We previewed last night at a Navy base in San Diego with Dotty Lamour and had a lot of fun. The previews are always more fun than the actual shows. Since the chips are not down, everyone is at ease and the audience senses it. We leave tomorrow morning for March Field, where we'll again get shoved around by the brass until midnight.

I met your old collaborator, Charlie Isaacs, and he is being shipped overseas. Pretty soon they will unquestionably grab off all the fathers in the draft and we will lose Artie Stander. I believe he is by far our best writer and I am trying to persuade him to puncture his ear drums. It's a fine state of affairs when the head comic has to puncture the ear drums of his writers so they can continue to grind out mouldy wheezes for the Pabst brewery.

How about a furlough? Don't you ever get enough time off to fly down here? I would pay your fare and you could live in your old room or you could sleep in the window of the English Bakery on Canon Drive.

Do you really have to wait until the Admiral gives you permission to leave? Why don't you just walk up to him as they do in the movies, and say, "Look here, old boy, who's running this show? When I say I want to fly down to Beverly Hills for a few days, that's exactly what I mean." Don't let old Mutton Chops start pushing you around so early in the war. Once you let those captains and admirals get the upper hand, there's no holding them.

Anyway, see what you can do.

Love and kisses,
Hugo Z. Hackenbush

February 16, 1945

Dear Art,

Your father was telling me that in the letters you receive, nobody mentions my name. This is not unusual; it happens to many dogs. You know, it's a strange thing, but once you walk around on four legs instead of the orthodox two, people begin to suspect that you don't know what's going on. I don't know whether you have ever been a dog—I know you look like one —but it has certain advantages and disadvantages. As you know, your father and I both live under the same roof. He is not a bad guy, despite the fact that he kicks me occasionally, especially those days when the market goes down. When he strokes me affectionately, I know that the stocks are on the upswing. I watch your old man very closely, although I don't imagine he thinks I do, and he is quite a character. He reads the paper every morning, worries about the war, and all the other problems that the morning paper presents. Your father and I have many run-ins these days. You see, he can't get it into his thick skull that I have come of age and that sex is just as important to me as it is to him. There's a beautiful collie in the 500 block on Palm Drive who thinks I'm a pretty hot dog. I'm crazy about her, and although it isn't good for my social prestige to be seen around with a bitch from the 500 block, I try to be broadminded about it and not too dogmatic in my views.

I've done considerable running away in recent months—sometimes for days! It isn't that I don't like your father but my freedom is terribly important and I am not going to relinquish it for that mangy pound-and-a-half of horse meat that he tosses at me each evening. I may not even go with him when he moves to Westwood. The backyard is exceedingly small and there is a hell of a high steel picket fence surrounding it. I am convinced that if I try to scale this enclosure I will probably be disemboweled, so I may solve the whole thing by just remaining in Beverly, feeding out of garbage cans and living a dog's life with my collie.

Well, I could go on and tell you many tales of my adventures in the hills of Beverly but I don't want to bore you. The only reason I wrote you at all was because I didn't want you to think that I was an out-of-sight, out-of-mind dog. As a matter of fact, I miss you a lot and if you could send me a few bones, even those of a Jap, I certainly would appreciate it.

By the way, when you write to your father again, remember, not a word about this letter—he doesn't know I can write, in fact, he thinks I'm a complete schmuck.

Well, take care of yourself. That's the leash you can do.

Your old pal,
Duke Marx

TO ARTHUR SHEEKMAN

July 27, 1942

Dear Sheek,

Dame rumor hit it on the head. Head over heels is right. I think it's wonderful too. She* is far too good for me, but you'll see her pretty soon and you can draw your own conclusions. This girl had two years at Stanford and a year at U.C.L.A. The only fly in the ointment is that she's 22 and I'm 97. It's quite an age margin. One day, without flinching, I told her how old I am. She said "Who cares?" and went right on talking. The suggestion that she go into your play came from Max Gordon. He was so impressed with her looks that he asked me why I didn't consider her for "Franklin Street." She has a tentative arrangement with Warner Brothers at the moment. I explain all this lest you think she is playing me for a part in the show. Once you've met her, I'm sure you'll realize that she doesn't go in for that sort of thing. This must sound exceedingly jerky. I'm sorry I brought the whole thing up. Thirty minutes with her will impress you more than my pages of drivel.

Love,
Groucho

* It is a little difficult to identify the young lady because Mr. Marx has since forgotten her name.

TO MEMBERS OF GROUCHO'S
POKER CLUB

March 25, 1944

To: Mr. Arthur Sheekman,
Mr. Harry Tugend,
Mr. Irving Brecher,
Mr. Harry Kurnitz,
Mr. Nat Perrin

Gentlemen:

As you know, the taxes today are as high as an elephant's eye (to coin a phrase that I just stole from Oscar Hammerstein) and, therefore, a single man has very little chance to lay anything aside.

I am writing this letter to you because you are the charter members of our poker club. In recent weeks, there has been a shocking increase in absenteeism and instead of the seven sad, familiar faces that I have grown to tolerate, a number of corrupt and unfamiliar pans have begun to appear around the green baize. Ostensibly, the original purpose of the Tuesday night meetings was to give us all an opportunity to see each other more or less regularly and incidentally to play a little poker. But now that our little group is at an advanced stage of decay, I, for one, want to confess that my purpose in participating in the game was to gather a weekly minimum of thirty nontaxable dollars. This nontaxable money meant a lot to me—it provided me with shelter and firewood; it clothed me and fed me and I needed every dollar of it desperately—but (to change the tense) eager as I am to get this money, I'm not willing to spend my Tuesday nights with a group of loutish and unkempt strangers. Therefore, gentlemen, for future evidence of your good faith, I would like some assurance that you will be present each week—either a deposit of a substantial sum, or, if this is not feasible, perhaps you would be willing to leave in escrow some small valuable piece of jewelry.

In closing, I want to say we are all lone travelers in a world bristling with enemies. We all need something spiritual to cling to. Not to get too sentimental, I sincerely believe that we need each other, just as man needs woman, and a cat, a cat house. The Tuesday night game should not be abandoned. I feel that it contributes something to our lives.

As you know, I am a single man and my tax is as high as an elephant's eye.

Sincerely yours,
Groucho Marx

THE CHILDREN:

1. *An Autograph Collector*

January 8, 1947

Dear Groucho Marx—

My Father met your brother Gummo here in Palm Springs, and he said that if I would write to you, he was sure you would send me an autograph. I like your shows a lot.

Yours very truly,
Marjorie Nedford, 11 years old

January 15, 1947

Dear Marjorie:

I think you should warn your father about this man Gummo. For years he has palmed himself off as one of the Marx Brothers and has made a good thing of it. Actually he is no more one of the Marx Brothers than Chico is one of the Dolly Sisters.

Confidentially, this Gummo comes from a long line of Rumanian Gypsies; he was deposited at our doorstep at the age of fifty, and there's nothing we can do about it.

Here is the autograph. I would send you a lock of my hair but it's at the barbershop getting washed.

Sincerely,
Groucho Marx

2. *Sylvia Sheekman*

January 3, 1949

Dear Sylvia:

I finally finished the gingerbread man. I didn't mean to eat him, but it was either him or me. The last thing I ate was his foot and this I didn't expect. Sylvia, you won't believe this, but on the way down my gullet he kicked me. This is a fine world we are living in when you can't even trust a gingerbread man.

I hope you have a very happy 1949 and that you are laying in a good supply of ginger for next Christmas.

Your pseudo-uncle,
Groucho

3. *His Grandson, Andy Marx*

July 30, 1963

Dear Andy,

Your mother tells me you're having a hot time at camp, and I thought that by this time you might have written me a letter describing your activities. What's the good of me being your grandfather if you don't send me any news about yourself?

How long are you going to be up there?

When you get back, be sure to give me a ring. I will invite you over to swim and throw water on the French poodles.

Hoping this reaches you by Pony Express, I still remain your grandfather,

Groucho

TO MR. AND MRS. ARTHUR MURRAY

May 23, 1951

Dear Katie and Arthur:

Your announcement that your daughter Jane is marrying an obscure quack named Heimlich on June 3rd saddened me considerably. I've had my eye on Jane for a long time and always hoped that some day you would wind up as my in-laws. Well, she made her choice—one that, I believe, she will ultimately regret. With me, each day would have been 24 hours of gaiety and laughter; with Heimlich she will have a life of viruses, vaccines, surgical instruments and rubber gloves. Only time can decide whether she made the right decision.

Even though I am a bitter, disappointed and disillusioned man I send them both my heartiest congratulations.

Best,
Groucho

P.S. Note to Jane: See that all his nurses are ugly.

TO MR. AND MRS. GOODMAN ACE

July 30, 1954

Dear Aces:

This is just to notify you that I got married.

Groucho

August 3, 1954

TO FRED ALLEN

Dear Freddie:

It's kind of nice to be married again, except that I can't stop making passes at strange girls. Of course this will eventually wear off, I imagine about the time I get divorced again. You know, with patience, I may become the next Tommy Manville.

Please pay no attention to what I've just written. I've been watching a lot of summer television and I'm not sure I haven't become mentally unbalanced.

Anyhow, I miss you and the kid in the black tights, and hope to see you in the not too distant future.

Eden also sends her love to you, Portland, and that great melting pot, New York.

Best,
Groucho

FROM ARTHUR SHEEKMAN

Rapallo, July 20, 1954

Dear Groucho and Eden:

Twenty minutes ago I bought the English newspapers in Santa Margherita; dropped them on the front seat of my car and, while driving home (around one of those narrow, curvy roads) my eye fell on Eden, smiling at me from the front page of the Daily Express. No thanks to either of you, I was not killed.

The headline says, "Groucho Weds Secretary," and I suppose that if I'd kept my eyes open, I wouldn't have been surprised. But why did you have to be so sneaky? In all the times I've seen you dictating letters to Miss Eden Hartford, it never occurred to me that your relationship was anything but "strictly business." True, she took most of her dictation on your lap, but I assumed that was because Italian chairs can be very uncomfortable.

I don't think I have to tell you that, except possibly for ourselves, there is no couple in the world for whom we wish greater happiness.

Next week Gloria and I will have been married exactly twenty years; and as I light my pipe (unassisted) and put on my own carpet slippers, I am inclined to agree with the philosopher who said that whether you stay single or get married, you're making a mistake. Of the two possible blunders, marriage is the least unsatisfactory—especially for so domestic an animal as you, Grouch.

As for news of Rapallo: Gloria burned a finger and then proceeded to get some cactus thistles into it. It is very painful. Sylvia has become friendly with the native girls, at the moment they are all very happy because the Italian Navy (one cruiser) is in the harbor. Tonight Sylvia goes dancing with the Navy and I have instructed her to get what military secrets she can. . . . My tobacco problem is no longer acute. As you know, the government here has a monopoly on tobacco and, aside from Revelation, it imports only Prince Albert, which is American slang for dried ravioli.

Our love to both of you.

Arthur

August 4, 1954

Dear Sheeks:

I received your letter and I was delighted to read that you finally discovered I was married. You say the heading said "Groucho Weds Secretary." If she was a secretary then why does anyone need a wife?

The Krasnas are throwing a big affair for us tonight (personally I like my affairs in private) but they are both very rich in their own right and they insisted on spending a substantial sum of money to show us off.

It's stale stuff I know, but women always seem so much more joyous than men when another schlepper gets hooked. I suppose this is their ultimate triumph and additional proof to themselves that the male is a dead pigeon and that eventually he will be trapped. I don't know what kind of bait they use* but it certainly is effective. If, in addition, you get one that can cook, well that's so much velvet and the husband should get on his knees every night and thank Allah.

Eden has gone quite domestic. Last week she baked a big chocolate cake, copied from a recipe in Good Housekeeping. I took one bite, got my car out of the garage, checked into the Beverly Wilshire hotel and stayed there for three days.

* I do know what kind of bait.

By an odd coincidence it took exactly three days to consume the cake.

I just finished the Hecht book and it knocked me flat. There's an occasional vacuum stretch, but on the whole it's a tremendous piece of work. I know he writes flamboyantly and is needlessly vulgar at times, but that's a big talent and a hell of a courageous one. I had forgotten just how courageous until I read the last hundred pages.

The book is selling well and I am sending you a copy. I don't care what it costs.

I am also sending you a book by E. B. White who, I think, is my favorite American author. I don't believe there are any two writers who are farther apart in style and viewpoint, but they both do something for me. I had no idea my taste in literature was so catholic.

I'm sure you know that the Tugends bought the Zeppo Marxes' menage. It's a beautiful but bizarre looking layout, and it seems to me that instead of being occupied by the Tugends it should be housing a couple like Lupe Velez and Gilbert Roland.

Kiss each other for me—all three of you—and have you thought at all about coming back to the United States, or do you want to wind up another Ezra Pound?

Love,
Groucho

TO DR. SAMUEL SALINGER

April 23, 1954

Dear Doc:

I have just returned from the desert. My younger daughter and I left Beverly Hills in perfect health. She came back with a sore throat and I came back with a cold. As soon as I regain my health I will be off to some other health resort.

I am glad you liked Melinda on the show. We received quite a lot of mail after her performance and I must say it's a responsibility. One has to be careful that the child doesn't lose her sense of values by being singled out at school and other public places as one who has appeared on TV. So far she has been very cute about it, but if she gets the least bit spoiled, I just won't allow her to appear any more.

Regards,
Groucho

P.S. You say, "Your stint on the Rodgers and Hammerstein General Foods program was up to standard." This is one of the least ambiguous insults I have ever received.

TO ALEX GOTTLIEB

September 17, 1962

Dear Alex:

With so many miles between us, I am reluctant to bring up an unpleasant subject, but my gardener informed me that before you scrammed the Garden of Eden for an airless flat in the slums of New York, you gave him carte blanche to proceed with the necessary planting on the hill above my mansion.

Many moons have slipped by and the rainy season, with its customary floods, is about to inundate us with enough water to make Noah (if he's anywhere in the neighborhood) start collecting two of each, again.

To get back to this accursed hill, I suggest you drop me a line authorizing the gardener (who can't read anything except the instructions on a package of seed) to proceed instantly with the project.

I need not remind you that our friendship has been a long and dubious one, and as I am friends of both you and your wife, Polly, it would take but a moment on the telephone to instruct my attorneys to slap a lien on your miserable hovel and, simultaneously, to garnishee Polly.

Remember, the grass is always greener where you don't happen to be the neighbor.

Respectfully yours,
Groucho Marx

September 19, 1962

Dear Groucho:

About your recent semi-illiterate letter concerning some hill you want planted with flowers that spell out your name and the channel on which your show is being rerun—it has arrived.

The letter was read with relish (and non-cholesterol mat- jes herring) at the breakfast table and brought a polite chuckle from the crowd gathered there: namely, my many-millioned brother-in-law (Billy Rose) and his sister, who happens to be my wife and your girl friend. Both of them pretended (1) to enjoy your letter, (2) to understand it.

Happily, I fell in neither group.

However, my interpreter says it means that you want me to pay for planting my own property. Isn't this contrary to all the rules of chicanery?

To get to a more pleasant subject like your gardener, what does he suggest we plant on the hill? How much will it cost? How much will he kick back to you? How much of your kickback will you kick back to me? Could you send me a check in advance so I can give the money to your gardener to plant the hill?

Polly and Billy join me in sending you our fondest and warmest regards.

Your friendly neighborhood neighbor,

Alex

TO NORMAN KRASNA

April 11, 1963

Dear Norman:

You ask about my family. Melinda has gone through a series of careers. A year ago she had just seen "West Side Story" and decided that she was to be the next Natalie Wood. But after a long talk with Dee (that's Howard Hawks's ex, and Eden's sister) she decided she'd be a fashion model.

Then, after I had sunk two hundred bucks in that venture, Melinda reached another decision. She told me that now that they have taught her how to walk (which I thought she did rather well prior to the expenditure of the 200 bucks), she is abandoning the modeling school and plans to embark upon a new career. It's called settlement work. What this consists of, I have no idea, but I'm sure it's going to run into money.

Eden is now a year older than she was last year. Today she had a birthday. She has reached the stage where she is beginning to lie about her age. Last week, in Phoenix, she told the guy who played Zwilling that next week she'd be twenty-four. Pretty soon I'll be able to introduce her as my great granddaughter.

Arthur has just sold another story to Bob Hope.

Thornton Wilder saw "Elizabeth" last Thursday in Tucson, came backstage afterward and told me he enjoyed it immensely. Later that night we had dinner together. I never met a man his age who was so full of joie de vivre. Like all the others, he didn't say it was a great play. No one has ever said that. But he did say he had a wonderful time.

I really have a problem. It's about a fellow who's retired and goes to Hillcrest. Since I don't play cards and I'm pretty well bored with golf (except at the Springs, where even golf is comparatively exciting) what to do?

Incidentally, when I do go to the club now, I go as a transvestite and sit in the women's dining room.

Melinda is going with a basketball player who is six foot four and can stop me in one round if he has to, so I try to keep out of their way. She has her own car, her own telephone, her own room and the last time I saw her was two years ago when she couldn't get the motor started one morning.

Perhaps next year I may sell the house, spend about eight months in New York and the other four in Palm Springs.

Fondly,
Groucho

TO HARPO

September 18, 1964

Dear Adolph:

Remember once, way back in '29, when I suggested a few stocks that would, in time, place you in the same class with Andrew Mellon and Diamond Jim Brady? It was but a few months after this that you were wiped out.

Yesterday at luncheon, your brother, Dr. Gummo Marx, had just returned from the dentist's where he had a few of his teeth filed off and, naturally, was in a more apprehensive mood than he normally would be.

Not knowing how much money you are worth, and seeing no reason why I should, it is difficult for me to give you the benefit of my wisdom. I can only tell you that as far as I'm concerned, if I were to invest $100,000 in a project, it would have to be something like AT&T or Standard Oil of New Jersey.

Take this for what it's worth, but remember, some day when you come creeping to my front door asking for alms for the love of Adolph, don't say I didn't warn you.

I'm glad you are in almost perfect physical condition, and not tossing that 100 grand into the crumbling sands somewhere east of Indio will surely help to keep you that way.

Sincerely yours,
Jeffrey T. Spaulding *

TO HIS NIECE, MINNIE MARX (HARPO'S DAUGHTER)

October 16, 1964

Dear Minnie,

I received your cute letter, and as a matter of fact, I got two letters from you. One was manila and the other was strawberry.

I certainly plan on giving you away to that handsome youth on the 28th of November. I not only intend to stand beside you when you get married, but intend to kiss you before that scoundrel gets a chance to.

You really fooled me. I always had the notion that you would eventually marry a horse. However, on thinking it over, I realize it wouldn't have worked out.

* Groucho's role in "Animal Crackers."

All my love to you and that handsome bounder who is going to steal you away.

Love,
Groucho

TO BETTY COMDEN

October 25, 1964

Dear Betty:

I want you to know how much I appreciated your lovely letter of condolence and love—

Having worked with Harpo for forty years, which is much longer than most marriages last, his death left quite a void in my life.

He was worth all the wonderful adjectives that were used to describe him.

He was a nice man in the fullest sense of the word. He loved life and lived it joyously and deeply and that's about as good an epitaph as anyone can have.

My best to your family and my love to you.

Groucho

P.S. This is a hell of a handwriting for a man who is old enough to be your father. I'm sure Melinda's cat could have done as well, but he wouldn't love you as much as I do.

TO ONE OF MELINDA'S BOYFRIENDS

1965

Dear Mr. Janneck,

John took me round to see his mother,
Then he introduced us to each other.

She put me through a cross examination,
I nearly burned with aggravation.
Then she shook her head, looked at me and said,
Poor John, Poor John.
                    (First sung by Vesta Victoria, in about 1910.)

I received your cute little letter, and I must say, you are a cute little man. I had a cute little letter from my daughter Melinda, which I get every eight weeks, in which she wrote she had thrown you out again and was now going steady with your father. This will come in very handy, if some time in the future she wants to get her ears bobbed. This won't make any difference to me because with the way she now arranges her hair, I'm not sure that she has ears. Do you realize that I have been supporting her for almost nineteen years and that in the last three I couldn't tell you whether her ears stick out, or if they lie close to her face (such as it is) or even if they're clean?

How are you getting along at U.S.C.? How is your I.Q.? Is it as low as it used to be when I first met you? You asked me whether I had seen the queen. I have seen one. It was in a ginny rummy game and it was the queen of Spades.

It was nice receiving your letter. But for heaven's sake don't write me again, for I'll be home at the end of this month, and some night, when my madcap daughter is out on a date, you can come over with your guitar and serenade me beneath my window. This won't be easy, because my bedroom is on the ground floor and we may have to dig a hole so that you can look up to where I'm sleeping. My best to your family, and to whoever Melinda is going with. Your faithful friend, Old Dog Tray.

                              Typed by Eden—
                                    Groucho

P.S. I've just inquired. Melinda's ears are small, pretty and close to her face.

TO HARRY KURNITZ

October 12, 1965

Dear Harry:

. . . Like other friends, you seem concerned about my professional inactivity. You wonder how I make the days pass. Surely (you suggest) I must be bored. And I, in reply, can only say, How little you really know me!

Let me give you a sample day. I hop out of bed at the crack of dawn. At 7 on the nose I have prune juice, whole wheat toast, a touch of marmalade and a pot of Sanka. After brushing my teeth I watch "Woody Woodpecker" and "Captain Kangaroo." At 9:00 I take a nap until noon. Then comes lunch.

I have a can of Metrecal, and a slab of apple pan dowdy. After lunch I take a nap until 2; then I watch "Huckleberry Hound" and, if my wife is out shopping, I watch "Divorce Court." After that I brush my teeth and take a nap until 5:30. Five-thirty is the hour I look forward to. We call it the cocktail hour. We each have a glass of cranberry juice, a cheese dip and a package of Sen Sen.

At six we eat our big meal, Yami Yogurt, apple jack and a sprinkling of sunflower seeds. At 6:30 we watch Soupy Sales and his madcap friends entertain each other with zany antics. At 7 we take two straight-back chairs and face to face, give each other a manicure. At 7:30 we watch "Supermarket Sweep" and "Social Security in Action." Then we play some old recordings of Lawrence Welk and his half-man, half-girl, orchestra. At 8 we take two Seconals, three aspirin and a shot of LSD and fly to slumberland, eagerly looking forward to what thrills the next day has in store for us.

And now—I'm off to the dentist.

Be of good cheer and hurry home.

Groucho

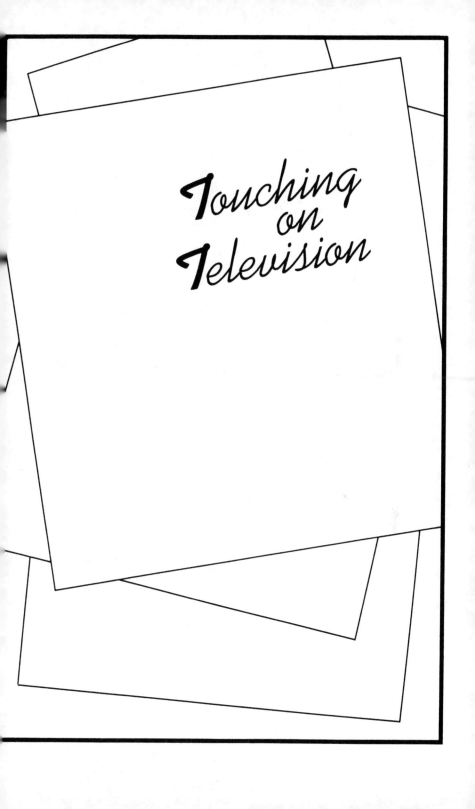

Touching
on
Television

TO FRED ALLEN

Dear Fred:

Well, Hooper is gone but he threatens to return again in the near future, this time with a polling device even more inaccurate then the one he palmed off on Nielsen.

I am beginning to regard myself as the kiss of death to any branch of the amusement industry. When I reached big-time vaudeville it immediately began to rot at the seams. During the days when I was a movie actor, no theater could survive unless it gave away dishes, cheese and crackers, and, during Lent, costume jewelry. I remember one midnight leaving the Marquis Theater in Hollywood after a triple feature with two pounds of Gold Meadow butter, a carton of Pepsi-Cola and 12 chances on a soft water tank.

And now I am having the same effect on radio. According to Hooper, I am now 5th in the national ratings, but who the hell is he polling? I can't find anyone who admits they still have a radio, much less listens to one. Luckily my sponsor's employees are on strike so he has no way of knowing whether I am selling his cars or not. The rich people, or potential car buyers, are the ones who have the television sets. The paupers, or schlepper crowd, still hang on to their portable radios, but unfortunately they're not the ones who buy Chryslers and De Soto station wagons. So my guess is that as soon as the strike is settled, the Chrysler Corp. will ask me to move over to television. Little do they know that in a few short months I will have this new medium croaking its death rattle.

I expect to be in New York around the middle of April and hope we can have one meal together even if it's only at the Automat.

Regards,
Groucho

march 31, 1950

dear groucho—

i do not think you are the asp that has bestowed the kiss of death on vaudeville, the picture industry and radio. vaudeville committed suicide, the picture business ran out of adjectives and radio was thrown to the cretin. at the present time, your radio show is the only one that is mentioned by critics and listeners who, because they have dirty windows and cannot see the aerials of their neighbors' roofs, do not know about television and still listen to radio. if you want to give television the buss of rigor mortis you had better hurry. after a few recent shows, dogs in this section have been dragging television sets out into the yards and burying them.

the paper claims that "the homosexuals in capital are estimated at 5,000." it looks as though garner was the only nance to ever leave washington. you may have read that arthur godfrey has a new plane. when godfrey isn't on the air he is in it. i still haven't seen ace to give him your regards. fortunately, i am not a card player. if i had to wait this long to see an ace i would be the talk of the friars. be of good cheer. if the chrysler workers get the pension fund you may be declared in. let me know when you will be here. regards—

f. allen

october, 1950

groucho—

every sunday, after mass, we stop for breakfast at the stage delicatessen. at this hour max, the proprietor, is host to a motley throng. horse players, bookmakers, cream soda lovers and sturgeon gourmets. how i, a gentile, get in there, i don't know. since the same characters meet every sunday there is a friendly atmosphere rampant that no airwick can subdue. when the lox is running good and the cream cheese is spreading easily those assembled, between smacking their chops and wiping their greasy fingers on their vests, will discuss some topic that is currently engaging the general public.

yesterday, the air conditioning was not functioning at the stage. there was a gamey flatulent essence dominating the room but the flanken was lean and spirits were high. talk turned to the tallulah show. every tout, every bookie and every questionable customer present had seen the program.

eating was suspended. chicken fat was shaken from fingers to point them. novy was shredded from snags of teeth to make way for encomiums. the countermen stopped slicing to mingle their opinions with those of the chef who looked out of the kitchen door while keeping his eyes on an order of scrambled eggs and onions not too brown. a fat man put down a dr. brown celery tonic bottle and emitted an effervescent burp while he paid his tribute to the hour. a man sitting on a toilet bowl swung open the men's room door and added his kudo to the acclaim.

everybody in the delicatessen agreed that the tallulah

show had been great. this is a cross section that the surveys never reach. i bring you this report to let you know how the man in the street reacted to the show.

i thought the show was excellent. the mechanical miss hurt a little and meredith was winded trying to get the panel bit off but over all portland and i agreed that it had taste, intelligent fun and stature. regards—

f. a.

october 13, 1950

dear groucho—

you realize, i hope, that it is a hell of a lot of trouble to go to to put on a so-called tv show just to arouse you to the point where you would write me a letter. i don't want to be in television. i met goody the other day and said that i never heard from you. now you have made a liar out of me by proxy.

you are right about the senator [claghorn] he was out with a show and couldn't be here for rehearsals. last spring norman krasna suggested that i do the alley with puppets. it was the only way we could use claghorn. he flew in from detroit the night of the show. his show is closing this week and i may try the original alley cast in the november show.

the revue type of show is the wrong approach. we have to work in a theater with an audience. the cameras can go noplace and the intimacy that is so important in the medium is totally lacking. i hope, after a few shows, to shed the audience and attempt to do something with more scope.

you are fortunate, i think, that your show lends itself so well to the alleged new medium. portland and i saw your first one. the film is good and it is a pleasure to be able to enjoy some good dialogue without having to watch a lot of broken-down small-time acts, burlesque bits and tired blackouts. all of

(74)

the shows here, the comedy shows i mean, seem to be using the same devices. this should make your refreshing half hour a novelty doubly welcome as the season goes along. at least you are spared all of the headaches we have. today, i was informed that midgets are scarce "all of the good midgets are working, etc." i am not going to be able to shake off too many of these crises.

meantime, thanx for your letter and regards.

f. allen

November 7, 1950

Dear Fred:

Thanks for the piece by Goody and the note which accompanied it. I thought it was a sensible and extremely complimentary piece. The fact that he lived at my house without paying for his room and board may have influenced him slightly, but on the other hand I have always regarded myself as a splendid fellow and a brilliant comedian to boot (make up your own joke).

Got quite a bit of you yesterday. I heard you on the NBC radio show and thought it was a mistake to do a sketch on Benny since he was the one NBC wanted the public to ignore. Other than that, you and the show were both good. Then, nothing daunted, I watched you on television and I must say the show was an enormous improvement over your maiden effort. I particularly liked the Titus Moody stuff, but the whole show was so much better balanced than the first one. You had close-ups and they also gave you a chance to talk and that's good enough for me. My guess is that your television problems are over and that you will eventually represent in television what you did in radio—the best what am.

By the way, Portland who, I understand, is your wife,

looked mighty sexy in those upper lengths. You better keep her out of California for this state is overflowing with Errol Flynns and, in a pathetic way, me.

Your friend, and all around good fellow,

Groucho

april 30th, 1951

dear groucho—

i spoke to goody this a.m., and dropped several hints that you would not be averse to getting a few laughs on the tallu-lah show come sunday.

they have margaret truman and when i left they were try-ing to book macarthur. if they get the general we may end up with all of the straight lines in the script. if macarthur refuses to do straight for truman i am sure that goody won't be able to talk him into standing around while you and i get a few snickers. they will probably flood the studio and have mac wade through the audience up to the stage.

i should warn you that this is the last show and from the writers' collective attitude i take it that they are not going to take any crap from any of us on the show. they have been tacit all season and i sense that a wrong word may stampede the writing staff and cause them to beat one of the guests to death with a straight man. i merely mention this so that you may be on guard.

mr. salpeter recently trapped me into investing in one of his ventures with the usual results. if you have any money i suggest that you leave it home. i believe mr. s is planning an-other venture.

portland joins me in best wishes. we will look forward to seeing you. regards—

fred allen

May, 1951

Dear Fred:

I was just about to answer your letter when word was flashed throughout Southern California that you were soon to arrive for one more assault against the motion picture industry, this time with Ginger Rogers. Well, if you have to go that's the way to go.

If you do come alone be sure to bring some fishing tackle, for my cellar leaks, and we can have a high old time down there, swapping stories and exchanging worms.

The weather here has been glorious. The pussywillows are in full bloom and though I am loath to say this, I think the little willows have been getting more pussy this year than ever before.

The May wine is just beginning to acquire its full body. You see, because of the difference in time, the wine you drink in the east early in the spring only comes into its full maturity out here during the winter solstice. And the crops have been beautiful. The Lord, Fred, has been mighty good to us. We harvested enough corn not only for us, but for the stock as well, and the syrup has been flowing as though it were possessed. Mother says I am blasphemous, but we all have to have our little joke. We look for a hard winter, for only yesterday I noticed an extra heavy growth of fur on the left side of my upstairs maid, and that means the storms will soon be upon us.

Other than this there is nothing to tell you. As you know, we miss the clump of your hobnailed boots on our eiderdown, and can only hope and pray that ere long Ethan Allen will give up that silly siege of Fort Ticonderoga and send you back to us. Well, I'm fagged out now so I guess I'll turn in. Last night I spent almost the whole night shucking corn and mother said I'm not shuckin' as well as I used to. I guess I must be getting on. Mother also said I'm not getting on as often as I used to. Well, that's the way it goes.

Love,
Groucho

P.S. The brood sow is with pig again.

August 30, 1951

Dear Fred:

It is very difficult to correspond regularly with one who is not a woman. This, in case you care, explains why my letters are so infrequent. If, for example, one is corresponding with an attractive female—preferably not too old—there's always the likelihood that, at some future date you might be able to get closer to her. Corresponding with a man—a man our age, at any rate—soon reduces itself to a mutual cataloguing of aches and pains, and the constant trials they are both being subjected to by the tax department.

Please don't assume from this that your letters are not worth receiving. The joy they give me can only be compared to the happiness I experienced years ago when a wire would arrive saying that we had received a year's booking on the Pantages Circuit. I cherish each letter as though it were "a gem of purest ray serene." This, in case you care, is lifted from Thomas Gray and can be found on page 262 of Bartlett's Quotations.

My friend Goody tells me that you're London-bound with the rowdy and predictable Tallulah. As one who has journeyed the high seas a number of times, I trust that you will beware of card sharks, pool sharks and, in case you should be lucky enough to fall overboard, just plain sharks.

I wish I were going with you. What high old times we could have—Goody, you and I. Three old biddies swapping aches and pains, telling tall tales of romantic exploits and cursing television. Yes, Fred, we could make the ship rock with our laughter.

So have a good time and my best to the Duchess.

Groucho

september 1, 1951

dear groucho—

i know that you must derive much more pleasure dashing off a note to some old bag you hope to tree on your next trip east than you do writing to goody or to me. there is an old legend written on the wall of the men's room at the martha washington hotel. it reads—it is better to marry a young girl and satisfy her curiosity than to marry a widow and disappoint her. when you write ace you know you are going to get an answer. when you write me you know that the letter will never show up in court with a request for a breach of something settlement.

goody sailed last week on the queen mary. several days later i read that the queen mary had the roughest august crossing in its history. if his dramamine didn't work we may have lost a citizen. goody will probably stay over there. portland and i are flying over sept. 9th. the last i heard at nbc was that they were trying to book bee lillie, gracie fields and the andrews sisters on the first show from london. that will be some novelty. you hear all of those people on the air over here year after year. if they would book british talent never heard here the venture would have novelty at least. if the show stinks goody can always blame the labor government.

meantime, hope that all goes medium rare. say hello to harry tugend and irving brecher and to the late mr. hutton. banzai—

fred allen

October 18, 1951

Dear Fred:

Despite the fact that I regard myself as an extremely glamorous figure, I rarely receive any mail that would indicate that the fair sex, as a sex, has any interest in me. No cravats, no Johnson & Murphy shoes, no expensive stogies ever darken my mailbox. The following is a brief sampling of what nestles in my wastebasket this morning.

The first envelope I opened was from a quack cruising under the pseudonym of Dr. Bendricks. Apparently he has seen me on tv, for he wrote that he could equip me with a new set of atomic glands. He calls his method the "Chemistry of Natural Immunity." He said he was confident that these new glands would do the trick. I am not sure what trick he was referring to but it certainly sounded encouraging. Unfortunately, I have no idea who Bendricks is. Is he a reputable scientist? The whole thing is too much for me. At any rate, temporarily I am throwing the whole thing in the lap of Dr. Morris Fishbein.

The next letter was from the proprietor of a Beverly Hills liquor store, and a gloomier prophet I have rarely read. He warned me that liquor prices were going sky high and that I had better lay away 30 or 40 cases of hard booze before war is officially declared. Since my drinking these days is confined to swallowing a thimbleful of cooking sherry each night before dinner, his letter left me in a fairly calm condition.

The third letter was from the Continental Can Company pleading with me to send in my proxy on my 100 shares of stock which, incidentally, have gone down seven points since I bought them. The letter pointed out, rather querulously I thought, that I was a stockholder in a giant and growing corporation, but that its officers were helpless to proceed with the business at hand unless I was willing to cooperate and send in my proxy, and pronto. The whole company, they implied, was going to hell. Thousands of stockholders were sitting in a drafty auditorium in Wilmington, Delaware, unable to unseat the present officials unless they were morally strengthened by my proxy.

The next letter was from the Electric Bond and Share Company (in case you've forgotten, this is the uptown equivalent of Goldman-Sachs). In 1929 this outfit reduced my bank account by $38,000. Unfortunately, through some confusion in the bookkeeping department, I find myself 21 years later, still the owner of one-half share. In case you are not too familiar with current Wall Street prices, an entire share can be purchased for $1.10. They, too, were after my proxy. I have tried many times to dispose of this shrunken security. One year in desperation I even sent them the half share, special delivery and registered, but a few days later it came back—this time to make matters worse, with six cents postage due. One year I destroyed the God-damned stock but it didn't faze EB&S one bit. I am on their books and apparently they are determined to keep me there—at least until the next market crash.

The next was a letter from AFRA. They pointed out that I was some months behind in my dues and unless the money was forthcoming in the near future they were planning on pulling out the musicians, stage hands, cameramen, electricians, studio policemen and an ex-vice president of radio who stands in front of NBC giving away free ducats for Spade Cooley.

So, Fred, I say to hell with the U. S. mails. I would be deeply indebted to you if you would write your congressman asking him to vote against any further appropriations for the post office. Without funds this monster would soon wither away and die and I could then spend my declining years with an empty wastebasket and a light heart.

Regards,
Groucho

november 3, 1951

dear groucho—

your recent letter, complaining about the quality of fan mail you have been receiving, has had to await a reply until your problem had been thoroughly mulled. unlike cider mulling, this takes time. the man bent on mulling a batch of cider merely heats his poker, or his shish kebab lance, over an open fire and plunges it into his cider. a man who mulls over a letter may be busy mulling for weeks.

it seems to me that your dilemma is posed by high standards. you cater to a class of radio and tv owner who can write. when you appeal to a literate element, people who not only own radio and tv sets but who also own pens and pencils and know how to use them, you have to expect mail.

if you are going to eliminate mail you cannot hope to do it through closing up the post office and the postal department. without the post office politicians would have no places to put their brothers-in-law. you can only stop this avalanche of fan mail through lowering your standards and going after the illiterate crowd.

i have become involved in a morris office package for tv. we have done one show which turned out badly. we are supposedly to dramatize old benchley, thurber, twain, etc., magazines pieces. most of the material i have seen won't come to life from the magazine page. the other stuff that might work has been stolen or the rights sold to picture companies for shorts. the shows that work once a month have no steady writing or production staffs. you get people who stop on their way to a danny thomas or jack carson show. i do another on nov. 11th and it, too, looks like a mess up to now.

regards—

fred allen

december 27th, 1951

dear groucho—

upon my return to new york i reported to the writers' galley at nbc. instead of flogging their wits i found goody and his merry men piling their money on a table in the center of the room. they were raising enough money to bail out the star of their program should the case take a nasty turn later in the week. with the bail money up i guess they will proceed with the script feeling a mite more secure.

i started "the later ego" * on the plane. i hope that you noted the item that involved the reshooting of a scene in the film "madonna of the seven moons." the scene was an attempted rape of the chaste angela and the actor kept forgetting that the british board of censors will not pass any seduction scene unless the seducer has one foot on the floor. apparently sex in england is something like snooker.

the bellboy, at the beverly wilshire, told me that my tv show would be on this coming sunday. nobody in the morris office knew what had happened to my kinescope. how this bellboy acquired his information i don't know. either he is the sponsor, plying his hobby, or he knows something. if you see it i will appreciate your reaction.

portland and i both appreciate your hospitality and we hope that you will have a vigorous new year. i have one more tv show, jan. 6th. after that, i may learn a trade or something. trust that all goes well.

regards—

f. allen

* Essays by the late James Agate.

January 8, 1952

Dear Fred:

I am glad to hear that you bought Agate's "Later Ego" and also that you liked it.

Tugend and I both watched your show last week and thought it was a substantial improvement over the ones that had preceded it. The part I liked best was the kidding of "I Remember Mama," etc. You undoubtedly know that you are at your best when you talk satirically. This you do better than anyone else and it is the kind of stuff you should bear down on.

I must point out, in advising you, that I picked the Giants to subdue the Yankees, Buddy Baer to beat Joe Louis, and Landon to be elected President.

I see in this morning's Variety that a certain performer is now giving out awards. Since it would be impossible for him to get one himself—other than for boredom—he simply locked himself up in a room and came out with the announcement that, in his opinion, Red Skelton was the best comedian in television. I don't object to Red Skelton being named the best comedian, but an award from this fellow is a little like the branch manager of a Nedick's orange juice stand announcing that Romanoff's is a good restaurant.

I hope you and Portland are well and that you have a sizable New Year.

Groucho

july 31, 1952

dear groucho—

in recent weeks i have been subjected to a chain of indignities, involving the removing of my appendix, that may cause my permanent undoing. i have intended to write you about my experience and how i missed part of the heat spell by purposely staying under anesthesia for an extra three hours. the reason i haven't written you is because i received a letter from harry tugend saying that he had just recovered from kidney stones, arthritis, pinched nerve, jaundice and hepatitis. i knew harry would be telling about his maladies when the round table met and the thought gave me an inferiority complex. "how can i write groucho," i reasoned, "about my stinking little vermiform lark when harry has practically had his entire anatomy in a sling?" i know how you californians think. after a recital of harry's ailments, a local boy, and then the man from the east with the lousy appendix. "we do things bigger in california, etc." i could hear the reaction. that is why you haven't had word from me. my complex has subsided a bit and i imagine that harry's triumph has died down around hillcrest. this may be the right time to get word through to you.

after all of these years i sure thought that i would arrive at utter mckinley's patio with all of my equipment. i guess the old saying is true. jesse crawford used to say "never trust an orange."

have started my book. one chapter finished. hope all goes well.

regards—

fred allen

june 12, 1953

dear groucho—

i have just returned from boston. it is the only sane thing to do if you find yourself up there. in the boston paper i saw two headlines. "groucho marx in hospital for minor surgery." (some under-age ailment, i assume.) the other headline read "eden coming to boston for operation." i thought that after your new york trip you and your wife, eden, were both exhausted. i later learned that it was anthony eden who was coming to the lahey clinic.

now that i know which eden is in an oxygen percolator the concern is about you. since i have been practically out of work for two seasons i have been able to get a little publicity collapsing and being taken to the hospital or giving out announcements that my blood pressure is worse and I will have to stop working. now that you are getting into my sick racket i am a dead duck. i will either have to go to work or get some exciting disease.

i have a new book. "encyclopedia of aberrations." there are some definitions of "head bangers," "philoneism" etc. there must be a million head bangers in show business. if i can't work later i think i will try to get a job in a psychopathic ward as the head banger pro. for novice head bangers i might be of some help. there is one definition in the book. an "afradisiac" is an afra member who chases dames. portland joins me in best wishes. we hope that everything is exaggerated and that you will be robust in short order.

regards—

f. allen

June 23, 1953

Dear Freddie:

I must say that when a man is flat on his back a letter from the Boston strong boy gives one a moral and spiritual uplift and makes one realize that all those that reside outside the hospital are not his enemies.

While incarcerated at the cold cuts emporium I received quite a lot of mail and oddly enough most of it from Baptists, Methodists and Catholics.

This morning, for example, I got a letter from a Rev. Pfister. He wrote me that someone had requested that he send me a booklet and a medal. The last medal I received was as a runner-up in a woman's tennis tournament some years ago in Far Rockaway, so I am going to hang this shrine of St. Jude around my neck. If it does nothing else, perhaps it will grow some hair to replace the foliage that was shaved away by a journeyman barber the night I entered Cedars of Lebanon. He came in and without any preliminaries grabbed hold of my feet, trussed me up in the air and scraped me to the marrow. There I was—an old Christmas turkey, in probably the most undignified moment of my entire theatrical career—hanging in midair being clipped by a total stranger.

Today I finally emerged from the land of the poached egg and tapioca pudding and I am slowly storing up strength for whatever Fate has in store for me.

I see by the papers that you are now a member of the Brandeis faculty and that Sid Perelman was made an upper classman. Variety says you were very good, but then you always are.

Best to both of you,

Groucho

july 5, 1953

dear groucho—

i have been concerned about your operation. it is a bit late, i know, but from your description of the procedure—"the crotch plucking," "the marrow scraping" and "the trussing up"—i am convinced that you were not delivered in pain to the cedars of lebanon. you must have been carried in to some poultry market in the neighborhood. i hope you are fully recovered and your parts restored to their potency.

sid perelman and i appeared at the brandeis university commencement week festivities. sid sucked me into the deal which leonard bernstein was promoting. brandeis has only been in existence for three years, not long enough to have any old grads to return to the campus. leonard invented something called the "fun festival." for our evening leonard hustled irwin corey, jack gilford, alice pearce, arthur kober, sid and me. it takes a bit of mental doing to conjure up an academic evening involving this all-star cast. sid and i made a two-man panel and discussed the development of the "comic performer" using the acts to illustrate the various types of comic characters. the audience enjoyed the evening and sid showed up with an opening monologue that was very funny.

we are leaving for maine tomorrow. we are going to stay up near doc rockwell's house for about three weeks. we are starting the tv show on aug. 18th and i will have to be back. portland joins me in best wishes. will contact you when we get back at the end of the month. carry on—

f. allen

july 22, 1953

dear mr. marx—

you were quoted in the dining room of this inn as of yesterday.

a thyroid housewife, sitting behind me, said, "it's like that funny story groucho marx told."

the funny story turned out to be the one about the man who was saying grace in a low voice—somebody at the table said, "i can't hear you." the man said, "i wasn't talking to you."

just wanted you to know that if you have the marx tradition under control along the sunny slopes of california we have the rock-ribbed coast of maine groucho conscious.

this inn is a rustic establishment. the outdoor life is over-done. at midnight the house detective makes his rounds of the grounds shaking the trees. this has kept monkey business down under the 1952 season.

there is a town so dull up here the tide went out one day and never came back in.

we are going back next week to start working on the new???? show. regards—

f. allen

July 30, 1953

Dear Freddie Boy:

I received a picture of a crab, which I presume was Dr. Rockwell thinly disguised. I also read Goody's piece about you and me and though I doubt whether there was any speculation on Madison Avenue about our relationship, it did make interesting reading. The line about the tide going out and never returning is a wonderful joke and was received with cheers at the Round Table at Hillcrest. It's the first clean line that has been uttered at that table in over three years.

I note what you say about Laurie doing a definitive book on vaudeville. I hope it's more accurate than his previous publication.

Anyway, the book I want you to write would be informative but also humorous, and in your own particular style. I don't know how to get this through your head, Fred. You are the best humorist of our time, and still you won't do a God-damned thing about it. Of all the millions of books, good, bad and otherwise, there isn't one by Fred Allen. I have lectured you about this time and time again and I will continue to do so until you capitulate.

I know nothing about your show. Is it going to be live, film, kinescope, and when will it appear out here?

I'd like to see it. And it had better be good because I just got a new 27 inch set and it reveals everything.

My vacation is about over and in another three or four weeks I'll be back hoodwinking the customers.

I hope you are well.

My best to Portland.

Groucho

august 21, 1953

dear groucho—

we finally foaled the initial show without benefit of midwife or dr. kinsey. harriet van horne and jack o'brien panned the hell out of it but nobody at the agency has thrown an executive at me up to now so perhaps we will survive.

goody called me up and said that he thought when we get the bugs out of it (i suspect that this is a nice way of saying a thing is lousy—when you get the bugs out of it) it should make a good vehicle for me. the first show the interviews were cut to nothing and the overall confusion made me nervous which certainly didn't help me with the ad libbing. actually there was no opportunity to ad lib. i had so many ad libs left over when the show finished i talked to myself for two hours.

you were right about film. you haven't a chance with any sustained comedy material with this sort of a setup. another factor is that with a quiz the comedian is in contact with the contestants during the game and can do anything he wants during the questions and answers. with this talent setup i am only in contact with the contestant for the short interview. when the act starts i disappear completely and have to start all over with the next contestant.

we are looking at the kine tomorrow and i will know

more about the problems. i think the show gets out there in two weeks. if you do happen to see the first one will appreciate your opinion and suggestions. if i can get enough time to ramble around and talk it may work out. but if we are saddled with the acts and the device i will be a grilled gander. hope all goes well.

f. a. (night clerk at the barthold inn)

September 4, 1953

Dear Fred:

I didn't see your first show, but I did see the second, and to get right to the point I would say that the chief trouble with it is the fact that there isn't enough of Fred Allen. Some way should be found to eliminate those three professional judges who have big reputations and do nothing. Besides, they look terrible.

If you are going to have a Fred Allen show, you had better have Fred Allen. God knows I am no play doctor; hardly know enough to get out of the rain (which, by the way, we could use desperately out here). But I repeat, your stuff was funny, but there wasn't enough of it.

As I told you last summer, the fact that you are on live will always be a handicap. It's a little like making a movie without previewing, editing or cutting it, but apparently there is nothing you can do about it.

I won't burden you with a long letter, nor do I expect an answer in the near future. I know you must be busy, nervous and tired, trying to whip this thing into shape.

I will watch the show again next Tuesday and will write you my views.

Best to you and Portland.

Groucho

March 17, 1954

Dear Fred:

I will be in New York the 25th of March. I am doing the customary unfunny guest shot, this time for General Foods. They may make him a lieutenant for this. Hope to see you.

Excuse brevity but I am taking some full-length pictures this afternoon for a calendar company and I have to rush over and get my clothes off.

Best to you and your nymph.

Groucho

august 6, 1954

groucho—

i have recently finished a book called "treadmill to oblivion." it will be published in november by little, brown and co.

apparently the morris office and all of the goodson and todmans not only couldn't put humpty dumpty back together again, they haven't been able to sell the new quiz show. if nothing happens i am thinking about trying to write an autobiography and incorporate some of the material you suggested about the vaudeville years. i can work on it all winter and when i get things organized i may come out and talk to some of the old vaudevillians. of course, if they cross me up and finally sell the show to some insane industrialist i will have to set back my literary plans. i hope to start the book, however.

portland joins me in best wishes to all marxes in and out of swimming pools wherever you are.

f. allen

August 16, 1954

Dear Freddie:

It's a little ironical, and certainly doesn't speak well for the television racket, when its only first-class mind is now looking for a sponsor. When I see the gibbering idiots on panel shows, quiz shows, and other half hours of tripe that infest this medium, it doesn't seem possible that you should be without a sponsor.

The other night I accidentally watched a panel show, I don't know the name of it, but boy, did they yock it up! The tiniest wheeze was received with gales of laughter.

In the old days the audience supplied the laughter; now the actors do it for them. This is certainly the era of Do It Yourself.

Before I'd yield to this sort of thing, I would retire and open a small hat factory in Danbury, Conn.

I see now that Cantor is starting a daily newspaper column for the Bell Syndicate. The only man in show business who should write a daily funny piece is a Mr. Allen, and why he doesn't do it I don't know.

I hope this letter doesn't sound as though I thought you were hungry, cold, and about to be ejected from the Mills Hotel for non-payment of rent. I know you don't need the money, Fred; it's just that I hate to see so much talent not being used.

Regards,
Groucho

October 11, 1954

Dear Freddie:

I am patiently awaiting the publication date of your book. I haven't written you for some time because I have been busy writing ad libs for next season. I have already written all my ad libs for 1954 and most of them are pretty awful.

To show you what an expert I am on sports, I won $100 on the Giants. Some charitable fellow, who doesn't want to die and leave all his estate to the mercy of the inheritance tax, paid me 100 to 50 that Cleveland would win the Series. So I won $100; $50 of this I promised to my wife, Eden, if she would sit and watch the games with me. After the first game, Eden, who likes baseball about as much as I like zucchini, offered to return the money if I wouldn't insist on her watching any more.

At any rate, I won the hundred; I gave Eden $50; and of the other $50 I spent $40 to get the main tube replaced in my television set, which had blown out the day Dusty Rhodes hit the pinch homer. This left me a total of $10 which went for hair dye; the nervous strain of watching the series had turned my hair snow white.

Are you reading my son's pieces about me in the S. E. Post? I had no idea I was such a nut.

Best to you and Portland.

Groucho

November 22, 1954

Dear Fred:

Thanks for the clippings on Arthur's book. Even the New Yorker praised it—that astonished and delighted me. As I said, it seems to me I come off as quite a nut in this book, I don't mean a deliberate one like Jack Rose or Coolidge . . . I realize now I've been crazy all these years without being aware of it. Well, enough of me. I'm pretty sick of the subject and hope this finds you the same.

I believe I told you how much I enjoyed your book. I

don't know whether it will sell because it's pretty special, but this should encourage you on to greater literary efforts.

I was on the Chrysler "Shower of Stars" last Thursday night. When I say I was on it, I mean it was a courtesy surprise visit. I had one line which was, "Let's get something we can all enjoy." The idea was that Betty Grable and Harry James were sitting in the front seat of a De Soto and I was hiding in the back, on the floor. Thus when Betty Grable pressed the radio on the dashboard, I would jump forward and press the radio dial again—tuning to my show—and then mouth that immortal line, "Let's get something we can all enjoy."

Right before the show, the producer asked me if I would eliminate the line. He said the show was running overlength. I argued stubbornly for a while but finally asked them if I could use half the line, "Let's turn on something." They said this wouldn't make any sense—so I said the hell with it and crouched back again in the bottom of the car. The big surprise was supposed to be me bouncing up from this into the scene. I guess I didn't crouch low enough. . . . Either that, or the cameraman was drunk. At any rate, the audience saw me all through the scene, although I was supposed to be hidden; and when I jumped up for the surprise, I guess I didn't jump high enough or I jumped too high, for I happened to wind up in a spot where the windshield blocked my face.

Gummo, unfortunately, forgot to get the contract beforehand for this show, so I doubt if I will ever get the pittance I was promised. As I was lying there in the back of the car, it occurred to me that in "Cocoanuts" and "Animal Crackers" I had about 90 sides of dialogue. Here I had only one line and they even clipped that. Well, I guess that's show business.

Best to you and the Stormtrooper.

love,
Groucho

november 26, 1954

dear groucho—

i couldn't see "shower of cars" up in boston. there was no
set available. there are sets in boston but you have to know
somebody. the reason the cbs goons tried to scrow your artis-
tic triumph was obvious. as one of nbc's giant men they were
out to get you. i am surprised that you were even able to get
your face in front of the camera let alone blow the one line.
columbia is a university and columbia is the gem of the ocean
but columbia is dedicated to knock off you nbc stars.

i spoke to a number of book people up there and they
said that arthur's book was doing very well. i thought the
magazine might hurt the book sale but one of the little, brown
co. executives told me that the magazine usually helps the book
sale. that should insure the book's success and some additional
dough for arthur. i thought he did a wonderful job. the book
has a nice quality and for a close relative you come off very
well. if arthur had called it "life with father" you could have
turned the book into a play and given lindsay and crouse
something to worry about.

as you say, "treadmill to oblivion" has a limited appeal.
the publisher feels that if they sell 25,000 copies it will be a
big deal. the one thing that i feel good about is that nobody
criticized the writing. i am thinking about starting the other
book after the first of the year. i would not want to do an
entire story of vaudeville but in some sort of an autobiographical thing i could use a number of vaudeville chapters as long
as the material i had would hold up. i have to wait for some
other business to slink away before i can really start. i will
advise you later on.

goody has a show that he wants me to try. he has probably told you about it. amateur writers send in material and
the scenes, bits, monologues, etc., are cast with the best talent
available. i don't see how you can sustain the idea. the standard

of the professional writing is low enough. depending on amateurs to send in playable scripts i think would be fatal. goody thinks i am nuts, i am sure, but i had stuff sent in to us for twenty years and i was never able to find a potential writer among hordes who were bombarding us with assorted funny stuff.

hope all goes well. portland, a former actress employed by mr. gordon, sends her tousled regards.

fred allen

December 23, 1954

Dear Freddie:

The Yule Season is once again upon us. Each year it seems to arrive a little faster. I note what you say about your personal mail piling up. This is one of the reasons I allow long intervals to elapse between our letters. You're busy. I'm lazy and the world is full of a low-grade virus. A small hunk of it attacked me last week and put me hors de combat.

As I lay there in bed with a hot-water bottle on my dogs, an electric blanket covering my hairy chest and a half dozen assorted antibiotics tossing around inside of me, I wondered what the hell the world was coming to. I wondered too whether I would ever again be well enough to stagger down to NBC in last year's De Soto, sans power steering, sans wrap-around windshield, and once again hoodwink the audience; and surprisingly enough I didn't seem to care much whether I made it or not. Geriatrics has become a wondrous science. The medics can now stretch your life out an additional dozen years but they don't tell you that most of these years are going to be spent flat on your back while some ghoul with thick glasses and a matted skull peers at you through a machine that's hot out of "Space Patrol."

Although I didn't feel much like writing I couldn't let

the holiday season pass without trying to spread a little cheer.
My love to you both.

Groucho

february 22, 1955

dear groucho—

since my book was published i have been busier than a
good humor man on a hot day. i have been appearing on radio
programs, tv shows, in bookshops, at seances and finally ended
up with a super-book plug on a spectacular a medium was presenting on a ouija board.

whether these antics sell books i do not know. it seems to
be the accepted practice in the book trade. the minute some
deluded juggins writes a book he is supposed to be on the de-
fensive. he is supposed to be at the beck and call of every dame
who is hustling a book club to say a few words or he is to be
available for window appearance at sundry bookstores. mail is
to be answered most of which comes from people who like to
read but who do not like to buy books, hospitals who have
small budgets but want the book for their libraries and church
bazaars who want autographed copies to auction off to raise
money to provide a low-hung deacon with a durable truss.

you touted me on to this writing thing. you are sitting
smugly on your wafer-thick prat making a fortune and meeting a nice set of people on the program. i am fending off the
dregs of the literati.

i went over to philadelphia recently. the sat eve post
people want me to do an autobiography. at the luncheon mr.
hibbs was bragging about a copy of arthur's book you had
autographed for him. i am considering the project. i have been
talking to a number of old vaudeville actors but the research
is too costly. i have been bitten during each interview. i got

nothing and so far i have gone for a suit, a winter coat and too much money. mulling it over i don't think i could sustain an entire book on vaudeville. i might make use of some extraneous matter to embellish the chapters that would concern my experiences in the small-time domain.

if you are tired of it all and want to make a fortune without working i will let you in on my invention. it is sweeping church parishes around the country. i have patented a pulpit that can be turned into a bingo table. don't let hope and crosby grab this off. get in on it. i am also working on a long fly for short-armed men's trousers.

life is uphill—don't put down the load. carry on—hope everything is okay. the rating is up. if you are at home i will call you when we get in. meantime—you name it—

f. allen

July 29, 1955

Dear Fred:

I was pleased to see you again last Sunday if only on a TV tube. I assume from this that you have partially recovered from that clip joint where you were incarcerated, and I am sure one of the reasons that you returned to work so swiftly was the size of the bill they slipped you when you staggered out of the ward.

At one point in the proceedings last Sunday, you wore glasses. I wish you would always wear them. They make you look years younger and give your face the same kind of softness that General Grant had at Appomattox.

Seriously, they do something for you.

Best to you and Porty from an old party named,

Groucho

august 2nd, 1955

dear groucho—

thanx a lot for the glasses suggestion. i always come off like a dufflebag with a nose, photogenically. i made a picture with jack benny. i had all of my hair, teeth, bones and blood. jack had a hairpiece that looked like a basset hound's rump, he was wearing hillard mark's teeth, his bones were rented from a chiropractor and his blood was borrowed from a hemophiliac who started bleeding suddenly and had forgotten to bring his pail with him. when the picture came out jack looked like a westmore dream. i looked like some fag caught in a revolving door at the sloane house.

i had a running gag to start with the woman who wrote me about wearing the glasses. she wrote me again saying that my glasses were old-fashioned and to get a new pair. it could run along with a few laughs for three or four weeks but on this show things get lost in the shuffle. it is difficult to get laughs. you can only pick points out of the conversation and some nights the conversation sounds like something you might over-hear in a morgue.

regards—

f. allen

September 12, 1955

Dear Fred:

I see that the Dodgers won the pennant. I don't care much either way. What startles me is the swiftness with which an-other year has rolled around. It seems only a few months since Durocher was a hero and Willie Mays was seriously being considered as a running mate for Stevenson. I must say that this new year has disturbed me only physically and mentally.

While you were basking in the cool, crisp autumn air of the eastern shore, we went through a week of temperatures that are usually seen only on a medical thermometer. I went to Vegas to cool off, saw Lena Horne there at a nightclub (I'd forgotten that she is a one-woman heat wave). At any rate, I got so hot watching her that I had to return to Beverly Hills.

I'm now involved in an escapade loosely called "Fifty Years of Show Biz." This allegedly will be the history of vaudeville from 1900 to 1950. It's actually a government project, for the revenue department will grab off about 85% of what I get. Why I persist in doing these shots baffles me. I guess it's a challenge. The last one I did was also a challenge. Halfway through, someone stood up in the audience and loudly announced that he'd be goddamned if he couldn't be funnier than that. I couldn't argue with him because I could see his point. Some day I'll get smart and just remain on my little stool, confusing and baffling the peasants.

Glad to see that you are working steadily—and hope you continue to wear the glasses.

Best to you and your honorable wife—from your honorable friend,

Groucho

TO GOODMAN ACE

August 9, 1950

Dear Goody,

Our friendship, a frail one at best, has reached an impasse. I dislike New York and don't want to go there, and you despise Hollywood and refuse to come here. Perhaps we could compromise and meet once a year in Kansas City. We could lunch at Nancy's, and in the evening, after an afternoon at

Johnny Kling's billiard emporium, we could dine at the kosher restaurant across from the Orpheum stage door.

I am delighted that you (unlike Variety) liked the TV spot I did for Popsicle. I didn't think it was too good, but it had value as a guide to what we can do once we find our way around.

Last week the Friars, having run out of theatrical celebrities, tendered a dinner to Harry Karl. Karl has a black mustache, is married to Marie McDonald (The Body) and operates 112 shoe stores. Not being a Friar and having always worn Johnson & Murphy shoes, I was asked to speak, but declined with the excuse that I knew very few shoe jokes.

However, all the regulars showed up—Jessel, Danny Thomas, Martin and Lewis, George Burns, etc., and I understand they put on a very good show. I had a little difficulty hearing them. For some unknown reason Krasna and I were placed at a table occupied by (1) a portly agent, who kept rubbing my leg with his, under the delusion that it was part of Mrs. Stebbins; (2) Eddie Small, who kept pleading with Krasna to go into independent production in southern Italy; and (3) Artie Stebbins, who kept insisting in a 20-year endowment voice that I wasn't long for this world and before it was too late, why not take out a big policy for my loved ones and previous wives.

All in all it was a pretty classy affair. There was hardly a shoe store in town that wasn't represented by its manager and you would have laughed your sides sore at the quips that flew around about soles and heels, people being on their uppers and, finally "Young Man with a Shoe Horn."

At the conclusion of the last speech which was Karl's he was presented with a pair of baby shoes and three new branch stores. The baby shoes made Marie blush all over the body.

At midnight I went home well shod, fully insured and

spent the night fitfully dreaming of independent production in southern Italy.

Love and kisses,
Groucho

Sunday, 1950

Dear Groucho:

I would have answered your letter sooner, but you didn't send one.

However, no matter.

Well, television sets were dark for an evening or two last week in New York, as conversation came back for a brief stay. There were the subjects of the H-Bomb, and Mrs. Peter Lindstrom.

The H-Bomb holds little terror for me as we live in a building formerly owned by Hearst, and there's an old electric sign on the tower which lights up in the blackout and says "No Bombs—W. R. Hearst."

As for Ingrid Bergman, the town is divided into two camps. This is the road company Mary Magdalene, and there are those among us who would stone even the FIRST cast, to say nothing of Miss Bergman. My own opinion has not yet been formulated. I have tried to reduce it to a lesser, and not quite so common, denominator. What would my own church do, I ask myself, if, say, Molly Picon had dashed off to England with Carol Reed? Would Second Avenue ban "The Shatchon and the Madel?" Would Lupowitz and Moskowitz serve black matzo balls?

These were the questions which tore at me when I went to see "Stromboli." As for the picture, I keep my opinions to myself.

Love,
Goody

January 18, 1951

Dear Goodman:

Your letter received and you certainly have your problems. For a miserable pittance I'll promise not to show it to Wald and Krasna.

Miriam had told me that she had spoken to you and that you were not going to do the Big Show the week I'm on. I then instructed Gummo to call McConnell and to tell them that without you I would not appear. Either you are a shifty crook, or you just don't remember what you say from time to time.

I had a very pleasant morning today. To begin with, it was raining. After reading the war news I went to my lawyer's, who immediately opened up with the news that the government didn't see eye to eye with your correspondent about some tax items back in 1946 and 1947 when I was a comparatively young man. This doesn't involve much, but what makes it even more pleasant is that the returns as yet have not come in for 1948 and 1949.

I only cite these annoyances to show you that it isn't necessary to have relatives in Kansas City to be unhappy. Frankly the whole thing doesn't disturb me too much and I snap my fingers at the Revenue Department. However, when you arrive on February 4th and you knock on my front door, if there's no answer you can always reach me at the Federal jail down near the Union depot.

Thanks for the dress for Melinda. She said she would thank you personally when you arrive. That is, if you are still working on the "Big Show." If not you can look elsewhere for your thanks. Most people that I speak to like the "Big Show" and most of them agree with me that it's too long by at least 30 minutes. I read the rating in Variety and if these ratings are to be taken seriously, I question whether it will continue into the next season. My predictions are usually accurate. I was the fellow who said there would be no market crash in 1929.

I await your arrival with a remarkable amount of composure.

Love from all.

Groucho

P.S. I saw Joe DiMaggio last night at Chasen's and he wasn't wearing his baseball suit. This struck me as rather foolish. Suppose a ball game broke out in the middle of the night? By the time he got into his suit the game would be over.

Groucho, Dear Sir or Madame:

I had a call from NBC today and they said Gummo had written them asking if I am now or ever had been a member of the writing staff of the "Big Show." So they asked me to write you that I am and will be.

This nasty canard going around that I am off the show has been most embarrassing. And I'll tell you how I started it.

I had to take some weeks off to write my movie. So far I have been off two weeks, with one day spent in going over what my writing staff has written. Last week I picked up a script, and started throwing up. So I started fixing the jokes up right and left. I fixed Fred's opening routine with Tallulah. The boys accepted some of my stuff—but they insisted that Fred would WANT to say "It was so cold down in Miami that I had to crawl in between a hot pastrami sandwich to keep warm."

That, they said, was Fred. That, Fred told me on the phone, was author Fred. So he changed it to an electric blanket with long sleeves, put in a joke about being a banana turner in an automat, and came off with colors flying and quite happy with the show.

The Marlene Dietrich–Tallulah Bankhead insult routine I threw out entirely. I went home and stayed up writing a classy routine of insults and came in and read them to the boys the next day. They listened in respectful apathy, and when I had finished my masterwork, they said that if Dietrich refuses to do their routine, they would put in a word for mine.

Luckily for them Dietrich loved the stuff they had written, and they went on with it and it got the biggest laughs of the show. And the show went down in history as one of the best shows of the ten. . . . To add to all this, many people called me during this week to congratulate me on it, and I meekly accepted their plaudits.

There was an editorial in Collier's last week which said that this was the show that proved that adult humor could bring radio back. Adult humor to me is a series of jokes a guy can quote around Toots Shor's to the wise guys—not just be able to say Marlene and Tallulah sure bawled the hell out of each other. In this opinion, I am sorry to report, I am an oppressed minority. But it is my opinion and I shall defend to the death my right to say it. And no doubt it will kill me.

I hope to see both you lovely people soon. If you can find time, I'd appreciate a few lines, even if they're only a short apology for Taft or anything you may have said about me you're sorry for.

Love,
Goody

April, 1951

Dear Groucho:

I was wishing all week you were here so I'd have somebody with whom I could discuss the MacArthur argument. My biggest argument, naturally, was with Jane. She only reads the News, and in the News anything that gets five stars can't be wrong. She wanted to send a wire of impeachment but she couldn't spell it. Personally, I feel his option should not have been picked up, because not only did he knock the product but he wouldn't stop ad libbing after the sponsor told him to stop.

I'm coming out to the coast again with the "Big Show" which goes on May 6—the last of the season. And since Jane isn't coming with me, and if Shoofly is out of the house, and there are no strange women and their sisters hanging around, I'd like to keep you pleasant company for a week or so. If not I can always go to a hotel on Fairfax Avenue, so please don't put yourself out. In any case you will let me drop in to watch television, won't you? It has been so long since I haven't heard a commercial . . .

Harry Ruby finally came to see me and we had a long short talk about the old days two months ago when I visited Hollywood, and it was sure good to sit around and chew the fat with good old Harry, and your ears must have been burning because we spoke of you quite often and you can bet your shirt we certainly did you up brown—ha ha ha, you old son of a gun.

May I wish for you and Melinda and Sarah and Mattie a joyous Passover? I shall think of you when I eat my first seder dinner to which a nice lady has invited us. She says they are going to ask the four kashos. So I am asking the Five De-Marcos. . . . Love, and stay well,

Goody

October 22, 1951

Dear Goodman:

Since there is an acute piano shortage in my house I was cajoled by Bob Braun of the Morris office to make one of my rare appearances on the "Big Show" on November 4th. The only reason my appearances are rare (and this is something I don't usually disclose) is because nobody asks me oftener.

In all the years I have been out here I have never yet had an offer to appear on the Lux show. Of course they may not be aware of it, but I have been using Lux soap for many years and you have no idea what it's done for my complexion. My skin is as fair and transparent as a sub-deb's. People marvel at it. Many is the time I have walked down Hollywood Boulevard and heard people say, "There goes Groucho Marx. I marvel at his skin. It's as clear and transparent as a sub-deb's." But despite all this, no emissary from the Lux show has ever communicated with me and offered me an engagement. Some weeks ago, I recall, they had a female movie star on the Lux show. Not a bad actress, as actresses go, but, Goody, compared to mine, her skin is as mottled as a tablecloth in a cheap cafeteria. I know for a fact she does not use Lux soap. I know definitely that she uses Brillo, but still they use her on their show, and she's shameless enough to accept these engagements, mottled skin and all.

So what the hell, I'll go along in my little old way collecting pianos from NBC and eking out a dollar here and there. It's my network and I love every inch of its coaxial cable.

If you should meet anyone from the Lux show please don't breathe a word of what I've written. This is for your ears alone. And while we are on the subject of your ears, perhaps you could use some Lux soap. Used faithfully it will make your ears as clear and transparent as Maxie Rosenbloom's.

Fondly,
Groucho

Dear Groucho:

You are my friend. And just because you're too busy or too illiterate to write more often is no excuse for dropping a friendship which began with "In honor of your fifty years with the railroad I present you with these ties"—and, which only last week was refurbished when a nice little eighty-year-old man said he was retired from business and you replied: "You mean you're a bum?"

Well, the radio business has entered a new era. First, there was the Crosley, father of the telephone call asking the listener what he listened to last night. Then there came the Hooper, father of the phone call asking the listener what he was listening to at the moment. And now it's the Nielsen, father of Anna Q.

The Times today (Sunday) has a piece on the operation of the Nielsen. Read it. Put a commercial before and after it and you've got a comedy spot which nobody could turn out. I like the paragraph which explains the modus operandi:

> Every two weeks the Nielsen home office mails a new magazine or film cartridge to the 1500 sample homes. As an incentive to the housewife to uphold her end of the deal, two shiny quarters jump out when she inserts the new cartridge and removes the old one, which is mailed to Nielsen for tabulation. When she pulls out the old cartridge, a buzzer keeps sounding off till she inserts the new one.

If the censors would ever let you do *that* on the air, huh? And get this paragraph:

> Nielsen's forty field representatives travel an average of sixty miles per home in calling on their constituents. . . . The field men never ask questions. They're concerned only with keeping the Audimeters in smooth working order and checking the food and drug items in the kitchen and medicine cabinets in each sampled home. . . . By a method which no layman would ever

understand, the products on the kitchen shelf and in the bathroom are correlated with the radio ratings of various programs.

Your sponsor will be delighted to hear about this. Imagine a field man looking into a medicine cabinet for some bicarbonate of De Sota.

Love,
Goody

Dear Groucho:

I know you're dying to learn how we made out on our first show for JELL-O (the little hyphen is for the whipped cream and sliced bananas, I suppose). Someday I'm going to write a book called "The Hucksters" and tell about my experience with the advertising agency that handles JELL-O. How for two weeks before our first show I tried to get in touch with any one of the executives there and every secretary I spoke to asked: "Which Mr. Ace?" and I replied "Mr. Ace of Amos and Andy," and for two weeks got to speak to nobody. And then on the day of the first show they called me to ask me if it was all right if on the sign in front of the theater Jane's name appeared in the same color red as the word JELL-O (I am not making this up) and later in the day—a couple of hours before the first show they cut out two wonderful jokes: To wit: Whenever I mention work to Jane's brother he says don't use that four-letter word in front of my sister; (2) Miss Anderson take a letter. To Mr. Norris—dash—Met our clients yesterday and I halfway convinced him. Period. I have invited him to the house for dinner comma—and will try my best to get him signed. Exclamation point. Even if it means upsetting my digestion. Colon . . . (JELL-O doesn't recognize the existence of a colon). And several other jokes too humorous to mention.

I am seriously considering giving up radio writing and taking a soft job. Writing concession telegrams for Norman Thomas. You're so right about men and women—the gulf is so wide—and the screwing you get isn't worth the screwing you get, and buying a funny mask to scare hell out of 'em when they wake up in the morning isn't the solution either, my naïve friend. Well to hell with it.

Say hello to Betty Blythe and the gang.

Love,
Goody

June 23

Dear, Dear Groucho:

It was so nice to get your letter. I thought you had completely forsaken me, not having received any replies to my many letters and precious gifts of frankincense and bonbons and Frezone, which I've wafted your way these many moons, wondering where you are, and how you are, and if you are. . . . However, the cheery news that you are coming here next month raised my hopes that once again very soon I may be having dinner with Max Gordon. . . .

As for me, I have been vegetating, as I realized that all too soon I've become a senior hack television writer, even to the point of permitting myself to be cajoled into doing the Como show again this coming season. I had made such splendid plans to stay out of television this year, when Jane took over and told me it was about time I gave up this preposterous idea of making $25,000 a week doing big shows like the late Revlon episodes. To quote her correctly (and I have witnesses): "Do you have to take those jobs for $25,000 a week? Can't you get a job like everybody else for five or six thousand a week?"

So it's back to Como. No chaos here. He has two simple rules which his doctor gave him and which he confided to me: "Don't worry." And "Don't be nervous." They work very well. All you have to do is stop reading newspapers. . . .

All my love to you, to Melinda, to Eden, to Miriam, and to Eichman when you write him,

Goody

Dear Comedian:

Enclosed are some jokes. More will follow. I beg to remain,

Sincerely,
Your writer

P.S. All I can say is that if you read these routines and you like them, then you are the easiest guy to write for since Moses wrote the Ten Commandments after that Short Story Conference with God. If you don't like them, I'll never stay at your house again. Our producer leaves for the Coast right after the first show Sunday night. (He doesn't know he can be extradited.) He will confer with you, and you can make any substitutions you want, except put in Gummo in your place. . . . Good night—don't write, don't telegraph. I'll call you. . . .

Goody

July 13

Dear Groucho,

I went with Fred [Allen] to see his first show. It was a huge success with all the NBC execs assembled. I found one tiny flaw which I didn't mention, and which nobody else seemed to mind. Fred's conversation with people seems to be geared only to their setting up the straight lines so that he can tell the joke. Whereas the pixy and impish quality that is solely yours seems to draw from them, in warm, human dialogue, conversation which while hilarious is not a joke per se. This is between you and me and Erskine Johnson I suppose but that's what I believe. Anyway Fred is quite happy with all his action, and for a guy who claims to be as sick as he is, he is taking to it like a colt.

I read you were doing "Time for Elizabeth" somewhere. How did it go—if we're still speaking. Of course if we're not I will kill myself. I've been looking for a valid excuse.

On this straight line I will now close. All my love and adoration which I suppose you are having plenty of if I am to believe some of the pictures which have appeared here with you and some ravishing gal.

Goody

July 17, 1953

Dear Goody:

I liked your piece [in the Saturday Review] on TV summer shows, particularly the line about turning the radio on and staring at it.

However, this is not what I am writing you about. I read this morning that the excess profits bill has been extended another six months, and therefore it occurred to me that you owe me $10. Normally I wouldn't dun you for the money but this has been a hard summer. I don't think I have ever told you, but during the dog days my salary is whittled down to microscopic proportions. Unfortunately, my expenses remain the same—if anything, higher, since there is chlorine to be added to the pool, outdoor ash trays to be installed at strategic spots, and food provided for the drop-in trade.

Naturally I don't expect you to write a check for a sum

as minute as this. Just place $10 in an envelope and send it to Groucho Marx, North Foothill Road, Beverly Hills, California. I'll repeat this address once again—Groucho Marx, North Foothill Road, Beverly Hills, California.

I beg to remain,
Respectfully yours,
Groucho

Dear Julius:

The magazine on which your daughter now works wrote me for references. And I replied that I had known Miriam Marx for many years, and have always found her to be five feet six and a half inches tall, and that I know her to have the integrity and potential ability of her famous father, Karl. P.S.: She got the job. I haven't heard, but I suppose she's still there.

I would have answered your letter of a year or so ago, much sooner, had it not been that Jane and I got mixed up with a television show—or as we call it back east here, TV—a clever contraction derived from the words Terrible Vaudeville. However, it is our latest medium—we call it a medium because nothing's well done. It was discovered, I suppose you've heard, by a man named Fulton Berle, and it has already revolutionized social grace by cutting down parlor conversation to two sentences: "What's on television?" and "Good night."

. . . But here I am telling you all about us, and not mentioning that daily I run into many many people who still cling to that old medium, radio—which back east we call AM —a clever contraction of Amos and Andy, I suppose—and they tell me you are their favorite show. Honest to God. So you see you still hold a great affection in the hearts of these true-blooded Americans.

Of course these people don't accept television (TV), because television (TV) is so confining. They are able to turn on radio and still play cards, sew, read a book, and listen to their favorite programs. But once you turn on a television (TV) set, you have to sit there glued to it. Of course this argument is entirely falacious, as many a night we have turned on our television (TV) set, and gone to a play, or even to bed . . .

If I sound bitter it is because nobody wants to buy our good radio show which we did with so little success for a year or so. I may even go out of the business and try another medium. There have been so many successes in the theater by converting things into musicals—"Regina," "Gentlemen Prefer Blondes," etc., I'm thinking of making a musical out of "Miss Liberty."

Love,
Goody

October 16, 1953

Dear Goody:

I saw the Berle show with Sinatra and Tallulah and thought it was very good. After which I missed a couple and saw the one with Dagmar, Cooper and the dame from Paris. I thought that, too, was good. Not quite as good as the opener, but worth watching. I must say you have done a remarkable job for Uncle Miltie.

I had contracted to do a guest shot with Caesar and Coca. One of the clauses I insisted upon—and got—was that I would have the material two weeks before appearing. This they agreed to. Later they wanted to eliminate this clause and I, still smarting from my shot with Tallulah last year, said no dice. So after a good deal of teletyping back and forth, we mutually agreed to dissolve the pact.

My girl friend of 1952 and part of 1953 is in Paris living with her sister and her sister's husband (according to the letters she sends me). She is going to appear as Gregory Ratoff's wife in some schnitzel they are planning to shoot in Egypt.

This will give you a fairly comprehensive picture of my status as a lover. The girl prefers a bit part in a B movie in Egypt to New York with the man she loves. She seems to forget the money I spent on her. Christmas, for example, I bought her six pairs of stockings. And later, for her birthday, I had all the stockings darned.

The way of a man with a maid is indeed a rocky adventure, but one must go on.

My best to Jane.

Groucho

Sunday

Fine Friend:

No letter.

I called Room 679 at the Waldorf this morning and was connected with a Mr. and Mrs. John Rodofsky from Cairo, Illinois, who now occupy it. Naturally I saw at once this is not their real name, which is no doubt Smith, but they didn't want to have any trouble with the house dick so they registered as Mr. and Mrs. John Rodofsky.

I asked for Groucho Marx, and a man said "Who?" And I repeated Groucho Marx, and he said there was nobody there by that name, and I told him Groucho Marx had been living there yesterday and he got quite excited because, he explained, once the Marx Brothers played a vaudeville house in Cairo,

Illinois, and there was no door to the toilet which was just off
stage, just a curtain hanging in front of it. And Harpo was
playing his solo there one night, when somebody flushed the
toilet, and Harpo arose in chagrin, and the audience, thinking
he was finished, applauded him loudly. And also on the bill was
a man who claimed you could tie him up with ropes, and he
could escape—but one night somebody tied him too tight and
he never got out, and that's how Olsen and Johnson got the
idea for their straitjacket gag. But the point the man made
was that he is in the piece goods business, and he had sold the
theater that piece of curtain which hung in front of the toilet
instead of a door. . . .

Today we're bundling up and going out to watch another snowball game between the Dodgers and Giants. We
miss you quite a while—love,

Goody

October 16, 1953

Dear Goody:

I was sorry I couldn't join you in New York for the
World Series and I regret even more that Brooklyn showed
up. I don't think I could have faced another week of that. If
Brooklyn wins the pennant next year, and there's no reason
why they shouldn't, I think it would be a good idea to split
the Yankee team in two and force them to play each other.

World Series week I was in Detroit delivering an unfunny speech at the Detroit Athletic Club for the De Soto
and Chrysler brass. I did all the things I was supposed to do.
I went through the plant wide-eyed and eager; admired the
machinery, asked questions and received answers that were
utterly bewildering to me, and was slapped on the back stead-

ily for four days. This is what happens when one has a high Nielsen.

I then went to St. Louis and joined my friend Krasna and watched his "Kind Sir." Boyer is wonderful in it and I guess Martin is too, but though she is unquestionably a good actress she appeals to me emotionally about as much as Abe Lastfogel would, were he to play the part.

They are sold out wherever they go, which is certainly the way for a playwright to enter a city.

My best to Jane,
Groucho

September 14, 1956

Dear Goody:

Just a line to warn you that I will be at the Savoy Plaza on the 28th of September.

I have a little matter to discuss with my fans in the internal revenue office. It seems that they would like my autograph —on a small check.

I won't be in New York long . . . eight or nine days at most . . . for I have to rush back to watch how deftly and professionally the architect and his henchmen are chipping away—not at the foundation of my dream house, but at the remnants of my bankroll. Churchill, an ex-bricklayer, could have done the whole thing much faster. Each time they lay 6 inches of pipe (something I haven't done for years), they send me another bill for a thousand dollars.

Melinda is coming east with me. She, too, will be there on business. The business consists of "Pajama Game," "Damn Yankees" and any other musical that's around.

Love to you both,
Groucho

Dear Groucho:

Last night we saw a preview of what will be the best comedy show on TV next season. It was a fifteen-minute program with a guy just sitting there saying funny but intelligent things, and smoking a cigar, and taking long, silent takes after his guests have answered a question, and there was no—and indeed there didn't have to be—lousy action and sight stuff, which is now the vogue (to hide a lousy script and bad jokes), and I think I can say, objectively, despite the fact the guy complained about my box at the Polo Grounds, and invited me to come live with him QUOTE for any reasonable length of time UNQUOTE, and despite the fact that I am preparing a show for this new medium where we call people on the phone to answer questions—a show to be called "The Medium and the Telephone"—despite all this—I say that this will be the best TV show this coming season. And if you don't believe me you can ask my wife, who is a sort of George Jean Nothin' of Everything—who likes nobody and vice versa—and she said, when the show was over, "Well, all right you can keep the set." Meaning she had been threatening to throw the set *and* me out of the house for some months, but now that something good came up, it was OK. But I must warn you that she is the one who, when television first came out, said the same thing she said when the first automobile came out—"Get a horse," she said. So they got Hopalong Cassidy.

My congratulations and I think you got gypped on that 3-million-dollar contract.

There are problems about my coming west. Jane has her hairdresser here who knows just where the gray streaks need the most touching up, and I've just begun a long series of dental appointments to rehabilitate my mouth. So between her hair and my teeth, we have our roots here in the east.

Oh before I forget, there is a new thing in TV around

here—everybody is on the lookout for a show like Groucho Marx's. A week doesn't pass that I'm not called by an agency or a network to preside over a gimmick show—"you know— like Groucho Marx." Yesterday it was a man from the Esty Agency: "How would you and Jane like to do a quiz show for us—you know, like Groucho Marx." And very seriously I asked him who would be Groucho—Jane or me? He replied just as seriously, "You, of course." In every case after I've turned the job down, I've suggested they call Fred Allen. In every case they already had.

My love and again my congratulations on your TV debut.

Goody

Dear Goodman:

It was nice to hear your voice again, double nice since I didn't have to look at you while we were talking.

I thought your piece on "I Love Lucy" was real George and I think you are crazy if you don't take up writing as a profession. You write rather well and if you are interested I think I can get you a job as a cub reporter on the Los Angeles Inquirer. This is a throw-away newspaper, but fortunately it works two ways. The newsboy throws it on my lawn, and I throw it back again. He doesn't always throw it on the lawn; only when it is raining. But since it has rained every day since you left, I am now a subscriber to what is unquestionably the wettest newspaper in California. In recent weeks I have led a life somewhat like those legendary copra traders who inhabit Pago Pago.

Regarding my trip East, I have made an about-face and have decided to return to the Waldorf. I have a very good reason.

I am a practical fellow, Goodman, and I want you and

Jane to know that my shifting to the Waldorf is no reflection
on either of you. My admiration and affection for you both is
bounded only by the Seven Seas. But hear my side. On those
many occasions when the three of us have returned from the
theater, you and your wife would scurry off to your hovel on
the Ritz roof and I would be left flat in the lobby, looking
hopefully in my mailbox for even the remotest contact with
femininity. The contents of the mailbox would invariably consist of two messages—one from Max Gordon; the other from
Miss Jinx Falkenburg with an invitation to do a benefit. No
indication that, waiting for me anywhere in New York, was
there a bit of fluff, accoutered with standard high heels, silk
stockings and, of course, knockers. No trophies of the chase
to gladden my late hours.

Left alone in the dismal lobby, I would totter into the
creaking elevator and, with a faintly arthritic walk, limp to
my suite of one room, there to fortify myself with a glass of
Dr. Brown's Celery Tonic double.

The Waldorf, at least, has female room clerks on each
floor; and, around midnight, even these elderly human com-
puters who suspiciously and reluctantly hand you your key,
add a note of hope and femininity to the last mile as you walk
alone to your room.

Love to you both.
Groucho

Dear $3,000,000:

Well since last we met you have become immensely rich
—knock wood; and the Giants are only 4½ games out of first
place—knock wood; and there used to be a director at MGM
whom I thoroughly disliked and I hope they never hire another like him—knock Wood.

Reports seeping through from the Coast say you are

taking your good fortune in your usual stride—perhaps a new beret, they say, and a pair of striped trousers and a cane (nouveau cane)—but still the same old Groucho, five foot eight, and wiry.

As for myself, I am turning to playwriting. Somebody told me I oughta do a play out of the Easy Aces characters; at any rate I've started mulling it about, and have several scattered scripts and pages of notes cluttering my desk, and if all goes badly I should have something written by the end of the summer. I have plenty of advisers, and Jerry Chodorov keeps calling me up from some shady dell to urge me on and be sure to have a good first act curtain. I think muslin will be nice, what do you think?

Meanwhile for the first time in our career we have no money at all coming in. Jane says we must cut down our standard of living, and we can do it, she says, if we cut down on our cigars, and calling my mother every Sunday. She has also stopped the Times.

So what's new?

Love,
Goody

September 17, 1957

Dear Goody:

It was nice seeing you in New Jersey. Now that I think of it, this is the first time I've ever seen you in New Jersey. Up to now I've only seen you in Missouri, California and New York. You haven't changed much, though, because I recognized you instantly.

I must say that I'm a bigger ham than I thought, for, much to my surprise, I enjoyed appearing on the stage. I'm sorry you didn't see the play the second week instead of the first. By that time the actors all knew their lines and it became a performance rather than a memory test. With the thought of doing "Time for Elizabeth" as a movie next year, I canceled the TV spec. They would have paid a lot of money, but it would also have killed the play's chances as a movie, the theory being that if people can see a thing free, they won't pay to see it later in a theater.

The house is gradually taking shape, just as I'm losing mine. By the time you come out here, it will thrill you to your tranquilizers.

Love from all.
Sincerely yours,
Ed Davis,* General Manager
Snow Drift Washing Machine Co.

29th

My Dear 17.7:

Yes, Jane and I have a television show, as you read "some place." Maybe you read some place what Harriet Van Horne said: "as funny as their radio show and that's about as funny as you can get . . ." Or what Ben Gross said: "and different from anything else on television . . ." Or what John Crosby said: " very . . ."

The show is all on film. It is not kinescoped for the west or any other coast, thank God. I'll tell you why "thank God." A sponsor was ridiculous enough to buy the show for a one-time showing, after which the film reverts to us and we can sell it for years to come in towns where television (TV) is blessedly late in coming. So you see, we will be receiving checks after we have finished the stint, checks addressed to our concentration camp which, by the way, we have already

* Groucho's role in "Time for Elizabeth."

selected—the Roney Plaza. In fact we may be going there next month for a brief vacation—long time no sea. The Ziv Company and I are partners in this annuity. We will probably never reach a 17.7 but a decimal point following a dollar sign is just as good to me . . .

The format is a simple one. Jane and I sit in front of a television set at home watching a television show. The show we watch is usually a sports reel, a travelogue, or a whatnot, and we make up funny jokes to say while looking at it. The viewers at home see on their sets what we're looking at on ours, with occasional cut-ins of Jane and me. Of course we have received many letters—all from my mother—complaining that we are not seen enough on the show.

. . . It will be a new kind of writing for me. We have to write jokes to fit the footage of the film shots. Like I need a forty-foot joke to describe what the man is doing when he examines the sheep's wool in Australia, so I say to Jane: "See, they examine the wool to determine if it's ready for shearing." And she takes the rest of the 40 feet to tell the joke. Which in this case turns out to be: "Oh yeh—they want to make sure it's a hundred per cent wool."

Hilarious, isn't it? And after writing 40-foot jokes, 75-foot jokes, and even 108-foot jokes, we have a nine and a half inch rating, and all is well.

Aside from that Jane's brother suddenly got himself engaged and created some excitement in our house. However, I take it with a cold, philosophical calm, and am not thinking of it as gaining a sister-in-law, but rather fondly as losing a brother-in-law.

Love,
Goody

June 1, 1960

Dear Mr. Ace:

Please don't be alarmed, I don't want any money. All I want is your love.

Even though I'm not looking forward to it, I expect to be in New York late in June or early in July. Why, I don't know, except that I'm married to an extremely young woman who is ready, at a moment's notice to gallop off to New York, South Africa and all the way stations in between.

The other day I facetiously announced that I might go to Kansas City for a couple of weeks. She was packed in seven minutes and had already sent for a cab.

I have already done four shows for next season and before I leave for the East I expect to have almost half the season wrapped up. Incidentally, this will be my swan song on this project. I don't know what I'll do to replace it, but I have seven or eight thousand residuals mouldering in some vault and I believe it's about time I gave the public an opportunity to see what I've done to them in the past fourteen years.

Please get Dr. Schechtel warmed up in the bull pen because I've never visited New York without Eden or me coming down with borderline pneumonia.

Love to you and Jane and all your money, and do let me hear from you even if it's only a twenty-page letter.

Fondly,
Groucho

Dear Christine:

It was reassuring to hear your soft pitched voice from the hospital where I had pictured you prostate on your bed of pain. By now the doctors must have removed the last of the instruments they forgot and you are well past the bad jokes about Operation Operation and into a speedy recovery, thanks to the sturdy constitution you have built up by walking once around the block past Van Johnson's house and back . . .

. . . Me and Jane went to see "Me and Juliet" the other night and we enjoyed it tremendously. From now on I go to see everything and will brook no interference from Atkinson or any of these other critics. You were as right about "Me and Juliet" as I was about the Ritz Brothers.

At the expense of incurring Jane's wrath, easily aroused at best, I have been praying for the Yankees to lose a game, knowing that it will help your recovery. No man can do more for the man he adores.

I will call you one night this week, dreading though I do the intimate details of the operation. I trust you had it kinescoped, and hope to see it assembled as a Grouchilu Production.

My love to Eden,
Goody

January 23, 1962

Dear Goody:

When I returned home one day last week after an arduous day at Hillcrest, I was notified that you had phoned and that sometime later, when dusk was settling over the city, I would hear from you again. This was a base canard (which is a pretty large ship that plies the Atlantic). Later dusk did appear, but the bell didn't toll.

I saw your show a few weeks ago. I don't see it often, for Wednesday is the night I do mine. This one included, among its other participants, Art Linkletter, and as they say in Kansas City, I thought it was "right good." I'd even say excellent. I think it's a much better show than it used to be and I suppose, much as I regret it, I will have to attribute this partially to you.

I only mentioned Mr. Linkletter as a means of identify-ing the show that I watched. See Mr. Linkletter on TV is hardly the bombshell of the year. I'm not referring to his talent, for I think he's warm, personable, able and rich. There is hardly a television show in which he won't eventually show up. He's on early in the morning; he can be seen at noon, all during the afternoon and late into the night. And if he's not on as a performer, he will be seen selling something from some other show. I envy his vitality.

As you know, I am doing a new show which is precisely the same as the old show except that we have traded Mr. Fenneman for a spritely young doll with oversized knockers who leaps around the stage with all the abandon of a young doe being pursued by an elderly banker.

Unfortunately, we have against us "Doctor Kildare," "My Three Sons" and the public. If we are unable to woo any listeners away from the other networks, at the end of the season I will again be out of work.

However this will not deter my partner. He will retain me, again change the name of the show and sell it to some new unsuspecting sponsor.

Fondly,
Groucho

Groucho
and
Other
Men of Letters

TO E. B. WHITE

Dear Mr. White:

I received your note. I am now willing to concede that you are a fairly migratory gent. When I arrived in New York I was told you were in Florida. When I called you again they said you were in Maine.

I went to New York ostensibly to do the Rodgers and Hammerstein festival. Actually I came to New York to cut up some touches with the author of "Charlotte's Web."

Some years ago I had a dinner date with you and Ross. He showed up but you failed to appear. It's strange—I have no difficulty meeting Nick Kenny, Toots Shor, and other minor luminaries in New York, but you have adopted the mantle of Garbo and to me you are just a wraithlike figure who lives suspended in a spirit world.

Sincerely,
Groucho Marx

April 12, 1954

Dear Mr. Marx:

Before our correspondence attains the intensity of the Shaw-Terry letters, I want to explain my suspension in the spirit world—which is sometimes misinterpreted. Ross had a theory that if he could throw me with a better class of people, I might be more productive. (Ross entertained some incredibly unsound ideas and at great cost to himself.)

At any rate, once in a while he would pry me loose, and on the whole they were miserable experiences for the persons who got involved. I think of an evening when he attempted to throw me with Ginger Rogers and we all went down to Chinatown for a debauch that should live forever in Miss Rogers' memory as an example of midnight stagnation. (Another Ross illusion was that he understood Chinese food.)

It is nice here in the spirit world and if you get here I would like to buy you a drink. Garbo is here. We maintain separate residences, for appearances' sake.

Sincerely,
E. B. White

30 September 1959

Dear Mr. Marx:

Thanks for the book and for including my name at the end of that long, dreary list in the front. Thurber says it is alphabetical, but he is full of all sorts of odd bits of information.

I'm enjoying the book, and it is one of the two books in my library in which the sentences seem to be uttered aloud by the author of the book. (The other book is Fred Allen's.)

My wife and I continue to watch your show with enjoyment, and the whole thing is better than ever now that the bittersweet vine has reached the top of our antenna, so that you come through the set looking more and more like Raymond Duncan, the goatherd. Keep up the good work, and tell Melinda I was enchanted with the witch doctor.

Sincerely,
E. B. White

October 13, 1959

Dear Mr. White:

Since your profession is writing I don't expect you to continue this correspondence, but I just had to let you know how delighted I was to read that you enjoyed the book and that you and your wife also watch my TV show.

I am sorry that to you, I now resemble Raymond Duncan, but on the other hand, if this is true, you must realize that he also resembles me.

It is not easy to write even a short note to a man who has just published a book on the pitfalls of the English language. You see, I write by ear. I tried writing with the typewriter but I found it too unwieldy. I then tried dictating to my secretary but after some months of futility I realized that she, too, was unwieldy.

Hoping these encomiums don't embarrass you too much, I am

Sincerely yours,
Groucho Marx

TO PHYLLIS McGINLEY

September 17, 1954

Dear Phyllis:

> This book inscribed
>   from Phyllis McGinley
> Is more precious to me
>   than a bust of McKinley.

Many thanks.

Groucho

March 3, 1961

Dear Phyllis:

A thousand pardons! (One, anyway.) I had instructed my secretary to send you a copy of my book "Groucho and Me," assuming she would forge my name with her customary facility and inscribe a warm and brilliant inscription on the flyleaf.

She was at the dentist's all of that day, and the man who delivers the bottled water was the only one who came into the office. He saw the instructions on my secretary's desk and wishing to save face he sent the book on, willy-nilly. He tried to send it through the post office but it was Lincoln's birthday; the post office was closed and the only mail going through was by willy-nilly. The following day Willy told my secretary that this was the biggest day's business willy-nilly had done since Dillinger was shot in Chicago.

I hope you are back on your feet again, at least during the day, and perhaps you can enclose this note in the folds of your book, along with a pressed rose.

Love,

Groucho

TO MRS. GOODMAN ACE

November 21, 1955

Dear Jane:

I haven't much to say because I haven't been doing much thinking lately, but it occurred to me that if your husband (Mr. Goody) could have Simon and Schuster place a small ad in the local trade papers, a lot of people might be persuaded to purchase his book. As you know, it's mostly for show people and, as you apparently don't know, most of the show people live out here.

His current piece about Noel and Mary was superb; and he seems to get better every other week. You are no doubt aware that I am not given to writing fan letters. I have my own fan club in Brooklyn, which consists of two girls and a bus driver. These three don't know each other, but they correspond regularly. Last Christmas they got together and sent me a box of Chanukah candles.

I hope you and your husband are both well and that the languid barber who employs him continues to slice down all his competition.

Lovingly yours—your old Florida friend,

Groucho

FROM JAMES THURBER

April 9, 1958

Dear Groucho:

I am now working on Ross Number 9, a long and, of course, penetrating piece about his friendship, or whatever it was, with the man he called "that glib son-of-a-bitch" and "that emotionless fish," the late Ross-hater and Marx-lover, A. Woollcott.

What I'm agoin' to do, pardner, is send you a carbon of this piece in its last, or next to last draft, in the hope that it might move you, through some emotion, or all emotions, or none, to write me a few comments on those two crazy and remarkable dead men, or on anything else. . . .

I would like to have your opinion, and Harpo's if he can still whistle and make signs, on both Ross and Woollcott, singly and together. You come from common stock, but you have a mighty uncommon mind and talent. I toss out these compliments to win your love and devotion. To me Woollcott was such a pompous Grand Marshal of his own daily parade that all men wanted to put banana peels in his path, and all the ladies he praised and insulted in the same sentence wanted to pick him up when he fell. The famous story of the Gibbs Profile is dealt with in my piece, with quotes from Gibbs. He didn't know the Lunts had stopped their subscription to The New Yorker when the Profile came out, but he did know that Coward turned against him and Ross and me, too, because I wore the red rose of Ross and not the white orchid of Woollcott, I guess. Gibbs was also bawled out by Beatrice Kaufman, Edna Ferber, and Neysa McMein.

Me, I don't care who attacked Ross, and I attack him some myself, the way I would any other pageant, or monument, or magician. And if Woollcott couldn't take attack, then nobody could. The letters of the glib son-of-a-bitch definitely prove to me that he loved the clashes and friction and insults in his life, because they gave him a chance to write letters which might just possibly live, like the ones Henry James wrote to H. G. Wells, and those that probably came out of such literary feuds as Dickens versus Thackeray, and Henley versus Stevenson.

Mercy, how I do go on, and the night is falling. Love to you and your ilk, if any, and to Dave and Nunnally. Tell

Nunnally Stanley Walker says that Nunnally meant more to him when he needed comfort or reassurance than anybody else in the world, and I'll send him the quote to prove it.

There will be ten pieces in the Atlantic, and five more in the book, together with 25,000 words of what I call "Odds and Beginnings," letters, prefaces, and the like, dealing with Ross and The New Yorker.

Affectionately,
James Thurber

P.S. I am dealing only lightly with the letters those fake old ladies wrote to Aleck, because this is not a part of The New Yorker or Ross's story. Old Sam Adams tells it in detail in his "A. Woollcott, His Life and His World," but he avoids naming the culprit, if he knew, and I think he knew who it was. We always heard Charlie MacArthur blamed for it, and if he did it I think Adams left that out in deference to Helen Hayes and her love for A. W. Anyway, to my mind, Charlie was basically a sensitive and gentle man, and if he wrote the letters he so identified himself with the old ladies he didn't realize what a boomerang effect A. W.'s reading of the 23rd Psalm would have on people. All those guys, including Ross, played pranks so elaborate and long they became burdens. And all this time they had a fine example of how to do it, set by you and your frères. For example, you did not have to build the house that wasn't next door and put the painting in it. They did, and that was what was the matter, in part, with the Round Table.

May 5, 1958

Dear Jim:

Over the past two months I've had two letters from you and you have no idea what this has done to raise my social position in Beverly Hills. I'm now considered almost on a par with T. S. Eliot, Swinburne and Burt L. Standish.

About Woollcott, I know very little. On the few times we met, we casually insulted each other and left. Harpo is the one who would have to provide you with information about flabby Alex. Harpo has left Beverly Hills flat and has become a part-time grapefruit farmer in Palm Springs.

I have written and asked him to jot down whatever anecdotes he can remember about Ross and Woollcott. Whether I will ever hear from him is extremely doubtful. If I do, I will report to you.

I am going to be at the Westport Country Playhouse beginning July 21st, in "Time for Elizabeth," and I expect you and your wife (the lady who has fond memories of me singing ribald lyrics to her in a shabby beauty parlor in Westwood) to be my guests. If you can come, and drag along E. B. White I could then die happy, knowing that I had encountered . . . if only briefly . . . the literary class of our time.

Your admirer and all around bootlicker,

Groucho

May 13, 1958

Dear Groucho:

Thanks, old fellow, as Ross would say, for your letter and for Krasna's too. It was good of both of you to go to this trouble for a mere shadow of his former self. Last night Helen, Mrs. T. Thurber and I ran into Sir Cedric and we mentioned the time of your dinner party, 200 years ago. The Ross book is shaping up well.

Andy White was delighted by your reference to him, and Elliott Nugent also enjoyed the letter, which is now in the Smithsonian Institute. Helen and I are sailing for Europe on the Mauretania on June 4th and so will miss you and Elizabeth, alas, and dammit.

My love to you, as always, and to Melinda about whom Helen was just reading me an article. Melinda is a lovely name and I'm sure she is a wonderful girl. My daughter's name is Rosemary and I have a granddaughter named Sara and a grandson named Gregory, aged 3 and 1 respectively, but never respectfully.

Affectionately,

Jim

FROM NUNNALLY JOHNSON

London, Monday October 9, 1961

Dear Grouch:

I was delighted to get your letter and very pleased about your new TV program—if you are. And I needed a little cheering up. Thurber is still alive as I write this but he may not be by the time you get it.

We saw a great deal of him and Helen, earlier this year. He was here for four or five months, waiting for somebody to tell him whether the "Thurber Carnival" was going to be put on here or not. It was not. Jim and I were on the N. Y. Evening Post together back in the 20's. In those days he'd get crocked (in these days too) and around 4 A.M., somebody's phone would ring and it would be Thurber. "Joe?" he'd say. "What's the trouble, Jamie?" "Nobody but me, eh, boy?" Sayre would say, "That's right, Jamie, nobody but you." Satisfied, Jim would say, "Thanks, boy, good night." That's all. Just wanted to be reassured.

But nobody had to reassure him these days. He was the God damnedest talker (look, I'm already using the past tense) but good, very good. I asked him once if not being able to see had given him more confidence. He said, "Hell, yes. Who's going to interrupt a blind man!" He insisted that he was the only man he ever heard of who had never had to undergo psychotherapy when blindness came on him. The first time he and Helen came to dinner with us, after the usual fumbling around he said to me, "This is always a little awkward for a blind man. I couldn't truthfully say it's been a long time since I saw Dorris, but then on the other hand it wouldn't sound right for me to say it's a long time since I felt your wife." He never harped on the point, he only joked about it, now and then, like when there was an audition in a theater here one morning, and a young lady, for reasons I don't know, didn't bother to leave the stage to change costumes. "When Helen told me there was a beautiful girl just about naked up there," he said, "I lifted my face and said, Lord, there are times when this goes just a little beyond a joke."

But no question about it, he used his blindness to get away with a lot of murder. For instance, nobody but a blind man is going to keep me up until 2 and 3 in the morning talking. But the more he drank, the more he wanted to talk. One night he made the flat claim that he was the finest actor alive and there was no part yet written that he couldn't play. I said, what about Ophelia? With a little preparation, he insisted, the part was not beyond him. (He was awfully pleased about your visiting him backstage in N.Y. and talked about it often. He also liked Harpo's book immensely, and that led us into stories about the Marx Brothers and Woollcott et al.)

He was very bitter about The New Yorker, and I thought with complete justification. He said they kept sending his stuff back, not by the editor but by young fellows who he said wrote him little lectures on comedy and humor. The important editors wouldn't even answer his letters. This astonished me. He said it was on account of the Ross book. He said nobody on The NYer liked it.

Oh, well, this is beginning to sound like an obit. But you know Jim, and a shock like this makes me want to talk about him. Next time I'll be cheerfuller.

Nunnally

P.S. Oh, yes. Helen [Mrs. Thurber] said some drunk dame told Jim at a party that she would like to have a baby by him. Jim said, "Surely you don't mean by unartificial insemination!"

TO ELAINE DUNDY

September 30, 1959

Dear Mrs. Tynan:

I don't make a practice of writing to married women, especially if the husband is a dramatic critic, but I had to tell someone (and it might as well be you since you're the author) how much I enjoyed "The Dud Avocado." It made me laugh, scream and guffaw (which, incidentally, is a great name for a law firm).

If this was actually your life, I don't see how the hell you ever got through it.

Sincerely,
Groucho Marx

23rd October, 1959

Dear Mr. Marx,

I have been carrying your letter around in my handbag for two weeks now, ever so, *ever* so cleverly working it into conversations ("Hey, guess who I *heard* from!") so that I can then produce it for my friends with a flourish. Unfortunately,

I'm going to have to put it away because it's getting all dog-eared and lipsticked and cigarette-tobaccoed in there and I want to save it for my grandchildren.

Thank you so very much for the delightful things you said in it. You simply cannot imagine what pleasure it gave me. I've seen practically all your pictures at least fifteen times and I even went to Paris to catch the one they wouldn't allow in England for a while because it was scripted by Mr. Ben Hecht with the Song in his Heart.

You don't happen to have an autographed photograph of yourself lying around, do you? I really would adore it! I am working on a book now—a comedy about an American girl trying to kill a middle-aged Englishman (as in the first one—only *slightly* autobiographical) and I know somehow that your photograph would help me keep the right, light, touch.

With great admiration,
Elaine Tynan

November 20, 1959

Dear Elaine:

I was delighted that you were delighted that I was delighted about your book.

I am sending you a photo of myself at the age of seven. You will probably say to yourself, "Why the cigar?" That's a very good question. Actually, the cigar is a phony. So is the mustache and, to wrap it all up neatly, so am I.

Yours until John McCarten gives some movie a good review.

I remain,

Abjectly yours,
Groucho Marx

P.S. I hope your old man doesn't get wind of this.

TO COLIN WILSON

November 23, 1959

Dear Mr. Wilson:

I just read a review of your newest book in the Los Angeles Times. Mr. Kirsch is a pretty tough critic, but I am not sure how much influence our local sheet has.

If you come to the States, as you threaten to in your letter from Tetherdown, Trewallock Lane, Gorran Haven, Cornwall (if I got nothing else out of your missive, the address is worth the price of admission), be sure to get in touch with me.

I am pleased to hear that you are writing a book about Jack the Ripper. He has always been my hero. I've always envied him and his activities, but physical limitations have prevented me from following in his footsteps.

Regarding the exclamation marks in "Groucho and Me," I assure you I had nothing to do with that. Some incompetent proofreader is the guilty party. My punctuation never goes beyond a comma or a period. Anything more complicated than that confuses me.

It was nice hearing from a successful writer. The only other one I've ever had any correspondence with was Somerset Maugham, who recently announced that he now considered himself an extinct volcano. Hoping this finds you on the top of one, I remain,

Cordially,
Groucho Marx

TO ALEXANDER KING

March 21, 1960

Dear Alex:

I continue to watch you on the Jack Paar show with openmouthed amazement. I've heard some pretty fair conversationalists in my time (and don't forget, my time is your time—and then some), but you are undoubtedly the best off-the-cuff speaker I've ever listened to. For God's sake, stay well and don't stop slashing away at all the things that displease you.

With the current administration largely composed of ineffectual chowder-heads, it is inspiring to hear a still, small voice shouting the battle cry for freedom.

Best to you and to your wife.

Regards,
Groucho

FROM LEONARD LYONS
OF THE NEW YORK POST

October 26, 1960

Dear Groucho:

You may remember that when I introduced you to Brendan Behan at the Algonquin, you spoke of "Finnegans Wake." Behan said that in the Algonquin at the time was a man who really understood the Joyce book—Thornton Wilder.

I mentioned this to Wilder. Yesterday, after he evidently did some research, Wilder wrote me:

Re Groucho and "Finnegans Wake"—I have long thought he was in the book. Weren't the Marx Brothers once in a skit about

Napoleon? I seem to remember them wearing tricornes, etc. Anyway, on pages 8 and 9 there is a visit to the Wellington Museum at Waterloo and I read . . . "This is the three lipoleum Coyne Grouching down in the living detch."

Wilder once tried to explain to me the key to "Finnegans Wake"—involving his constant use of puns. The three lipoleum Coyne must be a reference to the Napoleon-type hats. And Grouching makes you a verb.

On the authority of Thornton Wilder, the foremost Joyce scholar of the world, you can be assured that you are in "Finnegans Wake."

Congratulations and Mazel-Tov.

> With best regards,
> Leonard Lyons

November 4, 1960

Dear Lennie:

There's no reason why I shouldn't appear in "Finnegans Wake." I'm certainly as bewildered about life as Joyce was. Well, let Joyce be unconfined.

Tracing this item down from the "Wake" could be a life project and I question whether I'm up to it. Is it possible that Joyce at one time was in the U. S. A. and saw "I'll Say She Is!"? Or did a New York policeman, on his way back to Ireland to see his dear old Mother Machree, encounter Joyce in some peat bog and patiently explain to him that, at the Casino Theater at 39th and Broadway, there were three young Jewish fellows running around the stage shouting to an indifferent world that they were all Napoleon?

Anyway, thanks for the research, and if you run into Mr.

Wilder (and wouldn't I love to!) give him my love. If there's any left, take it for yourself.

Regards,
Groucho Marx

TO PETER LORRE

October 5, 1961

Dear Peter:

It was very thoughtful of you to send me a book explaining James Joyce's "Ulysses." All I need now is another book explaining this study by Stuart Gilbert who, if memory serves, painted the celebrated picture of George Washington which hangs in the Metropolitan Museum. I realize that there is some two hundreds years' difference in their ages, but any man who can explain Joyce must be very old and very wise.

You disappeared rather mysteriously the other night, but I attribute this to your life of crime in the movies.

Best to you both.

Regards,
Groucho

FROM FRANK SULLIVAN

January 9, 1960

Dear Groucho,

Your letter about that Moose book warmed the cockles of my heart and it was about time something warmed something around this burg. It has been very wintry here but that should not surprise anybody, as it is winter.

Well, I have a trade last for you. I have been delighted to see "Groucho and Me" right up there on the bestseller lists in the Times and Herald Trib every Sunday, and I had a fine time reading it, too. It warmed the cockles of my heart. I think those cockles are just about cooked now, and I better take them off the fire.

The attached clipping * from Variety reached me via Rome, Italy, where that oppressed and downtrodden share-cropper, Massa Nunnally Johnson, is hellin' around with Ava Gardner, making a picture. I begin to suspect that maybe I made a mistake back in 1931 when the world folded and I turned down an offer of a job in Hollywood from Winnie Sheehan. Who knows, I might be in some nice warm country today, directing Thelma Ritter. Nunnally writes that the Orson Welles clipping can't touch an item he once saw in a Hollywood trade paper that read, "H. B. Walthall has been signed for the role of the district attorney in Dante's 'Inferno.'"

My television is busted and I have been listening to you on radio, which is not as good as seeing you but better than not hearing you at all. Last night I caught the "solder" program with Emma the aged hiker and Max Shulman and I may say that I was rooting mentally for Max to answer "Mikoyan" to the big-money question. And he did, and it was wrong. I don't know the strength of my own extrasensory perceptions. I will send Max a check for the money he didn't win.

Happy New Year to you and the Missis and Melinda.

Yours,
Frank

* The clipping reads: "Orson Welles expected in Zagreb, Yugoslavia, to play Robert Fulton in "Napoleon at Austerlitz."

October 25, 1965

Dear Groucho,

Not all your letters are in the Library of Congress. At least two are in the Cornell University Library in the adjoining collections of mss., letters from famous people, incunabala, minutiae and lacunae donated to their alma mater last year by the Messrs. E. B. White and F. Sullivan. You are in company with about 300 letters to me from H. W. Ross, some of them hilarious, some of them uproarious and all of them enlightening. I could have contributed more Groucho letters to raise the literary tone of Cornell except two is all I ever got from you. At that you were a more prolific correspondent than Benchley. I could only find one from him, enclosing a check from his film company for some idea I contributed, and telling me in No Uncertain Terms, what I could do with it. If some serious-minded, prayerful candidate for a doctor's degree ever pores over that letter from Bench, and over Ross's and some of O'Hara's, he is going to be set right on his ass. Which, after all, is where we all are nowadays, isn't it.

Your true friend,
Frank

November 1, 1965

Dear Mr. Sullivan, or Frankie boy, as you prefer:

You could have knocked me over with a feather when I opened your letter this morning and discovered it was from the sage of Saratoga Springs. I don't know who addressed the envelope, but from the handwriting I would have guessed it was from some six-year-old fan of mine who couldn't live without my autograph. For a man who was employed years ago by a certain Mr. Ross, an irate bastard if there ever was

(148)

one, your handwriting has certainly deteriorated. Assuming that you addressed that envelope, my suggestion is for you to go back to Cornell University and take a refresher course in addressing envelopes. Years ago I used to have a girl friend who made a pretty good living addressing envelopes for a mail order firm in Hollywood. She used to get five dollars a night for a thousand envelopes and she would knock them off by midnight. The most of the night she spent in the sack with various men friends. She averaged about a hundred dollars a night, five dollars from the mail order business and ninety-five from the female order business. Well, that's about all there is to the story, it was only a brief romance, but I did salvage some of the envelopes for myself. Ah, youth, that it should be wasted on addressing envelopes.

My best to you and all the little Sullivans if there are any romping around the Springs.

Groucho

TO JOHN MASON BROWN

June 26, 1963

Dear Mr. Brown:

I'm halfway through your book and it's unquestionably the best thing I've read this year. And that goes for last year, too.

I think you made a mistake with the title.* I mean commercially. The average book buyer, as you know, is not a student of Latin, and the ones who can pronounce dramatis personae (or even corpus delicti) are few, indeed. Therefore, when one goes into a bookstore, fearful that he will mispro-

* "Dramatis Personae."

nounce the title, he usually abandons the whole project and winds up with a copy of Hedda Hopper's bestseller.

Don't be offended by the following suggestion. I know how your conversation sparkles. Why don't you make some personal appearances on the Tonight show, the Garry Moore show, Hugh Downs's early morning show and other national television shows that emanate from New York?

If you want a big seller (and with the exception of Proust, I don't know of any author who didn't), you'll have to get out and plug it just as we ordinary mortals do.

It would be a genuine literary loss if this book doesn't find the wide audience it deserves.

Regards,
Groucho

P.S. As Brooks Atkinson says, somewhat facetiously, "Why isn't it the book of the month?"

July 1, 1963

Dear Groucho,

I can't say "Mister." Everybody in this country knows you too well for that kind of formality. Now Karl is a different matter, but I have never been on speaking terms with him.

My sixty-third birthday is coming up this week, and even without your permission I am going to claim your letter as my most treasured present. It is a damned friendly, sensible, and helpful letter, one of the best epistles since St. Paul's, and with him I did not correspond.

Naturally what you say about the book sets me up no end. The publisher and I did have several talks about the difficulty of "Dramatis Personae" as a title. But we thought, perhaps too optimistically, that, since every high school student has had to read "Julius Caesar" and has encountered those words above the list of characters, it ought to be fairly clear. I knew we had been wrong when, a few days after the book came out, I went into a local bookshop and the nice man who runs the place asked me what it meant. The title I first suggested was one we obviously couldn't use, i.e., "The Portable John," and no doubt just as well. Even so, the book for that kind of book is really doing very well. It will never compete with Hedda Hopper and never be a bestseller. But there is some life in it, and I am pleased.

Thank you for your most considerate suggestions about the TV and radio appearances. I have already been on the Hugh Downs TV show and the Martha Deane radio program, and have some others coming up.

Needless to say, I am still dizzied by your saying it would be a "literary loss" and your agreeing with Brooks about the Book Club.

Again my deepest gratitude and thanks.

Cordially,
John Mason Brown

TO M. LINCOLN SCHUSTER OF SIMON AND SCHUSTER, PUBLISHERS

September 13, 1963

Dear Lincoln:

How you ever came by that name is certainly beyond me. Not that it isn't a good name, but you must admit it is far removed from your last name.

Would you by any chance have the original manuscript of "Many Happy Returns," a brilliant tome on the evils of taxation? It might have been the book of the year, except that shortly after it was published those little men in Tokyo blew Pearl Harbor to smithereens. (Frankly, I'm not sure what smithereens are, but it's a nice, long word and it gives even the most pedestrian letter (which this certainly is) a touch of class.)

Thanking you in advance, even if you can't find the manuscript.

Yours until hell freezes over.

Groucho

September 24, 1963

Dear Groucho:

Because of our abiding affection for you and a passionate devotion to your deathless prose, we organized a special archeological expeditionary force to dig up the original manuscript of "Many Happy Returns." We gave it the old college try, Groucho, by night and by day, by land and by sea, but alas, we hit solid rock below our warehouse, and found that a mass of old files had been completely destroyed by fire and flood a few years after your historic book was published. In other words, it was an act of God, and we beg your forgiveness for not being able to complete this search successfully. We throw ourselves on the mercy of the court.

As to my name "Lincoln," it all goes back to my lifelong devotion to the Gettysburg Address (not Ike's) and the Emancipation Proclamation, plus a childhood obsession with collecting Lincoln pennies, which enabled us eventually to finance the publication of your immortal masterpiece on the income tax, not to mention your son Arthur's classic biography, "Life with Groucho."

Sorry we couldn't comply with your wish. Your merest

whim is for us here at S&S a "command performance," which reminds me: Do you recall the cable that the Elman family sent out from Moscow when the great violinist was born? It read: "Mischa accomplished."

Devotedly, as ever,
M. Lincoln Schuster

TO BRYAN HOLME
OF THE VIKING PRESS

April 30, 1964

Dear Mr. Holme:

Mr. Hoffman (Irving, that is) must have been taking it in the arm when he told you I would do a front piece for Ronald Searle's collection.

Mr. Searle is unquestionably a genius, but for me to write the foreword would not only kill the sale of the book, but also ruin what is left of my vanishing career.

My knowledge of art is infinitesimal. I know that Rembrandt was deaf (no, that was Beethoven). I know that Van Gogh got hungry one day and cut off his own ear and that Toulouse Lautrec walked around on his knees. And that's about it.

What you need is the curator of the Museum of Modern Art or Peter Arno or Whitney Darrow or Rube Goldberg.

If there is anything I've written here that is usable for a quote, take it from there.

Sincerely,
Groucho Marx

P.S. The book is being returned under separate cover.

FROM T. S. ELIOT

26th April, 1961

Dear Groucho Marx,

This is to let you know that your portrait has arrived and has given me great joy and will soon appear in its frame on my wall with other famous friends such as W. B. Yeats and Paul Valery. Whether you really want a photograph of me or whether you merely asked for it out of politeness, you are going to get one anyway. I am ordering a copy of one of my better ones and I shall certainly inscribe it with my gratitude and assurance of admiration. You will have learned that you are my most coveted pin-up. I shall be happy to occupy a much humbler place in your collection.

And incidentally, if and when you and Mrs. Marx are in London, my wife and I hope that you will dine with us.

Yours very sincerely,

T. S. Eliot

P.S. I like cigars too but there isn't any cigar in my portrait either.

June 19, 1961

Dear T. S.:

Your photograph arrived in good shape and I hope this note of thanks finds you in the same condition.

I had no idea you were so handsome. Why you haven't been offered the lead in some sexy movies I can only attribute to the stupidity of the casting directors.

Should I come to London I will certainly take advantage

of your kind invitation and if you come to California I hope you will allow me to do the same.

> Cordially,
> Groucho Marx

January 25, 1963

Dear Mr. Eliot:

I read in the current Time Magazine that you are ill. I just want you to know that I am rooting for your quick recovery. First because of your contributions to literature and, then, the fact that under the most trying conditions you never stopped smoking cigars.

Hurry up and get well.

> Regards,
> Groucho Marx

23rd February, 1963

Dear Groucho Marx,

It seems more of an impertinence to address Groucho Marx as "Dear Mr. Marx" than it would be to address any other celebrity by his first name. It is out of respect, my dear Groucho, that I address you as I do. I should only be too happy to have a letter from Groucho Marx beginning "Dear T. S. E." However, this is to thank you for your letter and to say that I am convalescing as fast as the awful winter weather permits, that my wife and I hope to get to Bermuda later next month for warmth and fresh air and to be back in London in time to greet you in the spring. So come, let us say, about the beginning of May.

Will Mrs. Groucho be with you? (We think we saw you

both in Jamaica early in 1961, about to embark in that glass-bottomed boat from which we had just escaped.) You ought to bring a secretary, a public relations official and a couple of private detectives, to protect you from the London press; but however numerous your engagements, we hope you will give us the honour of taking a meal with us.

Yours very sincerely,
T. S. Eliot

P.S. Your portrait is framed on my office mantelpiece, but I have to point you out to my visitors as nobody recognises you without the cigar and rolling eyes. I shall try to provide a cigar worthy of you.

16th May, 1963

Dear Groucho,

I ought to have written at once on my return from Bermuda to thank you for the second beautiful photograph of Groucho, but after being in hospital for five weeks at the end of the year, and then at home for as many under my wife's care, I was shipped off to Bermuda in the hope of getting warmer weather and have only just returned. Still not quite normal activity, but hope to be about when you and Mrs. Groucho turn up. Is there any date known? We shall be away in Yorkshire at the end of June and the early part of July, but are here all the rest of the summer.

Meanwhile, your splendid new portrait is at the framers. I like them both very much and I cannot make up my mind which one to take home and which one to put on my office wall. The new one would impress visitors more, especially those I want to impress, as it is unmistakably Groucho. The only solution may be to carry them both with me every day.

Whether I can produce as good a cigar for you as the one in the portrait appears to be, I do not know, but I will do my best.

> Gratefully,
> Your admirer,
> T.S.

June 11, 1963

Dear Mr. Eliot:

I am a pretty shabby correspondent. I have your letter of May 16th in front of me and I am just getting around to it.

The fact is, the best laid plans of mice and men, etc. Soon after your letter arrived I was struck down by a mild infection. I'm still not over it, but all plans of getting away this summer have gone by the board.

My plan now is to visit Israel the first part of October when all the tourists are back from their various journeys. Then, on my way back from Israel, I will stop off in London to see you.

I hope you have fully recovered from your illness, and don't let anything else happen to you. In October, remember you and I will get drunk together.

> Cordially,
> Groucho

24th June, 1963

Dear Groucho,

This is not altogether bad news because I shall be in better condition for drinking in October than I am now. I envy you going to Israel and I wish I could go there too if the winter climate is good as I have a keen admiration for that country. I hope to hear about your visit when I see you and I hope that, meanwhile, we shall both be in the best of health.

One of your portraits is on the wall of my office room and the other one on my desk at home.

Salutations,

T. S.

October 1, 1963

Dear Tom:

If this isn't your first name, I'm in a hell of a fix! But I think I read somewhere that your first name is the same as Tom Gibbons', a prizefighter who once lived in St. Paul.

I had no idea you were seventy-five. There's a magnificent tribute to you in the New York Times Book Review Section of the September 29th issue. If you don't get the New York Times let me know and I'll send you my copy. There is an excellent photograph of you by a Mr. Gerald Kelly. I would say, judging from this picture, that you are about sixty and two weeks.

There was also a paragraph mentioning the many portraits that are housed in your study. One name was conspicuous by its absence. I trust this was an oversight on the part of Stephen Spender.

My illness which, three months ago, my three doctors described as trivial, is having quite a run in my system. The three medics, I regret to say, are living on the fat of the land. So far, they've hooked me for eight thousand bucks. I only mention this to explain why I can't get over there in October. However, by next May or thereabouts, I hope to be well enough to eat that free meal you've been promising me for the past two years.

My best to you and your lovely wife, whoever she may be.

I hope you are well again.

Kindest regards,
Groucho

16th October, 1963

Dear Groucho,

Yours of October 1st to hand. I cannot recall the name of Tom Gibbons at present, but if he helps you to remember my name that is all right with me.

I think that Stephen Spender was only attempting to enumerate oil and water colour pictures and not photographs —I trust so. But, there are a good many photographs of relatives and friends in my study, although I do not recall Stephen going in there. He sent me what he wrote for the New York Times and I helped him a bit and reminded him that I had a good many books, as he might have seen if he had looked about him.

There is also a conspicuous and important portrait in my office room which has been identified by many of my visitors together with other friends of both sexes.

I am sorry that you are not coming over here this year, and still sorrier for the reason for it. I hope, however, that you will turn up in the spring if your doctors leave you a few nickels to pay your way. If you do not turn up, I am afraid all the people to whom I have boasted of knowing you (and on being on first name terms at that) will take me for a four flusher. There will be a free meal and free drinks for you by next May. Meanwhile, we shall be in New York for the month of December and if you should happen to be passing through there at that time of year, I hope you will take a free meal there on me. I would be delighted to see you wherever we are and proud to be seen in your company. My lovely wife joins me in sending you our best, but she didn't add 'whoever he may be'—she knows. It was I who introduced her in the first place to the Marx Brothers films and she is now as keen a fan as I am. Not long ago we went to see a revival of "The Marx Brothers Go West," which I had never seen before. It was certainly worth it.

Ever yours,
Tom

P.S. The photograph is on an oil portrait, done 2 years ago, not a photograph direct from life. It is very good-looking and my wife thinks it is a very accurate representation of me.

November 1, 1963

Dear Tom:

Since you are actually an early American, (I don't mean that you are an old piece of furniture, but you are a fugitive from St. Louis), you should have heard of Tom Gibbons. For your edification, Tom Gibbons was a native of St. Paul, Minnesota, which is only a stone's throw from Missouri. That is, if the stone is encased in a missile. Tom was, at one time, the light-heavyweight champion of the world, and, although outweighed by twenty pounds by Jack Dempsey, he fought him to a standstill in Shelby, Montana.

The name Tom fits many things. There was once a famous Jewish actor named Thomashevsky. All male cats are named Tom—unless they have been fixed. In that case they are just neutral and, as the upheaval in Saigon has just proved, there is no place any more for neutrals.

There is an old nursery rhyme that begins "Tom, Tom,

the piper's son," etc. The third President of the United States first name was Tom . . . in case you've forgotten Jefferson.

So, when I call you Tom, this means you are a mixture of a heavyweight prizefighter, a male alley cat and the third President of the United States.

I have just finished my latest opus, "Memoirs of a Mangy Lover." Most of it is autobiographical and very little of it is fiction. I doubt whether it will live through the ages, but if you are in a sexy mood the night you read it, it may stimulate you beyond recognition and rekindle memories that you haven't recalled in years.

Sex, as an industry, is big business in this country, as it is in England. It's something everyone is deeply interested in even if only theoretically. I suppose it's always been this way, but I believe that in the old days it was discussed and practiced in a more surreptitious manner. However, the new school of writers have finally brought the bedroom and the lavatory out into the open for everyone to see. You can blame the whole thing on Havelock Ellis, Krafft-Ebing and Brill, Jung and Freud. (Now there's a trio for you!) Plus, of course, the late Mr. Kinsey who, not satisfied with hearsay, trundled from house to house, sticking his nose in where angels have always feared to tread.

However I would be interested in reading your views on sex, so don't hesitate. Confide in me. Though admittedly unreliable, I can be trusted with matters as important as that.

If there is a possibility of my being in New York in December, I will certainly try to make it and will let you know in time.

My best to you and Mrs. Tom.

Yours,
Groucho

3rd June, 1964

Dear Groucho,

This is to let you know that we have arranged for a car from International Car Hire (a firm of whom we make a good deal of use) to collect you and Mrs. Groucho at 6:40 P.M. on Saturday from the Savoy, and to bring you to us for dinner and take you home again at the end of the evening. You are, of course, our guests entirely, and we look forward to seeing you both with great pleasure.

The picture of you in the newspapers saying that, amongst other reasons, you have come to London to see me has greatly enhanced my credit in the neighbourhood, and particularly with the greengrocer across the street. Obviously I am now someone of importance.

Ever yours,
Tom

TO GUMMO MARX

June, 1964

Dear Gummo:

Last night Eden and I had dinner wth my celebrated pen pal, T. S. Eliot. It was a memorable evening.

The poet met us at the door with Mrs. Eliot, a good-looking, middle-aged blonde whose eyes seemed to fill up with adoration every time she looked at her husband. He, by the way, is tall, lean and rather stooped over; but whether this is from age, illness or both, I don't know.

At any rate, your correspondent arrived at the Eliots' fully prepared for a literary evening. During the week I had read "Murder in the Cathedral" twice; "The Waste Land" three times, and just in case of a conversational bottleneck, I brushed up on "King Lear."

Well, sir, as cocktails were served, there was a momentary lull—the kind that is more or less inevitable when strangers meet for the first time. So, apropos of practically nothing (and "not with a bang but a whimper") I tossed in a quotation from "The Waste Land." That, I thought, will show him I've read a thing or two besides my press notices from vaudeville.

Eliot smiled faintly—as though to say he was thoroughly familiar with his poems and didn't need me to recite them. So I took a whack at "King Lear." I said the king was an incredibly foolish old man, which God knows he *was;* and that if he'd been *my* father I would have run away from home at the age of eight—instead of waiting until I was ten.

That, too, failed to bowl over the poet. He seemed more interested in discussing "Animal Crackers" and "A Night at the Opera." He quoted a joke—one of mine—that I had long since forgotten. Now it was my turn to smile faintly. I was not going to let anyone—not even the British poet from St. Louis—spoil my Literary Evening. I pointed out that King Lear's opening speech was the height of idiocy. Imagine (I said) a father asking his three children: Which of you kids loves me the most? And then disowning the youngest—the sweet, honest Cordelia—because, unlike her wicked sister, she couldn't bring herself to gush out insincere flattery. And Cordelia, mind you, had been her father's favorite!

The Eliots listened politely. Mrs. Eliot then defended Shakespeare; and Eden, too, I regret to say, was on King Lear's side, even though I am the one who supports her. (In all fairness to my wife, I must say that, having played the Princess in a high school production of "The Swan," she has retained a rather warm feeling for all royalty.)

As for Eliot, he asked if I remembered the courtroom

scene in "Duck Soup." Fortunately I'd forgotten every word. It was obviously the end of the Literary Evening, but very pleasant none the less. I discovered that Eliot and I had three things in common: (1) an affection for good cigars and (2) cats; and (3) a weakness for making puns—a weakness that for many years I have tried to overcome. T. S., on the other hand, is an unashamed—even proud—punster. For example, there's his Gus, the Theater Cat, whose "real name was Asparagus."

Speaking of asparagus, the dinner included good, solid English beef, very well prepared. And, although they had a semi-butler serving, Eliot insisted on pouring the wine himself. It was an excellent wine and no maitre d' could have served it more graciously. He is a dear man and a charming host.

When I told him that my daughter Melinda was studying his poetry at Beverly High, he said he regretted that, because he had no wish to become compulsory reading.

We didn't stay late, for we both felt that he wasn't up to a long evening of conversation—especially mine.

Did I tell you we called him Tom?—possibly because that's his name. I, of course, asked him to call me Tom too, but only because I loathe the name Julius.

Yours,
Tom Marx

FROM A LETTER TO RUSSELL BAKER

January 21, 1965

"I was saddened by the death of T. S. Eliot. My wife and I had dinner at his home a few months ago and I realized then that he was not long for this world. He was a nice man, the best epitaph any man can have . . ."

(164)

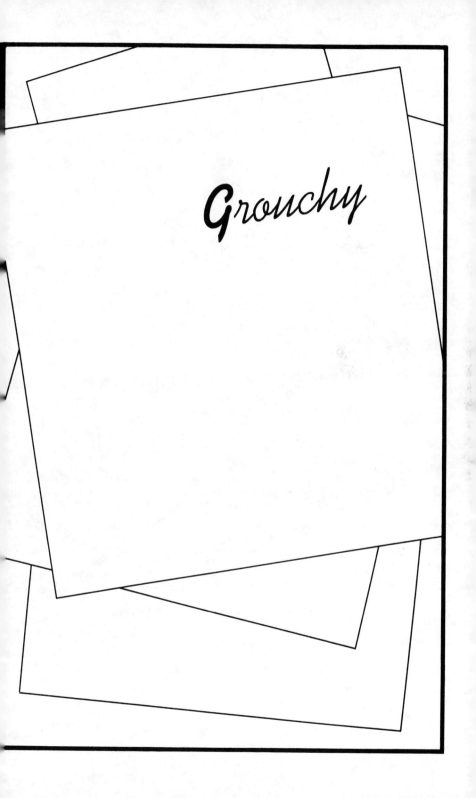

Grouchy

TO JACK GOULD
OF THE NEW YORK TIMES

December 28, 1949

Dear Mr. Gould:

I was really impressed by your analysis of the show not only because of its complimentary tone, but because it so accurately described so many of the evils of radio. I must say that originally I approached the job of radio quiz master with all the enthusiasm of a man about to handle a dead snake. I pointed out, rather querulously, that there were hundreds of quiz shows on the air and what would be the point of throwing another one into this quivering medium. I added, too, that by and large they all sickened me and I stipulated that if I were to accept this job I would insist on reasonably difficult questions, no toadying to the contestants, no false hysterical laughter and the rest of the childish claptrap that quiz masters, with few exceptions (names on request), are addicted to.

I could go on and on but I realize that getting out the Sunday Times all by yourself must be quite a chore so I'll sign off and wish you a snowy winter, a rainy spring and a wet summer.

Sincerely,
Groucho Marx

TO BETTY FORSLING

December 6, 1950

Dear Betty:

I have solved the television problem by having a remote control installed on the ugly box. As soon as the first word of the commercial is heard, bang goes the little switch and the idiot barker bellowing the virtues of Odorono, Lifeguard tubes, Mohawk carpets or Halo shampoo is silenced into instant oblivion. Of course it would be embarrassing if my sponsor should get wind of this device but they are so busy in Detroit converting from automobiles to five passenger cannons that I think I can continue to play with my luck.

I still think you should come to the coast, even if only to get away from the Long Island Railroad. It's lovely this time of the year—the fake snow on Hollywood Boulevard, the fakes on Sunset Boulevard, and the studios bursting with pictures that can't be released. Speaking of pictures that can't be released, I did one two years ago with Jane Russell, she of the noted bust, which for some reason or other Howard Hughes has hidden in the vault. And now I have signed to do one with Marie Wilson. Apparently there's something about me that attracts these remarkable features. Some day I expect to do a picture with Mae West if, in the meantime, she doesn't die from curvature of the bed.

I hope you are well and adore me as much as ever. If you want to come out I'll pay your fare as far west as Schenectady —they're not going to get me under the Mann Act.

Groucho

TO EDWIN K. ZITTELL
OF LOOK MAGAZINE

February 1, 1951

Dear Mr. Zittell:

Mr. Leo Rosten writes dazzlingly and engagingly, but unfortunately inaccurately about Miss Bankhead. I know because some weeks ago he wrote about me, and described me as a harum-scarum clown willing and eager to commit any kind of mayhem to gain a laugh. Actually I am an elderly student thirsting for learning and solitude, leading an exemplary and sedentary life in a bookish and cloistered atmosphere.

I know Miss Bankhead very well and this full-blown act that she assumes for the press is completely phony. To them she presents herself as a carefree gamin, a social rebel kicking up her heels, frantically dashing from one hot party to another, flouting all the conventions of civilized society just for the hell of it.

This is not the real Tallulah. The one I know is a small-town girl trapped in a profession she loathes, yearning for a touch of the soil; dreaming of a little farm in the backwoods, the gurgle of well water, perhaps a cow or two, a few chickens cackling in the sun, the smell of new-mown hay, and a mate, sunburned and raw-boned, by her side.

In the not too distant future if you happen to drive down Highway Seven between Little Rock and Van Buren and you are hungry for fried possum and corn pone, stop awhile at Bankhead's Beanery. Yes, the motherly little introvert bending over the old wood burner will be the erstwhile madcap Tallulah. And at the cash register you will see the shadow of what was once Groucho Marx. Tell Leo Rosten, your bewildered Boswell, to come down and visit us. He'll get no fried

possum and corn pone, but we'll fry the February 13th issue
of Look and make him eat it word by word.

Sincerely,
Groucho Marx

TO ABEL GREEN

June 7, 1951

Dear Abel:

I believe the emphasis on popcorn and other noise-making
foods has helped to drive many people away from the movies,
and I think the commercial pounding that the television listeners are subjected to will eventually drive many of them away
from their sets.

Where they will go I don't know. Perhaps they will take
up fox hunting or glass blowing, or maybe they will just roam
the streets at night searching for peace and quiet.

My comments are necessarily brief and cautious, for in
my profession it is extremely hazardous for a comedian to
outrage the sponsor, for without the commercial he hasn't got
a job and without a job he is hardly a comedian.

Sincerely,
Groucho

TO THE PRESIDENT OF THE CHRYSLER CORPORATION

December 1, 1954

Dear Mr. Colbert:

My mother always told me that if I had anything of importance to discuss, to go to the top.

Each year the motor manufacturers hammer home the idea of more horsepower. I realize a reasonable amount of power is necessary, but I think it would be much smarter if emphasis were placed on safety rather than on additional speed. Perhaps the ads next year should read, "prettier, faster and safe." I also think that if a device could be installed on the carburetor (I understand there are such things) that would eliminate the belching of carbon monoxide through the city streets, the Chrysler Corporation could create an enormous amount of good will, particularly in big cities where the carbon monoxide problem is especially acute.

Every morning the front page reports of people killed in auto accidents. A good percentage of these fatalities could be eliminated if the motorist had a reasonable amount of protection. The average car driver in a modern automobile is a sitting duck. There is nothing to protect him. The records show he would be far safer on a battlefield.

Your new cars look good, but the fact of the matter is that all the new cars look good, and I firmly believe that the first automobile company that starts stressing safety instead of speed will win far more than its share of the business.

Sincerely yours,
Groucho Marx

TO HARRY KURNITZ

February 3, 1956

Dear Harry:

Now that you are published regularly in Holiday Magazine, there really isn't much point in continuing this correspondence. I liked the piece in the January issue very much, and as soon as I go to the dentist I will read the February issue.

Incidentally, this dentist of mine is a gay fellow, a bachelor. Instead of stocking his anteroom with the National Geographic and articles on Soil Conservation, he has Confidential, Rave, Holiday, "Fanny Hill," "Call House Madam," and "A House Is Not a Home."

His assistant (who cleans the teeth before the master deigns to step into the horror chamber) is a part-time whore, and can be seen soliciting between Burbank, Glendale and Maywood on Wednesdays, Saturdays and Sundays. On those days the dentist is absent. He has either winged to Las Vegas to lose the exorbitant sums that he has extracted from me, along with my teeth, or is surf-riding in Acapulco.

The whole dental profession, in addition to being corrupt, is a dubious one. When you open your trap in a dentist's office, and he seems to peer down your gullet, the chances are he's not even looking there. He's trying to estimate (rapidly) who made your sport coat and whether the jewelry you're sporting is the real thing or some thin plate you borrowed from your wife.

I heartily disapprove of dentists going to Vegas, Acapulco or any other fancy resort. A dentist should stay in his office with his part-time whore, his glittering machines, his inlays and that goddamned abrasive that he slaps on your fangs at the end of a day's grinding.

Love,
Groucho

P.S. How would you like Knowland for President?

TO FRED ALLEN

March 4, 1956

Dear Fred:

I don't know about New York, but out here Spring is right around the corner. In the offing are Emmy awards, Look awards, Redbook awards, Academy Awards, and all the various TV and radio medals and scrolls that TV actors keep handing to one other. It's pretty tiresome and slightly nauseating.

This year I surmise that overexposure will be the death of many a half-hour show. I'm surprised I've lasted this long and I attribute this to the fact that nobody sees my show. By comparison, what a leisurely business vaudeville was! TV is the rat race of the century. The sponsor on my show now has a commercial which shows De Sotos flying in the air. Why this should make it a satisfactory vehicle in which to drive to the supermarket, is beyond me, but I have a remote control on my set and I just don't listen to anything.

My best to the juggler's delight—and take care of yourself.

Regards,
Groucho

TO GOODMAN ACE

September 16, 1960

Dear Goody:

Now that the winter solstice is rapidly approaching, here you are back cracking barbershop jokes for the Italian barber; I am making my annual farewell appearance for Kintner, Sarnoff, etc., and things seem to be back where they were when Coolidge was President, and boy, couldn't we use him now!

I have again decided to forsake the Savoy, and for sound reasons. The hotel, as you well know, is across the street from Schwarz's toy store and I suddenly realized some weeks ago that I don't have to buy toys any more. Melinda is now 14 and my guess is she's out after much larger and livelier game. She has just started Beverly Hills High and that's where life begins. Despite this she still watches TV with a religious fervor.

I didn't like the play, "Anniversary Waltz," but there was a scene in it where one of the characters, after a particularly long commercial (for B.O. soap, I think it was), raised his right foot and kicked the set to small pieces. A child's mind must inevitably rot, looking at this dreary procession of nonsense night after night, and I think that the next ten years will produce a population composed entirely of goons. I would kick Melinda's set to small chunks, but there's one in every room and I haven't got enough character to destroy six sets, two of them in color. I'm not trying to be comic about this. It disturbs me deeply that the TV set has become such an integral part of her life and the life of all her friends.

When I was a kid, we used to read. I keep throwing books into Melinda's room but she keeps throwing them out. Last night she threw me out as well. For me, the only good thing about TV is that it has allowed me to earn far more money that I deserve.

Your letter was very funny and long; and since I will be seeing you in a fortnight, we can then talk until the cows come home. (I think there's still one in Central Park.)

Until then, so long, skol, arrivederci, prosit, salud, hasta la vista, à bientôt and ciao. (Ciao, in case you don't know, is an Italian salutation. It is also a breed of dog that will bite your ass off for no reason at all.)

Fondly,
Groucho

December 13, 1960

Dear Mr. A:

When you called me last Tuesday at 9 o'clock Pacific Standard Time and told me I looked absolutely beautiful on the Susskind show, I immediately knew that the hour was lousy. Any time a man calls long distance to emphasize the fact that an ancient comedian looks enchanting, the comedian —unless he is a full-blown jerk—realizes instinctively that he has failed in his mission and that all he is getting out of it is a comparatively large sum of money which, come April 15th, he will reluctantly hand over to the tax department.

I think Mr. Susskind made a great mistake in the kind of questions he asked. There he was, sitting in the seat of mighty, surrounded by five broken-down ex-vaudevillians girding themselves for convulsive laughter, and his first question was something like, did we think it fair for Germany to refuse to give us the six hundred million that Secretary Anderson went over to collect? Halfway through the question Durante's body slumped sideways, his eyes became glazed and it was only quick action by George Burns that prevented Jimmy from falling off the chair. Now this is a hell of a way to start a rip-roaring comedy show—and so it went. I must say, however, that the camera work was magnificent. Every time I spoke, the camera was on someone else. Since this show I have been called (among other things) "the ghost comedian." I might just as well have been on radio.

The hour draws late and my domestics are champing at the bit. They have chilled the rare wines, warmed the ambrosia and I can only tell you that another indescribable evening awaits me.

Love to you and that kid you're living with.

Groucho

TO PETE MARTIN OF THE
SATURDAY EVENING POST

December 21, 1960

Dear Pete:

I saw you on "Open End" last Sunday, and it's about time someone spoke up about Freud and his disciples. I'm so sick of that nonsense. To wit: (a) Parents are responsible for all children who turn out badly. They hated either their mother, their father, or both. (b) All people in show business had unhappy childhoods and compensated for it by going on the stage.

Take my own case, for example. I loved my mother and my father. They were wonderful people and we had great times together. I went into show business because my mother's brother was Al Shean. He was netting $250 a week (sans taxes) and I quickly decided that if this kind of money was laying around in show business, I was going to get a piece of it.

I don't doubt that analysis has done some good for a few people. I have no way of knowing, but I wouldn't be surprised if it's hurt more people than it has helped. If analysis did nothing else, it left a lot of people with a hell of a lot less money than they started with.

I hope you are well and enjoying the holidays.

Regards,
Groucho Marx

EXTRACT FROM A LETTER
TO NORMAN KRASNA

July 5, 1961

. . . The other night I went to see "The Balcony." This is another slice of avant-garde that is polluting the side streets of every major city. I don't know if you are familiar with this opus but it was written by an angry old or young man named Genet. His thesis is that the entire world is a vast whore house and everyone residing in it is corrupt, one way or another. I don't argue with this idea but most of the language is in symbols. For example, if you think one of the characters is a policeman, it turns out later that he's a newsboy. I didn't stay for the second act but I was told afterward that the woman who plays the madam in the first act turns out to be a bus driver in the second act. The madam may have had some interesting things to say, but she was lying on a bed with one of her girls (or, I guess you could call her an "employee"), and in this scene they spent about twenty minutes mumbling to each other in words that didn't reach the fourth row— which is where I was hibernating.

The following morning I received a phone call from Jim Henaghan who told me that after the play, he was standing in the lobby when the producer of this turkey asked him how he liked it. Henaghan, who talks in a very loud, heavy baritone, told him what he thought, not only of the show but of the producer as well. The police finally came and hauled him off to the local pokey. It took a few hours before he was able to get bail and he is now suing the producer, the author, the director and the madam of the whore house (who, for all I know, is still lying on the bed with her girl friend).

I spoke to Polly Adler in the lobby before the curtain went up, hoping she could brief me on the authenticity of the locale, but she refused to talk on the grounds that it might incriminate her. She did say that she has some money in the play and if it goes over big she may open up again. (What, she didn't say.)

This play is now in its second year off Broadway and it is absurd for me to say it isn't any good. For all I know it might be the greatest play that's ever been written but I didn't understand it, just as I didn't understand "Krapp's Last Tape." If you turn that title around you will have an idea of what I thought of that one. I'm an old-fashioned man and I dig "Bye, Bye Birdie" and "My Fair Lady," and the only reason I go to these others is to please my wife, Eden, who has a passion for any form of show business. Well, if this is show business, I'm glad I'm getting out . . .

TO EARL WILSON

January 17, 1962

Dear Oil:

The last days of the newspapers seem to be rushing toward us with frightening speed. This past week both the Examiner and the Mirror disappeared into limbo and news from the outside world is shrinking rapidly. No more will I know what Taffy Tuttle did to Alice G. Whiz, and with the absence of your column I won't even be sure what I did in New York the last time I was there. Even John Crosby will have to hate Hollywood in some other section of the country. It's all too sad.

I predict the time is rapidly coming when there will be but one newspaper in the United States and that will be published around Emporia, Kansas or Pierre, South Dakota.

Should you journey this way, hell-bent for sex or gambling, I'm not very good at either but I'd be very willing to take you around.

My best to you, the B. W. and Slugger.

Cordially,
Groucho

TO ROBERT RUARK

June 26, 1963

Dear Mr. Ruark:

Thanks for your piece on dirty comedians. It blew a fresh breeze across a smutty section of America.

Freedom of speech is one thing, but these gents are overdoing it. And when I say "gents," this is where most of them should be doing their act.

Sincerely yours,
Groucho Marx

Broadway
and
Hollywood

FROM HARRY RUBY

Dear Groucho:

Thanks for the cabled good wishes. I'm sorry you asked how the show ("Helen of Troy, New York") opened out of town, but I'll answer your question as soon as I can stop crying.

To begin with, I believe we had a right to be optimistic. After all, two of the brightest men in the theater, Kaufman and Connelly, wrote the book; Bert (Kalmar) and I turned out, I believe, a pretty good score; and George Jessel and Rufus LeMaire dug up some very nice dough for the production; and a cast that includes such worthies as Helen Ford, Roy Atwell, Paul Frawley, Queenie Smith and Tom Lewis.

As for the out-of-town opening, it occurred in Fairmont, West Virginia. It was the very first time a Broadway show opened in the fair town of Fairmont, West Virginia—and, I suspect, the very last time.

As you may know, the plot revolves around the trials and tribulations of the president of a collar factory in Troy, N.Y., Tom Lewis, who is around seventy and usually has trouble remembering his lines during the first few weeks of a new show.

In the second act there is a scene that is supposed to be the turning point of the show. It turned out to be the turning point of the evening.

Tom was presiding over a conference with three of his top executives. They were having one hell of a time trying to agree on a name for a new collar that was about to hit the market. And they weren't getting anyplace.

Just as they were about to call it a day, Tom rose, called for quiet, and was supposed to say, "Gentlemen, I think I've got it. How about calling the new collar Tamerlane?"

But poor Tom couldn't remember the line. He stuttered, paced to and fro and gesticulated. Then, walking down front, he went smack into a vaudeville monologue he used to do before he clicked as a legit actor on Broadway.

As I need not tell you, Tom's monologue had nothing whatever to do with the plot of the show. The customers out front were completely bewildered. The actors on the stage just stood there—speechless, motionless, dazed.

Kalmar, Jessel, LeMaire and I, who were seeing the show from the last row, got panicky. We went looking for Kaufman and Connelly, who were nowhere to be found. The four of us dashed down a side aisle, went backstage, stood in the wings and—at the top of our voices—kept yelling the line at Tom. This confused him and the audience even more.

Whether or not Tom heard what we were yelling from the wings, I don't know. But just about ten minutes after he started his monologue, he stopped abruptly and, turning to the bewildered actors on the stage, said: "Gentlemen, I think I've got it. How about calling the collar Tamerlane?"

When the final curtain descended about twenty minutes later, the applause was anything but deafening. There were no curtain calls.

Anyway, we'll be on the road for another ten days, trying to get the show ready for Broadway.* Whether we'll be ready, I don't know. That opening night did nothing for the cast's morale. Or mine.

However,

Sincerely,
Harry

TO ARTHUR SHEEKMAN

November 4, 1930

Dear Grant:

There are three reasons why I haven't written to you. First, I wasn't sure where I was going next week, second, four leaps a day leaves very little time for a letter writing, and the last and most important reason was, that I could not think of anything to say.

This is a very unsatisfactory and trying existence, and if continued for any length of time will probably lead to suicide. I arise in the morning and before I have had my clothes on ten minutes, I am over at the theater doing the ordering scene. Then follows thirty minutes of Harpo climbing up Dumont's leg, and the shirt scene, and then to the dressing room for what I imagine is going to be a good long rest. I am no more than seated with the Morning World, when the buzzer rings and I am downstairs again doing the ordering scene, and Harpo is back again at Dumont's leg. After four shots of this, I stagger to my hotel, go to bed, and the alarm rings and I rush over to the theater and do the ordering scene again.

* The following footnote was supplied, 43 years later, by Mr. Ruby: "On the night of August 27, that very same year, 'Helen of Troy, New York,' billed as 'The Perfect Musical Comedy,' opened (and it closed the same way, six weeks later). H.R."

I am sorry now that I urged you to come to New York; if it wasn't for that you would be back in Chicago and could interview me for the Daily Times. I can't write any more as I have to go, the buzzer has just buzzed and I have to go down and do the ordering scene.

Love from
Groucho

P.S. Palace Theater Chicago next week.

June, 194?

Dear Sheek:

I realized you had no news to tell me when I read your letter and found it was full of your daughter's witty sayings. I am very fond of your daughter and think she is bright, precocious and pretty, but if your letters are going to consist of retailing Sylvia's remarks, I don't see why I can't eliminate the middle man and correspond with her directly. I'm really not complaining; as a matter of fact, what you told me about Sylvia was much more entertaining than what you told me about yourself.

A play, called "Heart of the City"—a big hit in London that skidded badly in New York—was purchased by Lester Cowan. He is producing it as a movie with Merle Oberon, Gracie Fields and, if the part can be sufficiently built up, I'll project my scintillating personality into it.

With love to all,
Groucho

Skowhegan, Maine, 194?

Dear Sheek:

I am slowly regaining my strength, and in a short time will be up and about. This is really silly. I haven't been sick, but I think that if one is living in the country, a line like this doesn't do a letter any harm. It arouses sympathy. In other words, it gives the audience someone to root for.

I read a piece in the American Mercury not long ago, about the harmful effects that tennis can have on a middle-aged man, so I gave my racket to Miriam for six dollars (it cost me nine when new) and am back in the rough on the golf courses, kidding myself into the belief that it interests me, and that I am having a good time. This is a lovely spot up here, but it is inhabited mainly by octogenarians, and I am beginning to yearn again for the tattle of little children.

Among the little kids that enter into the evening's small chitchat here are William A. Brady (71), his wife Grace George, who claims fifty, talks like sixty and is really seventy, Owen Davis who's a good sixty-five (if there is such a thing as a good sixty-five), John B. Hymer whose last theatrical claim to fame is a collaboration with Samuel Shipman (66) on "East Is West" (1909), and a legit who played with Booth and Barrett, and gives Max Gordon a rubdown for five dollars a week.

In the evening we sit around a fireplace with nothing to drink (unless it's my house), very little to smoke (unless it's my house) and nothing to eat (unless I buy it), and discuss what's the matter with the theater. Is it dead? and where is the road gone to.

Brady makes a three-hour speech against Equity, and then I defend it in a speech lasting not over five minutes. I would make a longer speech but I am two years behind in my dues and I can't seem to get my heart into it.

Then Davis, in a high quivering voice, tells about the

good old days when he wrote "Icebound." By this time the fire has died down and Hymer is feeling Grace George's leg with his foot under the delusion that it is Ruth's (this goes on under the table). Then the clock tolls ten, and with a shout we all get up and beat it for bed as fast as our little legs will carry us. Davis and Brady are carried to bed by the legit and are just revived in time for the golf game the next day.

What a time the senior Rockefeller would have up here, and what a time I am having! It's a great little place and you can visualize it by just imagining three thousand George Arlisses running around.

Write me soon with love.

Yours,
Groucho

TO IRVING BRECHER

New York, December 16, 1940

Dear Brech,

This is either a day for writing, the early stages of a honeymoon, or fifteen grains of opium. It's raining, a very pretty rain; not the spasmodic kind that we get in California, but a long steady one, the kind they show in the newsreels with the natives sitting on the rooftops with their cattle, wives and chickens.

I know nothing about the radio situation, and I presume you know about as much. I thought the show we gave that night was good, but I have a hunch there is a deepseated aversion to accepting me in any role other than the one I have always played.

Our tour east was uneventful and fairly strenuous. We stopped off in Washington to see President Roosevelt and the

Spewack show. Roosevelt was out of town. It would have been just as well if the Spewack show had also been out of town, although it had a lot of very funny stuff in it.

Wednesday night I saw "George Washington Slept Here." Very amusing, and the critics ought to be ashamed of themselves for the knifing they gave it. Thursday night I saw "Hellzapoppin'," second time for me. I found it just as dirty and unfunny as I did last year. However, they are still selling out, and I'm sure they're not interested in my opinion. Friday night, the Ed Wynn show. Utterly delightful, a master comic, not a dirty line or joke in the entire two and a half hours. Saturday night, Al Lewis's "Cabin in the Sky." Good singing, dancing, Ethel Waters in top form, and a quaint story. Sunday night at the Garden with Morris Ernst. Rangers and Americans, ice hockey, tickets two-twenty, ice fine, track fast. Met Ira Gershwin this morning in the coffee shop at the Essex. He had three newspapers under his arm, and four bags under each eye. He told me he hadn't slept all night. Not worry, just keyed up. I'm sure you know the condition by now. I understand the show "Lady in the Dark" is great. It's the story of Moss Hart's psychoanalytical career, and I probably will go to Boston for the opening.

I'm leading a luxurious life. I'm sitting in the front rows at all the hits. I'm dining at the finest restaurants, and drinking choice wines and liqueurs. The whole thing is costing me a fortune, and I doubt if I will have enough money to return west. My daughter Miriam has been sitting in her ski clothes for the past three days. She imagined New York was something like Switzerland, and that she would be streaking down long, snowy inclines as they do in the advertisements for the Alps. If it doesn't snow in the next two weeks, I probably will have to take her to Lake Arrowhead when I return.

Regards,
Groucho

FROM S. J. PERELMAN

April 7, 1943

Dear Groucho,

Your initial broadcast reminded me that I was long over-due on a reply; and not to wear out my welcome, thank you for that splendid bit of sewage about Leo (Sunshine) Fon-a-Row and a lot of laughs (spelled "laffs") on the Blue Ribbon show. By now you have probably seen John Hutchens' piece in the radio section of last Sunday's Times, which shows that your fans are still legion. I really thought you goaled them and especially loved the business of playing straight to your-self on puns like "aria."

I have been tied up since mid-January on a musical with Ogden Nash and Kurt Weill ("One Touch of Venus") which we finished the end of this past week. Nash and I did the book (based on a short story by F. Anstey, who was the editor of Punch back in the eighties), and Ogden's now finishing up his lyrics for Weill's music. It's the story of a small schnükel of a barber who accidentally brings a statue of Venus to life, and it has turned up a lot of pretty funny and dirty complications. The music and lyrics thus far (about two-thirds finished) are grand, and we're dickering with several leading women cur-rently. Rehearsals start about August 1st. . . . All this happened as I was concluding work on the revue; I have six of the seven sketches finished for that, and the present design is to do it in the fall.

Also, just to make everything really giddy, I've been taking a course in bacteriology in my spare time, and if you need a fast Wassermann any time this spring, mail me the bottle. I'm putting up posters in subway washrooms after June 1st: "MEN: Why worry? See Dr. Morty Perelman, night or day—no more expensive than any quack."

Well, cuddles, my best to yourself and all the pretty girls

on the bridle path, and let's know the news. Did you, or are you still planning to, make "The Heart of a City"?

Love,

Sid

June 26, 1948

Dear Groucho,

Your letter was a kind deed in a naughty world (a phrase I copped out of Bartlett's book of quotations years ago and have been trying to work in ever since). It was particularly heartening since it arrived at one of those moments of self-laceration that free-lance writers sometimes experience (never more than eight hours a day, however). In these rare moods the subject is given to regarding himself through the wrong end of a telescope and inquiring through his teeth, "Too proud to stay in your father's dry goods business, eh? I told you that you'd rue the day." None of this, of course, would have happened had I actually stayed in my father's business, where my superb acumen would undoubtedly have made me the uncrowned king of the gingham trade.

This is an ideal opportunity, incidentally, to tell you that I enjoyed a considerable social success up and down the China coast after we saw each other last by merely mentioning that I knew you. In fact, in one or two tight spots, I took the liberty of actually pretending to *be* you, so if you are visited by any slant-eyed Celestials from Chefoo or Macao who present IOU's and request that you honor them, I beg your indulgence.

The soothsayers inform me that it's more than likely I may get to the Coast in the next few months and I look forward to sharing a convivial glass with you. Why don't we meet at Jerry Rothchild's barber shop on Beverly Drive, have our hair cut together, and then run over to Armstrong Schroeder's for some little thin hot-cakes? Are you game?

With Laura's tenderest regards, and the sincere assurance that your letter really touched me.

Yours,
Sid

TO ABEL GREEN
EDITOR OF VARIETY

July 27, 1948

Dear Greeney:

The Marx group photo arrived for which many thanks. I must say I was amazed and horrified at the quantity of hair we dragged around in the old days. It is not generally known, but now that it is in the dim past I don't mind confessing that as young men the Marxes were never a spectacular success either socially or romantically, but until the photo arrived I never knew why. It's all as clear now as tea room soup. I am convinced that the burden of dragging those hirsute mattresses around for three decades withered us body and soul.

Now, however, on a smogless day our gleaming skulls can be seen as far east as Cedar Rapids.

Well, anyway thanks for the memory. The whole thing is too disgusting for words, especially the words I would have to use to describe our present appearance.

Regards,
Groucho

November 10, 1948

Dear Abel:

I am slowly recovering from the lacing we received from the New York critics. I think, with few exceptions, they are a sorry lot. Gibbs, for example, in The New Yorker: "There wasn't a joke in the show." Either he was stewed or he neglected to turn on his hearing apparatus. So many of the reviews were of a personal nature. Lardner, in the Star, lampooned me because I had co-authored a play that wasn't sardonic, sarcastic or bitter. Krutch, in the Nation, chided me for departing from the character I always portrayed on the screen and stage. Gibbs also had to drag in Hollywood. Judging from the fury with which most of the critics attack the authors, one would think that presenting a play in New York was a criminal offense.

Well, the hell with them. I have two soft rackets, namely movies and radio, and they will never get another chance to slay me.

Regards,
Groucho

February 11, 1949

Dear Abel:

It may be just a coincidence, but the moment you screwed out of here (which, I am sure, is more than you did while here) the weather became as mild as a review in a trade paper after you've taken an ad. The trouble with you effete easterners is that you always journey out here during the rainy or snowy season instead of waiting until the cloudbursts and monsoons disappear.

I don't know why you don't quit your job on Variety and become a pensioner. Under this new set-up California will pay an indigent $70 a month. You can supplement this with a diet of frozen oranges, and wax fat and happy. If you weary of this you can have fat wax happy for a while. Even suicide is cheaper out here. The California motorist will, on the average, knock off three pedestrians a month.

Give it a thought. Die in the West and you're halfway to Heaven.

Regards,
Groucho

TO ABE BURROWS

January 18, 1951

Dear Abe:

I can't tell you how happy I am that you have finally become a big-shot author. I always suspected you had hidden talent, back when you were doing the parlors of Hollywood, and it's gratifying to see it finally emerge. Of course you wouldn't take my advice. Do you remember how vehemently I urged you to become a nightclub entertainer? Had you listened to me you could today conceivably be the top entertainer at Joe's Chez Paree in East Liverpool, Ohio, instead of being an author of a lousy Broadway hit "Guys and Dolls" which, according to the weekly Variety, did a shabby gross of $46,000 last week. Nobody ever takes my advice. I remember in 1932 telling Truman to stick to the haberdashery business, that there was a fortune in shirts and jockey shorts. But no, he ignored me and looked elsewhere for counsel.

Give my regards to your beautiful wife and take care of yourself.

Groucho

FROM HARRY KURNITZ

February 17, 1951

Lieber Groucho:

Last night I saw a broad we had both pursued during moments of our more active lives, when that sort of thing seemed a matter of life or death, and for one transfigured moment a bridge seemed to rear across the chasm of time and I saw you as you used to be, the golden boy, the child of the twenties, the man whose fame echoed from Moscowitz & Lupowitz to the Cafe Royale, a distance of 18¼ linear feet. What happened to us? Why couldn't we keep the dream alive? I would like to do a biography of you in this spirit but frankly, Groucho, you don't drink enough. If you think you can manage to become a sobbing alcoholic in the years yet allotted to you, let me know at once because a lot of people who have already qualified are clamoring for my attention.

Meanwhile I am doing a show, a musical, no less, based on Fowler's "Modern English Usage." Offhand, this may not seem like much of a boygirl plot but my guess is that the trend is away from that sort of thing. Rodgers & Hammerstein, for instance, are planning a musical adaptation of the famed Smythe Report: "Atomic Energy for Military Purposes" and Mike Todd is working on Carver's "Contract Law for First Year Students," a volume I remember from scholastic days, and which would be much improved by the incorporation of a few acres of tit.

When are you coming to N. Y.? Soon I hope. The coffee-house set languishes for you. The theater has been fun, in an in and out way. The international homosexual conspiracy to dominate the stage in N. Y., London and Paris makes the Comintern look like a road company of "The Student Prince." George and Leueen Kaufman had their heads knocked off last night. Anyway, it's still a great season for him because in "Guys and Dolls" he did a great job of directing and Abe Burrows says he was a tower of strength on the book. Still, he could have used a hit . . . as who could not?

Kurnitz

TO GEORGE S. KAUFMAN

September 5, 1951

Dear George:

I have been in show business man and boy for over forty years (seventy, to be exact), and up to now the only free tickets, or Annie Oakleys as they say in the show game, I ever received were from an uncle of mine named Julius who unfortunately lived in Weehawken. He had a shoe store on the main street and some local advance man had presented him with two ducats for "Across the Pacific" starring Harry Clay Blaney. In return for this he had promised to hang a lithograph in his window. This served a double purpose. This not only advertised "Across the Pacific," but also served to hide the shoes that Uncle Julius was foisting on the good people of Weehawken.

Thanks again, and if you ever come west I will slip you a pair of passes to "She Lost It in Campeche" which I understand may come back to the Mason Theater.

Yours,
Groucho

TO PHIL SILVERS

November 15, 1951

Dear Phil:

I won't bore you with the details of how happy I am over your success. You've had it coming. You have been scrambling around near the top for many a year and now at long last you've broken through. The critics called you a major comic. Well, it couldn't have happened to a nicer guy.

(196)

But I must warn you. In a musical, as you know, there are temptations. Thirty or forty beautiful babes in back of you kicking up high—so high that they frequently display sections of their anatomy that in other circles are carefully reserved for the man they ultimately marry. Phil, steer clear of these man-traps. Marry, if you must, but don't marry a chorus girl. As the years roll by you will discover their high kicks grow proportionately lower, and their busts sag just as much as the busts of girls who have never seen the inside of a dressing room.

You may ask then what is the difference? As a veteran of three Broadway musicals, I can quickly tell you chorus girls are notoriously pampered and insolvent. No matter where you take them, they order champagne and chicken à la king. This can be very embarrassing if you are in the Automat.

However, if you must marry, I suggest you look in other fields. In a city as big as New York I am sure there are pants manufacturers, wholesale delicatessen dealers, and various other merchants who have daughters who conceivably have virtues even more indispensable to a nearsighted major comic than a talent for high kicking.

So steer clear of these coryphées. This doesn't necessarily mean that you have to snub them. Remember they too are people, even though they spend most of their waking hours grinding and bumping. I suggest that when you arrive at the theater give them a hearty but dignified greeting. You might even toss in a low, courtly bow. Under no circumstances shake their hands, for the slightest physical contact can lead to disaster.

If there are not too many in the group, you might inquire solicitously about their health. If you are in a particularly gracious mood, you might even give them a brief résumé of *your* physical condition. The social amenities out of the way, walk quickly to your dressing room, and unless there is a fire backstage, don't emerge until the call boy has notified you that it is time to make your entrance. Your behavior on the road we can discuss at some future date. You realize, or course, that once you get to Altoona, Sioux City and other way stations, you may have to modify your attitude, but judging from the reviews this is a problem that need not concern you for some time.

So look smart, be smart, and remember . . . in Union there is alimony.

Love,
Groucho

TO LEO ROSTEN

December 14, 1951

Dear Leo:

"It's Only Money" is now called "Double Dynamite" as a tribute to Jane Russell's you know what, and will open around Christmas at the Paramount in New York.

The fact that your children want photographs comes as no surprise to me. You apparently have been living with your head in the sand and haven't the faintest idea what is going on in the world. Practically all children are crazy about me, particularly girls. Unfortunately, as soon as they emerge from adolescence, they look around for facsimilies of Jeff Chandler and other bounders who, I am sure, do not possess the wisdom and charm that make me so attractive.

I hope this answers all your questions.

Regards,
Groucho

TO ARTHUR SHEEKMAN

New York, April 11, 1952

Dear Sheek:

I am on my way to the Yankee Stadium to watch the Yankees murder the Brooklyn Dodgers. The weather is ideal for baseball so I am taking a horse-blanket with me, a vicuña overcoat, two sweaters, a flat bottle of Old Taylor, a Bunsen burner and a pint of cough medicine spiked with benzedrine.

I have become a regular fan of the theater and I think it's a great idea. I don't know if you've ever witnessed any of it, but you know how we go into a picture theater and see pictures of the actors on the screen? Well, you won't believe it, Arthur, but here in New York they have real people up there on the stage. Why, you could almost talk to them! It's uncanny. I don't think it'll replace the movies, but it certainly strikes a new note in American Art.

For example, I saw "I Am a Camera" last night, the John Van Druten play, and we sat in the first row. And Julie Harris (she plays I guess they call it "the lead" in the theater), you could see the scratches on her legs. At first we thought this had something to do with the plot and we waited for these scratches to come to life. But Arthur, it was never mentioned in the play and we finally came to the conclusion that either she had been shaving too close or she'd been kicked around the dressing room by her boyfriend. Now honestly, could anything like this happen in the movies? Think of it—here you see a girl's real scratches! It was great fun.

I will be home in another ten days and will reveal many things that will make your hair stand on end—assuming that you still have any.

Yours sincerely,
Groucho

May 14, 1957

Dear Sheek:

This white elephant that I'm building on top of a hill uses up most of my time. I had no idea, when I embarked upon this extravagant folly, that it would consume so much of my time and money. On an average day, there are at least twenty workmen up there, each one carefully cleaning his fingernails while looking at his watch. Overtime starts about fifteen minutes after they arrive in the morning. However, one day it will all end, and I'll be cursing the day I ever had air conditioning installed as it blows on me from one end of the room to the other. I'm sure that "My Fair Lady" didn't require nearly as much preparation as this Alamo North of Dougheny.

We all send our love and wish you were here—(from the play of the same name).

Fondly,
Groucho

September 11, 1957

Dear Mr. Sheekman:

I don't know whether or not you know that I played the Straw Hat Circuit in "Time for Elizabeth" this summer. It consisted of Andover, N. Jersey, and Matunuck, Rhode Island. As Martha Raye would put it, "I was very large." Their top price normally is $4. They charged $5 for me, and sold out.

Actually, because of the tax situation, it didn't make much difference. But when you play to a free audience all year, it's good for the ego to know there are people willing to part with five smackers to see you "live." (And when I say "live" I mean as live as a man can be at my age.)

Since we're closing in Matunuck, Rhode Island, your

chance to see a great performance was lost. I now know how the people feel who never saw Sarah Bernhardt—and don't forget, one of her legs was wooden.

What are you up to? News about you is as scarce as hen's teeth. Normally, I don't use this phrase, but we happen to have a hen in our backyard and she has only one tooth. I'm sure you're familiar with the rest—"The whole tooth, and nothing but the tooth."

Had lunch with George [Kaufman] in N. Y. For a man who is rumored to be knocking on death's door, he seems to be pretty active. He is staging the Peter Ustinov play which opens in Boston on the 9th, and after that he is directing a new turkey that Max Gordon is springing on the American public.

Give my love to your charming wife, and tell her I saw her in "Shark Island" on TV not long ago. She gave a right good performance.

Your loving friend,
Groucho

P.S. Are you planting much winter wheat this year?

FROM BROOKS ATKINSON

November 25, 1953

Dear Groucho:

Since I am in an invidious position about your television broadcasts, let me say that I am following your example in the style of haberdashery. My mother always gets me a tie for my birthday. The one that came today is a narrow bow tie. My mother tells me that she doesn't like it, herself. But she notices that you wear a narrow bow tie in the photographs in the paper and she naturally assumes that this must be high style. As a matter of fact, I suspect that you copy the narrow bow tie from me rather than the other way around. But the evidence goes to show that my mother regards you as the center of fashion. Just be careful that you act in an appropriate manner from now on.

With best wishes,
Brooks

December 8, 1953

Dear Brooks:

Perhaps our little discussion about television has had a civilizing effect on you. I told you, that night at the theater, that there were more things on television than stale jokes and weatherbeaten movies. If you take this monster in moderate doses, you can learn how to remove hair from your legs without a razor; how to tenderize meat without a concrete mixer; how to be alluring to your girl friend without an aphrodisiac; what kind of beer has the fluffiest head; what brand of cigarettes will definitely not give you cancer, etc. etc. Plus all this, as a sedative it has no equal.

Apparently your mother is far more hep sartorially than her bewildered son, and knows where to look to be up on the fashions. Since you are one of a dwindling minority who boast that they don't have a television set, I suggest that you drop in at your mother's house every Thursday night at 8, turn to NBC, and discover for yourself what the well-dressed man is wearing.

Regards,
Groucho

TO JERRY LEWIS

April 5, 1954

Dear Jerry:

I've been reading in columns that there is ill feeling between you boys and that there's even a likelihood that you might go your separate ways. I hope this isn't true for you are awfully good together, and show business needs you. I don't mean to imply that either of you couldn't make a living on his own. I am sure you could. But you do complement each other and that's one of the reasons you click so successfully.

I am sure you have had disagreements and arguments, just as all teams, trios and quartets have had since the beginning of the theater. In the heat of working together there's inevitably a nervous tension and frequently it's during these moments that two high-strung temperaments will flare up and slash at each other.

There may be nothing to the rumors of your separation. However, if there is any ill feeling or bitterness between you, it will eventually affect your work. If that feeling does exist, sit down calmly together, alone—when I say alone, I mean no agents, no family, no one but you two—sit down alone, and talk it out.

Cordially,
Groucho

April 28, 1954

Dear Groucho:

I want you to know how very thrilled I was to receive your very nice note. It is most gratifying and heartwarming to know that a guy as busy as yourself cares enough about my problem to take the time to sit down and write. Believe me, I deeply appreciate your interest along with realizing the sagacity of your words, and have every intention of following your advice. I want to assure you that I will do the right thing in this matter.

Please convey to your family my warmest personal regards and again my many thanks for your letter. I hope someday soon I will see you so I can thank you in person. Until then, I will close with "the secret word—is thanks."

Sincerely,
Jerry

P.S. You're a nice man!

January 14, 1962

Dear Groucho:

Thank you for the General Electric show tonight. I derived a double pleasure from watching it—one, your performance, naturally . . . two, the delight and surprise that came over the guests in my home, and listening to comments such as, "He's very good as an actor," or "Isn't he believable?" or "I never knew he could be serious."

Well, it wasn't any surprise to me, nor do I think to anyone who does comedy, or for that matter, everyone who does anything in our business.

It really was a beautiful show, and I was completely enthralled with your warm and tender approach.

Always sincerely,
Jerry

January 23, 1962

Dear Jerry:

Do you remember some years ago when I wrote you and Dino a joint letter pleading with you not to go your separate ways? I said the separation would mean disaster for both of you. Since then you have made $18,000,000 (net) and Dino, I imagine, has made about the same. Therefore I will abstain from giving you any more advice.

However, I do want to thank you for your complimentary letter. The big surprise of my performance Sunday night in "Time for Elizabeth" on television was that it created so much surprise, despite the fact that good dramatic performances have been delivered by Cantor, Benny, Wynn, Berle and, of course, you.

One elderly member of Hillcrest stopped me the other day, shook a quivering finger in my face, and in a voice choked with emotion said, "That's the first time you've ever been any good!"

I think that dramatic acting is a comparatively easy racket, and I only wish I had discovered this twenty years ago.

I hope your suit with Paramount turns out more successfully than the one I'm wearing.

Regards,
Groucho

TO MAX GORDON

December 1, 1954

Dear Max:

I went to the opening of "Sailor's Delight" at the Huntington Hartford Theater. It's all about a mermaid with Eva Gabor, and it's a good unadulterated turkey. . . . Luckily they had a bar in the mezzanine and although I'm not a drinking man, after the first act I repaired to the distillery and tried to drink myself unconscious. Every theater should have a bar.

After the show I ran into the assistant manager and I told him they would make a lot of money if they would eliminate some of the cast and put on two extra bartenders.

I read that Sir George Kaufman has another big hit which makes me very happy, if for no other reason than it proves that us old boys are still in there putting it over the strike zone.

Love from all.

Groucho

TO GODDARD LIEBERSON

December 9, 1955

Dear Goddard:

It was nice of you to send me the recordings of "The Mikado." They were extremely interesting and I'm sure they will make very little money.

Unless you get out here within the next few months, I will see you in New York. I am going to New York to see the plays—and also to defend myself in a tax rap. The government has some curious notion that I owe them $1,000,000. I claim I owe only $3.85.

I admit now that I was wrong in writing off the $3.85 as a tax exemption. I said it was a business deduction, but it wasn't true. What actually happened was that I took eleven of my relatives to dinner at the Ontra Cafeteria on Vine Street. Since none of these relatives have any business, I can see where the government was justified in rejecting this exemption. However, the $1,000,000 is something else again. On this I expect to fight them tooth and nail (nail more than tooth, only because I have more nail than teeth).

I hope that you and your ballet dancer wife [Zorina] are flitting around happily together, like the moth and the flame in that old fairy tale.

Lovingly yours,
Groucho

June 19, 1956

Dear Goddard:

Well, the world has indeed revolved! When I last saw you in New York, you were a nondescript Vice President of a recording company. Yesterday, I stumbled across your photo in (of all places) the financial section of the New York Sunday Times. According to this piece, you are now a President, a Vice President, a Secretary of State—and all around Poo-bah.

I trust there is a commensurate increase in salary that goes with these various offices. Otherwise these are empty honors, and will ultimately land you on the relief rolls of N. Y.

Love,
Groucho

June 20, 1960

Dear God:

I never thought I'd be communicating with the Almighty.

Thanks for the albums. I agree with you that whatever chance Columbia Records had of making any money on the "Mikado" recording, the free gift of a dozen records certainly knocked it into a cocked hat. Actually, there hasn't been a cocked hat around since the revolutionaries fought King George and his Hessians for their freedom, but all my friends say "cocked hat" and who am I to duck the obvious?

I had hoped to be in New York late this month but Eden has signed on with some moth-eaten group of hams to appear nightly as Columbine with some seedy and half-assed Pierrot. As is her wont, she's doing this for free. I read somewhere that the strolling players of the Shakespearean era began this way, but in those days pumpernickel wasn't thirty-seven cents a loaf and a man could enter a cat house and while away an evening playing solitaire for thruppence-ha'penny.

Let me know if you are serious about coming out to the Coast this month. If so, I will be serious about remaining here.

My best to all.

Fondly,
Groucho

In celebration of Goddard Lieberson's twenty-fifth anniversary at Columbia Records, his friends compiled a scrapbook of greetings and comments. Included was this contribution from Groucho:

May 8, 1964

It is hard to realize that tall, spare, Machiavellian, sinister Mr. Lieberson will be honored by Columbia Records on his twenty-fifth anniversary.

Over the years I have listened to many of the recordings that Mr. Lieberson has endorsed; some of them so meretricious that I am amazed that the postal authorities allowed them to be sent through the regular mails.

Choosing a hit record is, admittedly, a difficult assignment, and I can only assume that swarthy, decadent Mr. Lieberson was chosen for this job because of his position—which is invariably horizontal.

Apparently it never occurred to those criminally responsible for elevating him to this high office, that a flair and instinct for music was a necessary requisite.

It is tragic to think that one who guides the destiny of a

worldwide music organization should be unable to distinguish between Mozart's Jupiter Symphony and "Tomorrow Night at the Darktown Strutters' Ball."

Despite his obvious deficiencies, I can truly say that his entire organization (to say nothing of me) loves him with the same fervor that is usually reserved for men like Stalin, Hitler and Torquemada.

Groucho Marx

TO IRVING BERLIN

April 4, 1956

Dear Irving:

I have taken to singing songs on my show; cute or funny ones, preferably. A few weeks ago I did "I Love a Piano" with Liberace, and last week I did "Cuba."

I know that you have many songs of this type and if, one of these days, you could stray far enough from your money to peruse your catalogue, perhaps you could instruct one of your hirelings to send me a few of them. They don't seem to be available in the music shops. I did get "I Want To Be Lazy" —but that's about all I could find.

Regards,
Groucho

April 6, 1956

Dear Groucho:

Your letter was read to me over the telephone in Florida.

My office has chosen some songs and are sending them to you but I also instructed them to send you a catalogue so you

(209)

can roll your own. If there's anything you want that we haven't got in stock, I will have it made up for you.

Outside of "The Cocoanuts," I'm still grateful to you for doing "Simple Melody" with Bing Crosby which ended up in its revival.

I see your show often and you remind me very much of the fellow who came to Atlantic City and heard George Kaufman read the first draft of "The Cocoanuts." I'm delighted with your success.

As always,
Irving

April 18, 1956

Dear Irving:

First of all, thanks for the parcel of songs, plus the catalogue and your invitation to "roll my own." Little did you know! While perusing it, I found some fifty-odd pieces (list attached) that I'd like to add to my repertoire.

Next time let me have your address so that my thanks can reach you directly, rather than be strained through a telephone wire from New York.

Warmest regards,
Groucho

April 23, 1956

Dear Groucho:

Frankly, there are some songs I would be tempted to pay you not to do. For instance, "Cohen Owes Me $97" would not be taken in the same spirit it was when I wrote it for Belle Baker when she opened at the Palace many, many years ago.

"The Friars Parade" is a bad special song I wrote for the Friars Club and you certainly would never have occasion to use that.

But why mention individual titles? Let me tell you of my favorite Groucho Marx story the way I tell it: "There's a song I wrote during the First World War called 'Stay Down Here Where You Belong' of which Groucho knows all the lyrics. Any time he sees me, when I am trying to pose as a pretty good songwriter, he squares off and sings it. I've asked him how much money he will take not to do this but so far he will not be bribed."

Always,
Irving

TO THE LUNTS

August 15, 1956

Dear Alfred and Lynn:

You will notice that I put Alfred first because he's the tallest.

I thought I would be able to take you up on your kind invitation, but things have piled up unexpectedly from many quarters, and luckily for you, I won't be able to come to Wisconsin.

You have no idea how fortunate you are, because I'm a particularly loathsome guest and I eat like a vulture. Unfortunately, the resemblance doesn't end there.

Maybe next summer, when I'm older and less complicated, you will extend this invitation again.

Love to you both—and it was wonderful seeing you on Broadway.

Best,
Groucho

FROM BERGEN EVANS*

March 25, 1957

Dear Mr. Marx:

I understand there is a faint and tremulous chance that you might join us some Sunday on "The Last Word" to discuss English grammar and usage and flog the pedants and goad the smug and épater the bourgeois and écraser whatever of l'infâme we can root out in half an hour. And the purpose of this letter is to add my personal beseechings to the more official requests you will receive.

We are an educational show and (as yet) unsponsored. So I am afraid the fee they can offer you can't be very impressive. If it will help sway you—though I doubt that it will—I will certainly add whatever I am paid for that show to whatever they can offer you.

If you can't come to New York, we can probably come to Los Angeles. Television magnates seem favorably impressed by someone who gets up suddenly and disappears over the horizon with a hell of a clatter.

Sincerely yours,
Bergen Evans

April 12, 1957

Dear Professor Evans:

An actor should always keep his mouth shut. I had to open mine and announce that I would like to appear on your show. Since it is on a competing network, I was under the impression that NBC would oppose this strenuously. Imagine my

* Author, Professor of English at Northwestern University, and moderator of such television programs as "The Last Word."

horror when they informed me that they didn't care too much, since it was on at an odd hour and nobody watched it. So here I am.

At the moment, I can't give you a precise date. I am presently building a house and doing my own show, but sometime within the next two months I'll make it—no matter what it does to my reputation as a semi-illiterate.

Sincerely,
Groucho Marx

May 8, 1957

Dear Prof:

I received a wire from some shifty character named Weinstein, who claims he is the Producer of "The Last Word." Personally, I always thought Webster was. But at the moment, I am in a state of innocuous desuetude. (I stole this from President Wilson some years ago, when he was writing stern notes to the Kaiser.)

I believe I told you that I'm moving from my old house into a new one, and until all the sordid details are ironed out (now there's a fine business for somebody) I don't know where I'll be—or why.

Kindest regards,
Groucho Marx

May 15, 1957

Dear Groucho:

. . . A sponsor isn't likely. Who in God's name would sponsor the split infinitive? And except that it might give us the means of persuading you to join us, I would rather not have one. There's less money, but lots less bother. This way I don't have to hack every discussion down until it fits the comprehension of an agency man or listen to his teeth chattering as he wonders whether the double negative isn't a reflection on (or of) the Republican Party.

Bertrand Russell has accepted an invitation to be a guest and so has Aldous Huxley. We won't despair of you until you tell us we must, but we will stop intruding on your privacy.

Moving into a new house is hell. When we passed simultaneously into suburbia and insolvency I had a terrible attack of shingles—and I couldn't even use them on the roof!

Kindest regards,
Bergen Evans

March 3, 1958

Dear Bergie:

A moderately erudite friend of mine has investigated the "Lay an Egg" and "Turkey" reference. I must say that you were much closer than we were in your surmise . . . or guess . . . or whatever it was.

I had a wonderful time on the show, and if I hadn't received either the money or the Encyclopedias, the hour I spent with you at my apartment would have been worth the trip. My only regret is that the session didn't last longer.

I don't know why you don't come out here this summer and see how the other half lives.

Cordially,
Groucho

November 7, 1958

Dear Bergie:

What has happened to my favorite show? A number of people out here are bitter about its disappearance.

See if you can't pull some strings (or whatever one pulls in this sort of situation) to get it back on.

Another thing, with "The Last Word" off the air, where is John Mason Brown going to throw his cigarette butts?

I miss seeing you, and hope I will get a chance to look at you again this summer.

Regards,
Groucho

February 13, 1959

Dear Groucho,

"The Last Word" seems to have been revived in order to give someone the satisfaction of killing it. The ways of TV add a fourth inscrutability to the three basic mysteries which the author of Proverbs couldn't fathom. Out of the opening 13 weeks we are to be pre-empted five times and then, I gather, canceled. Faulkner thought he'd reached the ultimate in having his heroine screwed with a corncob. He didn't know TV.

Along with millions of others, I'm looking forward to "The Life of Groucho Marx." I differ from the millions, however, in that I expect to buy a copy and not wait in line at the library.

Let me know if good fortune brings you to New York or bad fortune to Chicago. I'd like to see you.

Best wishes,
Bergen Evans

April 13, 1959

Dear Teacher,

For your information I will be in New York around June 10th, and in Chicago (at the Edgewater Beach Hotel) sometime in July.

If you again desire to view my well-worn carcass, this brief missive will inform you of my whereabouts. If you don't care to see me, just send ten cents in stamps and a quart bottle of Arpége.

I beg to remain . . . (Someday on your show I wish you would discuss the inanity of this cringing, archaic phrase. I can think of only one sensible use of "I beg to remain." Let's say I'm giving a party and it's late; I want to go to bed. But one guest is an alcoholic who refuses to leave. When I threaten to boot him out, he gets down on his knees and pleads, "Groucho, I beg to remain.")

There is no point to continuing this discourse for I have many letters to write to my betters, who number in the millions.

Regards,
Groucho

April 18, 1959

Dear Groucho,

"I beg to remain" is a piece of detritus from the days when a merchant was expected to show his inferiority to his customers. A book of instructions for the young shopkeeper in the eighteenth century tells him that he must "be master of a handsome bow and cringe." "I beg to remain" is part of the cringe. English tailors still keep it. It's part of what Max Beerbohm called "crawling on their knees and shaking their fist in your face." And I suppose it was an improvement on "Your humble and obedient servant." Now *there* was a subscription! Samuel Johnson, in that wonderful and terrible letter to Chesterfield—after he had taken the noble lord by the weazand and then kicked him squarely in the crotch three or four times—solemnly signed himself "Your Lordship's most humble, Most obedient servant." For a parallel to *that* sort of humility, the world had to wait for Arthur Godfrey.

Best wishes,
Bergen Evans

May 8, 1959

Dear Bergie:

I'm glad you explained what detritus means. I always thought it was some part of a horse, and rarely used it unless I was making a personal appearance at a livery stable in Kentucky. Since you wrote me, I looked it up in the dictionary, but have already forgotten what it means. If we are going to continue this correspondence, I think you should define it each time you write.

If I don't see you in New York I will see you in Chicago.

I beg to remain your humble servant,

Groucho Detritus

TO NORMAN KRASNA

June 6, 1957

Dear Mr. Krasna:

I'm sorry I couldn't come to your party the other night, but in my declining years I've become a social butterfly. Take the other evening, for example. I donned evening clothes (which took considerable preparation as the suit doesn't fit too well) and went to a very lavish, flower-bedecked party at Romanoff's. It was predicted that this would be one of the social events of the season. Even George Raft would be there. Well, to make a short party long—there were beautiful women all over the place, champagne was flowing, and I wound up with George Raft.

Regards,
Groucho

(Copy to Harry Ruby)

Beverly Hills,
September 3, 1961

Dear Norman:

I'm worried about Harry Ruby. He's taken to writing his letters in verse. Being a song writer,* that in itself would be understandable if he'd properly confine his subjects to such matters as moon in June; dolls who are both glamorous and amorous, or even—since he's still an incurable baseball nut—to Dizzy Dean's earned-run average.

But no; Ruby is now writing verses *about* verses. Explaining that "Writing Poetry Is for Those/Who Can't Express Themselves in Prose," he goes on to say:

> When I consult Roget or March
> For Words to weave upon my loom,
> My eyebrows testily I arch
> And order Junior from the room.
>
> I run my fingers through my hair,
> I pace the floor and curse my luck
> As I imagine Baudelaire
> And Shelley did when they were stuck.

But that, Norman, is not all. The man who wrote the memorable "Hurray for Captain Spaulding" now comes up with:

* "Three Little Words," "Who's Sorry Now?" "I Want to Be Loved By You," etc.

It isn't for the dead I grieve,
It's for the living whom the dead bereave.

And

This creed Death uses for his text:
"No one is better than the next";
So Death is, quite ironically,
The only true democracy.

See what I mean? My best to you and the family.

Groucho

P.S. I was needlessly alarmed. Last night Ruby and I went to the ball game. When he yelled for the Dodgers, it was in 100 per cent prose.

TO EDDIE CANTOR

July 3, 1957

Dear Eddie:

I liked your book "Take My Life." Some of the last parts —particularly the philosophy—I found a damned sight more satisfying than that religious confusion emitted daily by eminent churchmen. It made me think—something I haven't done in years.

Congratulations and take care of yourself.

Regards,
Groucho

July 8, 1957

Dear Julius,

Your reaction to "Take My Life" is most heartening.

You are not the easiest guy in the world to please and if you like something, it must be pretty good.

Ida and I have had to dine out on several occasions where a check was handed to me by a waiter. Naturally I had to pay it as I hate fights in public places outside of the Olympic Stadium and the Hollywood Legion Stadium.

Both Ida and I recall the joyous moments which came in Las Vegas when you and I would be introduced, take a bow, and that took care of the check. Now then—what do you propose to do about the future eating? Shall Ida and I continue to go out and keep paying and paying, or can you give us a date for our next Las Vegas meeting?

While awaiting your word, Ida and I send you and yours our love.

Affectionately,
Eddie

September 3, 1959

Dear Julius,

We have two of your books in our home—one I got for free from your publisher and one Ida (she never can wait) bought at Martindale's. I sat up late last night reading her version—the four dollar, eleven cent one.

"Groucho and Me" is funny, humorous, warm, and is typically Groucho. Unless the American public has forgotten how to read or laugh, it should have a tremendous sale. I have only one criticism to make.

Beginning with page 188 and speaking about the stock market, why, even for fun, do you have to lie? First of all, all my friends know I was never in the market. Being close to Bernard Baruch, I advised him to stay out. "Bernie," I said, "the stocks are too high and first thing you know it will be Bernie burny."

Now let's get back to the Palace—and don't you wish we could. It was not I who was appearing at the Palace, it was you and those three other boys. I came back to see you and you tried to talk me into buying something, and I said to you— I remember the words as if it were this morning—"Groucho," I said, "keep your tips. If these companies are so good, why do they want me for a partner? Why should I buy their shares? Why don't they give it to some relative, somebody closer to them than Eddie Cantor?" I remember how you applauded. It was heard by all the actors in their dressing rooms and they started taking bows—I could tell because heads were bumping walls.

Now as the comedian who had just laid a big egg said, "but seriously folks," it's a hell of a book. Before the week is out I want to buy a half dozen copies and send them to friends. Lucky that's all the friends I have—six.

Congratulations and much love.

Affectionately,

Eddie

FROM WALTER KERR

April 14, 1958

Dear Groucho Marx,

The fact that the Marx Brothers only get six lines in "Pieces at Eight" is an historical accident compounded of two parts: (a) the pieces are all collected from stuff seen and written in the past seven years; (b) you and your brothers, being intolerably lazy, have done nothing to assuage the loneliness and grief of those abandoned people who go to the New York theater during all that time. (That last sentence isn't quite in English, but I'm rattled today: I've just had a letter from a high school girl who explains that she and her class are reading "Hamlet" *in English* and can't I help her?)

Sure, your movies were wonderful. (One of these days I'm going to steal prints of the lot of them and try to do an in-depth study that will chill your blood.) But I got started in my theatergoing late, and only saw all of you in "Animal Crackers," plus a performance at the Chicago Palace in which Zeppo appeared, for reasons never explained, as you. Therefore, I feel deprived. In fact, I feel deprived practically every time I *go* to the theater. It isn't going to be the Marx Bros. tonight. The man I envy is Brooks Atkinson, who goes right back to "I'll Say She Is" (or was, or whatever the hell the name of that one was). Is television really necessary?

As for my own private feelings, I'll give you a hint: of all the unsolicited letters I ever got (excluding my wife's), yours was the one I was happiest to get.

Loyally,
Walter Kerr

TO DAVID SUSSKIND

February 20, 1964

Dear Dave:

Corresponding with you is like writing letters to an empty coal mine or an aching void. However, despite the fact that you choose to ignore my correspondence, the following may be of interest to you.

There is a new book out by Philip Stern called "The Great Treasury Raid," and it would make a very interesting subject for discussion on your show. I suggest you get Caplin, the tax collector, and a Texas politician who holds the 27½% oil deduction more sacred than the Old and New Testaments combined. Well, no need for me to tell you. I'm sure you know what the cast of characters should be.

Regards,
Groucho Marx

March 26, 1964

Dear Groucho:

I suspect the reason I am such a miserable correspondent where you are concerned is that I go into the letter form with you with a desperate inferiority complex. You are a notorious wit and take special pride in the bulk and merit of your correspondence, very much in the Shavian tradition. (At least, I read that somewhere, perhaps in Who's Who or The Police Gazette.)

I have read "The Great Treasury Raid," by Philip Stern, and I do intend to schedule an evening on tax deductions and inequities in the tax system. Every time I become irritated with the burdensome tax structure, I stop and think—where else could a young chap do so well with only modest equipment and burning zeal?

I miss John F. Kennedy, but have begun to reconcile to the homey-folksy ways of Lyndon Johnson. For a brief time it seemed as if literacy, intellect, sophistication and style were going to become respected aspects of American life, but I guess it was not to be. I find it more than passingly interesting that the first foreign dignitary received by President Johnson, President Segni of Italy, was entertained by the White House with an evening of hootenanny. Anyway, I am rambling like crazy and with no provocation whatsoever.

Please keep watching "Open End" for several reasons: 1) We need viewership very urgently. 2) It gives me great personal pride and pleasure to know that you are an avid viewer—as a matter of fact, I love you.

Best regards,
David

TO SIDNEY SHELDON

July 13, 1964

Dear Sidney:

I had lunch with Cooper (or Jackie, as we call him). It was very pleasant. He had cold salmon with a side order of cucumbers and I had turkey in honor of our new venture. Shortly after that he left for Honolulu, and he told me confidentially that this is the last I would ever see of him.

I'll be pretty busy in New York with the "Tonight" show, but I think we'll find time for some conversation.

I'm bringing Melinda and a girl friend (hers, not mine). The whole journey will be financially ruinous. I am allowing Eden to remain out here. She shed a bitter tear or two, then I belted her one. Curiously enough, this seemed to bring her around to my way of thinking. If a man isn't boss of his own castle, he might just as well pull in his oars.

Hope the Mets are not getting you down. As for the Dodgers, who cares? I wouldn't like this to be broadcast, but secretly I'm rooting for the Philadelphia club. They are a gallant crew and I'm sick of the Dodgers and the Giants and the Yankees—and of this letter, so good-bye.

Fondly,
Groucho Marx

TO MR. AND MRS. GARSON KANIN (RUTH GORDON)

October 2, 1965

Dear Gar and Ruth,

I was delighted to read Cecil Smith's review in the morning L. A. Times. I would have sent you one of those customary unfunny congratulatory wires, but because of the New York newspaper strike, I didn't know when the opening night would be. So please accept this as an opening night wire. I'm sure that you're both very happy with the results. I'm a little hurt that you didn't use me in the play. I could have played that elderly woman's grandfather.

My daughter Melinda is stabled at the Neighborhood Playhouse and I'm sure that if you phone her, she would be delighted to come to your house for dinner every night.

My love to you both and I hope you will have some time for an elderly comedian who, I would say off hand, is certainly as amusing as the late Kaiser Wilhelm.

Groucho

For Publication

TO THORNTON DELAHANTY
OF THE NEW YORK HERALD TRIBUNE

June 14, 1945

Dear Thornton,

I received your dignified letter and your not-so-dignified questions and I'll try to answer all of them in the order they deserve.

First, and farthest north in insolence, you want to know where we have been all these years. This is usually the opening line used in attempting to knock over a dame, or, to Emily Post it, "make a date." Well, Thorny, old boy, I have been many places in the past few years. I have been playing service camps for the Army and Navy and bond rallies for Morgenthau. I've even tried to go to Palm Springs a number of times but always ran out of gas on the outskirts of Azusa. Azusa, in case you don't know, has a drugstore where you can buy straw hats for horses and also for people.

As for the next question, "How does it feel to come out of retirement?"—what impudence! Why, I've been appearing publicly and shamelessly on the air for the past two and a half years. Through the ether, I've whooped it up for FDR, Pabst

(229)

Beer, General Foods (spinach), Chase and Sanborn's coffee and Kelvinator's iceboxes. I have been publicly seen at the ball park, moodily watching our inept Stars gracefully and inevitably slide into their accustomed spot in the cellar. Most any day, I can be seen on the main streets of Beverly Hills, buying insecticides, can openers and red meat points.

The next question is even more impertinent. "What about your public—where has it been?" Those of our fans who are still alive are temporarily marking time and peering with jaundiced eyes at Abbott and Costello, Danny Kaye and the rest of those current whippersnappers who are frantically trying to snatch the bread from the mouths of three lovable comedians.

You then ask, "What is it like to be back with Chico and Harpo?" I saw them yesterday for the first time in years. Chico I didn't recognize at all. For the past three weeks, he's been selling racing forms in Pittsburgh and he has a nut-brown look acquired hanging around the steel mills. Harpo is now a platinum blond and speaks only of his golf score and his wife and four children. He is loaded with dough and it only goes to prove that a man can make a fortune just keeping his trap shut. He doesn't have to build a better one—no, just has to keep it shut.

Next, you want to know how we look. We are all beautiful in a mildewed sort of way and, like Saroyan, enjoy each other enormously. On the set, waiting for the War Production Board to release film to the Independents, we sit and discuss the same old topic—it's always new and has many facets that I wasn't aware of in my younger and hairier days.

My favorite fan is a man in Willow Grove Park in Philadelphia, who is under the delusion that he is the ghost of Sousa, the band master, and at night as soon as the moon is up, he sneaks from behind a tree, and with an imaginary baton, directs an imaginary orchestra.

I have no advice to give to young actors. To young, struggling actresses, my advice is to keep struggling. If you struggle long enough, you will never get in trouble and if you never get in trouble, you will never be much of an actress.

Yours,
Groucho

In June 1947, Groucho wrote a column for Variety, which he sent to the editor, Abel Green, with the following note:

June 7, 1947

Dear Abel:

I trust this is illiterate enough even for your sheet.

Regards,
Groucho

GROUCHO'S COLUMN FOR VARIETY

Variety, which calls itself the bible of show business (actually it's the babel of show business) recently printed a news story to the effect that for "The Jolson Story," Al Jolson's cut—despite the fact that he didn't appear in the picture except for a brief moment—would amount to three and a half million dollars.

I have appeared in many pictures through the years (at the moment I can be seen in all my pristine loveliness in "Copacabana"), and I would swear on a stack of Bob Stacks that I have never pulled down any dough that has ever remotely touched this figure. Perhaps this is the signpost that show business has been waiting for. If a Jolson picture can roll up a ten million dollar gross without Jolson, how much more could it have made without Evelyn Keyes and William Demarest?

Maybe the studios have been going at it the wrong way. Perhaps they should stop the present custom of bunching seven or eight stars in one movie, and eliminate all the feature names in a picture.

I can just see the marquee at the local theater. Coming next week: "I Wonder Who's Hissing Her Now," without Olivia de Crawford and Clark Power. It can't miss. I am sure that millions of people stay away from the movies because they dislike the stars that are appearing at the local Bijou, but if they were assured that so-and-so wouldn't show his ugly kisser on the screen, my guess is they would tear the doors down to get in.

I am speaking from personal experience. In my time I have met hundreds of people who have said, "Hey, jerk, when are you going to quit the movies and get a job?" and if it's true of me, it certainly must be true of dozens of others whose talents may be even less than mine.

This system could also be applied to other fields of endeavor. I am sure that many political candidates are defeated because the public has been given an opportunity to see what they look like. The next great political victory will be achieved by the party that is smart enough to have nobody heading the ticket.

My theory is that there are too many people and too many things. Suppose you got that semi-annual card from your dentist notifying you that most of your fangs are about to drop out and you had better get up to his abattoir before you spend the rest of your life gumming your fodder. Wouldn't you rush up there with much more alacrity if you were certain that this white-coated assassin wasn't there to greet you with his chisel in one hand and his pliers in the other? Imagine if horse racing had no horses—thousands of people could go to the track each day and save millions of dollars.

Years ago, there was a theory called Technocracy. Perhaps mine could be called the Theory of Scarcity. Take the actors out of the movies, take squash and rutabagas out of restaurant menus, take Slaughter and Musial out of the Cardinals, and take Gromyko out of the U. N.

As for marriage, I know hundreds of husbands who would gladly go home if there weren't any wives waiting for them. Take the wives out of marriage and there wouldn't be any divorces. But then, someone might ask, what about the next generation? Look, I've seen some of the next generation—perhaps it's just as well if the whole thing ends right here.

TO GUMMO MARX

March, 1952

Dear Gummo:

I'm not sure whether it's another cold coming on or my old aversion to making speeches—especially to an audience of comedians. When they laugh it's because (like me) they've just thought of something they're about to say themselves.

Anyway, here is my little tribute to a genuinely great man, George Jessel. If I remain chicken and fail to show, will you take over for me? Thanks.

Your big brother.
Groucho

P.S. And don't forget, Big Brother is always watching.

[Enclosed was the speech, which, incidentally, was delivered by Groucho.]

I never thought the day would come when I would be forced to sit on a dais to honor a movie producer. It's a disturbing indication of how rapidly class distinctions are breaking down throughout the United States. Fortunately I don't regard Jessel merely as a movie producer. Jessel is an orator—a great orator. Georgie has done as much for Pico Boulevard as Patrick Henry did for the Thirteen Colonies.

I am constantly astonished at the facility with which Jessel tosses the English language around. This is even more astonishing when one realizes that he doesn't know the meaning of half of the words he uses.

Nevertheless, George is unquestionably the most relentless speechmaker of our time. He gives of himself unremittingly. He speaks at weddings, funerals and bar mitzvahs. Speaking that often, it's only natural that he sometimes gets confused. On one occasion he married a thirteen-year-old boy to a woman who had been dead for three days.

Jessel is living proof that a college education is no requisite to success. As a young boy he was a precocious moron. His formal education consisted of standing in the wings and watching Gus Edwards' School act. At the age of fifteen he was as innocent of life as the Breen office. Why, he couldn't tell you the difference between Diamond Jim Brady and Lillian Russell. However, for some strange reason this was a subject that fascinated him. He plunged into research with all the enthusiasm of a potential sex fiend, and today—only forty years later—there is no one better qualified to explain the difference between Lillian Russell and Diamond Jim Brady.

In addition, Jessel has many other talents. He is without question the greatest off-key singer since Bugsy Siegel. His voice is as flat as the chest of a ten-year-old girl. George is a mortal enemy to the Hit Parade. He has been known to destroy a popular song in twenty-four hours. He is the only man I know who can take a beautiful love song, send it through his nose and have it come out sounding like an air raid warning. When Jessel sings, his voice has the mournful quality of a tom cat on a back fence. And I might add—when Jessel sings, it's usually for the same reason.

Georgie's career should be an inspiration to every red-blooded American youth. In a profession that, by its very nature, has more than its share of temptations, Jessel has never strayed from the straight and narrow. He has led a life as rigid and austere as any monk in a monastery. He neither drinks, smokes nor chews. Occasionally, for medicinal purposes, he will drink a gallon of whiskey, but only if there is no brandy available.

Next month is Jessel's birthday. It is no coincidence that his birthday is in the spring, for Georgie is the spirit of spring. An hour with Jessel is like two weeks in the country.

In closing, I want to point out that almost any day eight or ten major comics assemble at the Hillcrest Country Club for lunch—all willing and eager to get on, but when Jessel talks the others just sit there with their mouths shut.

Say—that's an idea.

TO HY GARDNER

October 26, 1953

Dear Hy:

I wish I could write you those seven or eight hundred words that you have asked for, but I know only six hundred. Then, too, there are other reasons.

For one thing, I have been having a frustrating time with my avocado tree. I planted it in high hopes that some day it would be heavily laden with fruit. Well, five years have passed and in all that time not one avocado has hung from its limbs. Deep in despair I went to a nursery and explained the situation to the head man. When I got all through he looked at me even more contemptuously than usual and said, "Mr. Marx, don't you know that avocados mate, and if you want to get fruit you have to have a male and a female?" Well, Hy, you could have knocked me over with a watermelon. I knew that movie stars had to go through something like this to bear fruit, but I had no idea that the male avocado needed the female avocado just as desperately as Lana needs Lex, Frankie needs Ava and Abbott needs Costello. On second thought strike out Abbott and Costello. Nature just doesn't work that way.

Well, to make a small saga even smaller, I bought the second tree and I now have both sexes in the backyard. They've only been together a short time and I guess it's too early to tell, but up to now I must say I haven't noticed any difference. What puzzles me is that they never look at each other. They just stand there—eyes forward, austere and aloof, never moving a leaf, never even cracking a twig. Who knows—maybe they're self-conscious when I'm around. Some night when the moon is full, and your correspondent is likewise, I am going to sneak out there, plant myself in the bushes, and stay there until I find out definitely whether I am ever going to get any avocados.

Regards,
Groucho

FROM SYLVIA VAUGHN THOMPSON (SYLVIA SHEEKMAN)

January 30, 1962

Dear Groucho—

Years ago I asked Mother if she could give me your recipe for pot roast for my cookbook "Economy Gastronomy" and years ago, she did. Now the book's publication is a reality (Atheneum is publishing it), and I want very much to include your pot roast. If I may, would you kindly double-check this recipe:

Groucho's Pot Roast
Brown in iron pot. Take out meat, add 2 large onions cut up, ½ green pepper cut up, 3 crushed garlic cloves, 1 small bay leaf, and 2 #2½ size cans of solid-packed tomatoes. Return meat, and simmer 4 to 4½ hours.

Mother thinks that with this you serve potato pancakes and onions with peas. True? I wouldn't want to belie your taste. . . .

Love,
Sylvia

February 2, 1962

Dear Sylvia,

Your mother told me that you had written a cookbook and I want to extend my congratulations.

I am not certain of my figures but my estimate would be that this will make 7,396 cookbooks on the market. However, I am sure yours will be on the bestseller list before the snow flies. (I mean before the snow flies in Palm Springs on July 4th). This is not meant to discourage you but just to keep you aware of the facts of life.

Now as to the recipe, if you must insert it in your book, it's called Brisket of Beef and is as far removed from Pot Roast as Eisenhower was from Lincoln. The directions you sent are correct as are the accompanying accoutrements.

Love to you, Gene and to that vast family you are raising up north.

More love,
Groucho

FROM KATHRYN MURRAY

November 19, 1962

Dear Groucho,

Arthur is dancing the Bossa Nova and I'm hitting a time clock. I am also collecting family jokes for an article . . . jokes with tag lines that have become family expressions.

The only Marx tag line I know is your father's: "What odds will you give me?" But, as I remember, your Arthur told us that one so I'd like to credit it to him. Will you give me another to use with your name?

Love,
Kathryn

November 21, 1962

Dear Kathryn:

My father, when attending the theater with my mother, had a habit of singing along with the actors.

During one performance my mother said, "Sam, if you want to sing, why don't you get up there on the stage?"

"No, Minnie," he answered, "I wouldn't do that unless they paid me."

After thirty years of this vocal audience participation, one night he said to my mother, "You know, Minnie, I've been singing along for thirty years and nobody's paid me yet."

"Well," she said, "I'm not a rich woman, thanks to you, but if you'll shut up I'll pay you!"

I hope this is fairly close to what you want.

Regards,
Groucho

FROM EDDIE CANTOR

January 9, 1964

Dear Julius,

Since being inactive as a performer I've done quite a bit of scribbling. This is my fourth year writing a column for Diners' Club Magazine.

Will you please send me as quick as you can two lines which have brought you the biggest laughs. I would appreciate it for my next column.

Gratefully,
Eddie

January 14, 1964

Dear Eddie:

Briefly (and quickly) the two biggest laughs that I can recall (other than my three marriages) were in a vaudeville act called "Home Again."

One was when Zeppo came out from the wings and announced, "Dad, the garbage man is here." I replied, "Tell him we don't want any."

The other was when Chico shook hands with me and said, "I would like to say good-bye to your wife," and I said, "Who wouldn't?"

Take care of yourself.

Regards,
Groucho Marx

Friends Abroad

TO HARRY KURNITZ*

October 3, 1950

Dear Expatriate:

I do miss you and I will welcome you back with open doors. My Cadillac particularly misses you. You see, you lived on the only high hill in town and my motor needed that challenge. Things are so different since you left.

My sex life is now reduced to fan letters from an elderly lesbian who would like to borrow $800; phone calls from a flagrant fairy with chronic low blood pressure (he'd like to get in pictures); and Pincus' dog who howls mournfully under my window every night. He is an old cocker named Jo-Jo and he's looking for something. The stupid mutt doesn't know that it wouldn't be in my room, even if he finds it. How to convey this news to him is beyond me.

A brief rundown on some people you know may be of interest. Krasna and Wald have taken over RKO and all the surrounding property as far east as Figueroa Street and have given Mayor Bowron two weeks to get out of town. Three musical shows, all rehearsing under the impression that they

* The playwright and screenwriter.

were replicas of "South Pacific," opened and folded in jig time. Harpo is making a tour of the sticks accompanied by three different kinds of opera singer, four semi-male dancers and, believe it or not, a crateful of snakes. Chico is in New York under the impression that he is an Italian and as he has already hooked a sucker sponsor he will be seen and heard this fall on TV.

I am going to the Bogarts tonight for dinner with the customary uneasy state of mind. Bogey, as you know, lives on a steep hill and when a little high (I'm not referring to the hill) thinks nothing of shoving a guest down a mountainside.

So, if you never hear from me again and you are interested, with the aid of a helicopter and an Indian trapper you may eventually stumble over my body in some lonesome ravine.

Hurry home before I go crazy and get married again.

Best,
Groucho

Paris, December, 1951

My dear Hackenbush: *

My plan in composing this letter was to invite you to retire from radio and TV and come to Paris to live with me. However, that was based on my firm belief that I was going to win first prize of 23,000,000 fr. in the lottery last night. Well, Hack, to make a long story short, I was nosed out and it is my sad duty now to tell you that you will have to make the trip on your own.

I am just back from the skiing country, where I spent Xmas with Irwin Shaw, the Viertels, Anatole Litvak and some

* In "A Day at the Races," Groucho impersonated Dr. Hugo Z. Hackenbush.

other assorted refugees. Our girl went to Rome to visit the Home Office of her church on this occasion but she is just back today having had her behind pinched by scores of degenerate Italian noblemen. She is well and happy and blooming.

Well, Hack, here we are, separated by one or two oceans (depending on whether you start East or West). Paris is expensive but I am in great demand to fill in with gypsy bands all over town (try making a living *that* way if you like life on the Seamy Side). Must close now as the man who owns this typewriter is just coming to work.

Much love, always,

Kurnitz

January 7, 1952

Dear H.K.:

I note what you say about Miss Delaney going to the Vatican and, on the way, getting her bottom pinched by itinerant noblemen. This is farther than I ever got with the young lady and maybe that's why I don't hear from her.

I sent her a letter around the 15th of December. I must admit it wasn't much of a love letter. It was fairly brief, moderately querulous and emphasized the fact that her handwriting was practically undecipherable.

This was unanswered. I then sent her a Christmas wire which got the same response. So my guess is that before getting started, the Affaire Delaney has ended with all the abruptness of seven martinis on an empty stomach.

I presume you've heard about the Wanger shooting. Quite a letdown. We expected a world war in 1951 and all we got was Wanger shooting an agent. If this is going to be the custom in Hollywood, someone suggested that the next head of MCA should be Sergeant York.

Your producer, who you say idolizes me, is obviously a brilliant fellow. Slap him on the shoulder for me and wish him Godspeed and good luck in whatever profession he has chosen for his life's work.

Regards,
Groucho

London, January, 1952

Dearest Hackenbush:

The sun is shining today in London, which calls for a certain amount of dancing in the streets. I am going to a football game, which I believe they call "cricket" over here and tonight I shall see John Gielgud & Diana Wynyard in "Much Ado About Nothing."

The theater here, in excitement and variety, makes our B'way institutions look a little pallid. They have the benefit, of course, of unbelievably low production and operating costs.

In the matter of the People v. Miss Delaney I will say briefly for the defense (or is it the prosecution) that this is an extremely flighty broad, hopelessly unreliable and very cute. I'm sorry your letters were ignored. It's barely possible, what with her progressive schooling, that she can't read or write.

I hope you will indeed come to Europe when your programs go off. My plan is to finish this picture in late April, then sling my Jaguar across the channel and tour. I can think of little lovelier than the two of us side by side, the wind in the pathetic remnants of our hair, a song ("Dr. Hackenbush," naturally) in our hearts and hordes of pretty French girls waving flags in welcome as we liberate town after town.

Much love,
Kurnitz

At sea (where else) S.S.
Ile de France, Nov. 15, 1954

Dearest Hackenberger,

I am going to London, not, as you may have supposed, to visit the Queen. The Queen wouldn't spit on me. I have given her every opportunity. I am going just to get the hell away from N. Y. and my typewriter. I think that in the last 12 months I have written as much as Chas. Dickens in his lifetime.

We opened (or did we?) to mixed notices but even the adverse comment wasn't too hateful and I am much encouraged. The Shuberts, a pessimistic crowd, I am told, believe we are set for this season, and slowly and painfully I have come to believe it myself. Naturally, I am working on another play. It's about a father who entrusts his child to a nurse telling her to bring his boy up to be a pilot. Well, the old broad is hard of hearing and what do you think—well I don't want to give away too much now but believe me it's hysterical.

I may go to Rome to visit your in-laws, the Hawks family, though it won't be nearly as much fun without Bill Faulkner to keep us all in gales of laughter. I'll tell you this in confidence, Grouch—he did not get the Nobel prize for laughs.

I hope you and Eden are well and happy. I hope you remain the King of TV for X number of years to come and wallow in money, affection and grandchildren in that order.

Love and love again,

H. Kurnitz

March 28, 1955

Dear Harry:

As you probably have surmised by now, I am not the correspondent that Emily Dickinson was, but she was a woman and I am a man, and women have more time for letterwriting because they are not busy chasing women—unless, of course, they happen to be lesbians. (Many years ago I chased a woman for almost two years, only to discover that her tastes were exactly like mine: we both were crazy about girls.)

Suffice to say (which is how a lawyer of mine used to begin all his sentences—but unfortunately he had nothing to say after that. And neither have I).

As for the lawyer, he eventually became our Mayor and, although he wasn't a great success, he certainly had the trains running on time. He is now hanging upside down with his Italian inamorata in Westwood.

This letter isn't really making much sense. I merely wanted to know how you are, whether you plan on remaining permanently in the Balkans or wherever the hell you are. Are you ever coming back? Or are you just going to continue wandering vaguely from country to country?

I never visualized our relationship this way. I always thought you and I and Krasna and Sheekman and Ruby and Nunnally and a few other loyal friends would end our days on some seedy back porch in some shabby town in Indiana with a gallon of Apple Jack, corncob pipes and me plucking a banjo against the mad wailing of your fiddle as Sheekman and Nunnally did a hoe-down.

I've been casing the northern end of the Caribbean in recent weeks. No royal dignitary ever was received with more genuflecting, groveling and full-throated admiration—except in Jamaica, where I was arrested for molesting a young native girl. I could write you reams about my triumphs—but until I find out where you are and whether this ever reaches you, I'll just wind it up.

Love and kisses,
Groucho

Berlin, December, 1955

My dearest Hackenbush:

It occurs to me now that in the old days when you wanted news of Miss Delaney and were using me as a Jewish John Alden, I used to hear from you fairly frequently.

Well, it isn't the first time a woman has come between two men, or vice versa. Personally, I wouldn't trade you for a hundred Miss Delaneys—not with the kind of dough you must be making nowadays. Pretty soft, eh, for you stay-at-homes while others are in the front lines of Europe holding the Red Horde at bay. When you see things here, at firsthand, it makes you want to get down on your knees and thank God for a man like Senator Nixon. (I'm taking it for granted that this letter will be opened by the authorities en route.)

Actually, it's very interesting here in a dreary sort of way. After a while, though, one ruin looks very much like another, an observation which is doubly true of the German broads. I've been in the Russian sector of Berlin a few times, which is just as dreary, but with posters. By the way, I don't want to hurt Irving Berlin's feelings, so don't mention this: not once, while I'm in the Russian part, have I heard God Bless America.

Unbelievable, eh?

I am here with Carol Reed, *Sir* Carol Reed to you, whipping up a schmierkase about light love and dark doings between East and West. It may ruin me with the left wing but it ought to square me with the Legion. The last word I had on my status quo was that I wasn't actually boycotted but I'd better come home with a damn good explanation of why I joined the Philadelphia Young Men's Hebrew Association. Actually, I joined because I had hot pants for a girl named Pearl who was in the Young *Women's* Hebrew Association, but go start explaining that today. Anyway, if I have to go to jail I'd rather go as a Red than as a sex-fiend.

In odd moments, some of them damn peculiar, I have written a play and when I finish this present schnitzel, I am coming to New York to have it mounted (and see what you can do for me—as a venerable comic once remarked to the college widow). When the momzerim in the aisle seats have finished clubbing me I will come to California to get my wounds licked.

H. Kurnitz

Paris, December 29, 1955

My dear Hackenbush:

. . . for fifty cents you can buy the January issue of Holiday Magazine and somewhere in the book is my opening essay on the cinematographic arts, a monthly feature, which is expected to rival Rev. Norman Vincent Peale in Look (Dear Dr. Peale: My husband is a sodomite and I know I ought to pray for him, like you advised me, but every time I kneel down, well, Doctor, you should only live so long how much your advice has helped me).

The Krasnas had a Xmas party with Chinese food, which sounded like a wonderful idea on paper but the trouble is that it was cooked by some Formosan tribesmen who had heard of Chinese food, probably even seen some in some distant age, but who had never actually tasted any. We are going off together, the Krasnas and some tomato and I, after New Year's to play golf or romp in the snow, we haven't decided which yet.

The peaceful, sleepy village of Klosters sounds like a suburb of Burbank with Irwin Shaw, Zanuck, Hawks, Pete Viertel, Spiegel and other such sports on the premises and it sort of scares me so I may head for the S. of France, a more temperate climate and a convenient golf course. . . .

A big kiss for you, my beautiful Groucho, and for your Eden and for any of my friends who may have survived VistaVision and Todd A-O. . . .

Love always,
Harry

London, January 8, 1956

Dearest Hackenbush:

Now that your wife has bought you a new suit I don't mind starting up a correspondence, in fact, I think we should be pen pals and I am sending you this to start the ball "rolling."

The reason I know about your new suit, Grouch, is that we were finally so desperate for reading matter in Klosters that I was reduced to reading your wife's letters to her sister. I am glad to be able to tell you that her spelling and punctuation are above par for one of her years; that she violated no confidences of the nuptial couch, that she betrayed no particulars of your financial standing (boy, that must be zippy reading nowadays), and in general conducted herself like a genteel young girl who has landed on her feet and doesn't care who knows it.

You are Uncle, by the way, to a very agreeable boy of some nine weeks, the pride and joy of H. and D. Hawks. Only nine weeks old, Grouch, and he gurgles! Think of that! When *I* was nine weeks old I knew all the Rasumovsky quartets, read and wrote Hebrew and could recite Lenin's Ode on the Death of Tchitchikov.

Klosters was nice, actually, though I don't ski and have no intentions of embarking on a sport where they give you morphine and splints when you buy the basic equipment. Just above Klosters is Davos, the Magic Mountain Country. All the sanitoria have runners on the streets and God help you, if you cough twice they throw a net over you. Hawks and I (and Irwin Shaw) gave a New Year's Eve party in Klosters for the local elite, a shabby lot of snaggle-toothed Swiss peasants. I take it you were at C. Lederer's. I had an invitation, forwarded to the Swiss Alps and thought seriously of running over for an hour or two but the pants of my dinner jacket were unpressed.

Hawks wants me to stay and do another picture with him but I am being coy until I see what happens in N. Y. If the play closes, I open; if the play runs, I don't. That is the creed and the testament of your old schlepper pal,

H. Kurnitz

March 19, 1956

Dear Harry:

. . . I was at a party with Bush-Fekete [the playwright] the other night. It seems he was a very close friend of Molnar's and can talk about him for hours. Among other things, he said that Molnar was very careful with his money. He advised Fekete, "always live at the best hotel in town—but in the cheapest room. This is much better than the best room in a cheap hotel, for it gives you prestige and distinction."

Molnar lived at the Plaza on 59th Street and used to go out the side door to a delicatessen that offered an entire meal for 89 cents. Finishing that, he would buy a carton of coffee and a doughnut and bring them back to his room. This was for his breakfast the next morning—with the coffee heated over a

Sterno stove. He died soon after—leaving over one hundred thousand dollars in cash and securities. Such is the power of fear.

Art Buchwald is in town and was at Hillcrest yesterday with Krasna. He's extremely talented and probably a wonderful guy, but he has a disconcerting way of avoiding your gaze when you're talking to him and at the conclusion of what you say, there is absolutely no change in his expression. There are people who do this only because they are thinking of an answer. He doesn't even answer.

Because of your column, I have now been sucked into a year's subscription to Holiday Magazine. However, it wasn't a complete loss, for in addition to your column there was a piece by E. B. White—I think. (I'm not sure about this because I subscribe to so many things that most of the time I don't know what I'm reading.)

Love from all.

Best,
Groucho

London, September 5, 1959

Dear Flywheel,*

You may or may not remember playing Loew's Chickenfat in Far Rockaway but if you do you will doubtless recall a second violinist in the pit band (there was only one violin—a second violin) and if you are the same sentimental vaudevillian you were in those days a tear will come to your eye and you will murmur "Ah, yes, Loew's Chickenfat." It's not much of a way to spend an evening but better than the low pursuits which normally take up so much of your time and when you

* When on the radio with Chico, Groucho was senior member of the law firm Flywheel, Shyster and Flywheel.

brush away that tear you will brush away the years and we will be young again, straight and tall, erect again (and I don't mean once a month and Jewish holidays) with eyes undimmed by pain, frustration, myopia and the vision of Big Money. Here I am in London, too old to be a beatnik and too young for Zen. The truth is I don't fit in anywhere any more, Hackenbush, and people are beginning to notice.

The last cotillion I attended, half my dance card was unfilled. The other half was filled in by Margaret Rutherford.

The reason for this letter is to congratulate you on your book and to assure you that I would run like mad to the nearest book dealer who has it in stock but that happens to be 3,000 miles away, over water, and I see no way out except for you to notify your publishers to send me a copy. Airmail.

I am writing some jokes for a Yul Brynner movie on a grant from the Guggenheim Foundation. I spent a pleasant summer on (1) Sam Spiegel's yacht, (2) Biarritz and (3) Deauville, and now I hope to clean up this Augean stable of a movie and get back to work on a new play of which I have 2 acts. Unfortunately it is a play in 14 acts so I still have a lot of work to do.

Much love, dearest Hackenbush, and a kiss for Melinda who must now be big enough for that kind of work. Do send me the book. I long to read it.

Ever thine,
H. Kurnitz

Rhodes, October 21, 1959

Dearest Hackenbush,

What, you may well ask yourself, is H. Kurnitz doing in Rhodes? Stanley Donen, ever a pioneer, has allowed me to try the 12-Tone Scale in composing some jokes for this movie involving the combined talents of Yul Brynner and Mitzi Gaynor. He is a gangster; she his warm-hearted moll. Name another writer, if you can, capable of such originality of plot and character. Anyway, the island of Rhodes is about as far out as you can get in Europe. From my windows I can see the coast of Turkey and at sunset the lamps of the Halvah miners glow with an unearthly light.

En route here, stumbling through London airport in the foggy, foggy dawn, a voice called out "Koynitz." I know that only you and one other living man have just that precise slum version of the Eton-Oxford accent and to be sure it was Krasna, en route to Switzerland with a couple of suitcases crammed with money. He gave me a dollar, I kissed the hem of his garment and we went our separate ways, moles struggling upward to the light. What do you think of Jews Without Typewriters as a title for my autobiography? Or a love song—"I Thought the Acropolis Was a Ruin, and Then I Met You."

I am coming to California in January, my beloved, to spend approx. 3 weeks huddled with Cary Grant on a new movie. I would be much obliged if you will give a very large party for me.

Meanwhile and thereafter I send love to you and to Eden and beg to remain ever your devoted friend and disciple,

H. Kurnitz

December 18, 1959

Dear Harry:

I saw a note from you to my publisher, telling him that you liked my book. Even if it's a goddamned lie, I appreciate it.

What really horrified me was to see your picture in the

Hollywood Reporter last Tuesday. Times have certainly changed. In the old days, when reading the trades, we could always count on seeing a picture of some cute little tootsie garbed in less than nothing. Now we see you, which may be one of the things that's wrong with the movie industry.

With the possible exception of Shakespeare (I mean when he was alive), nobody ever rushed into a theater to look at an author. The tall, concrete doll to the rear of you in the picture is, for some curious reason, fingering her bust. Either that or she has had a sudden heart attack.

If you will tell me precisely when you are coming to Hollywood, I will arrange a party, something small but select, for your degenerate friends. I need an exact date, for the Ontra Cafeteria is very sticky about these things. They can serve the ham and spinach dinner on ten days' notice, but coming as you do from the land of the gourmet, I told them I didn't think you would be satisfied with ham and spinach. "Well," said the manager hopefully, "do you think your friend would be happier if we put sliced, hard-boiled eggs on the spinach?" So, at the moment, I'm leaving the food up in the air—where I'm sure it will be after you eat it.

Fondly,
Groucho

June 11, 1963

Dear Harry:

As usual, I ignored your advice and journeyed to the Huntington Hartford Theater to case your turkey. Everything you said about Elizabeth Seal was true. To think that this gamine, with whom I was so madly in love when she appeared in "Irma La Douche," could single-handedly foul up an entire evening, convinces me that Shakespeare was hitting the bottle when he said, "The play's the thing." It probably is, but you'd better have somebody to play it!

Your old friend, Lennie Spiegelglass, apparently has inherited the mantle of Anne Nichols, for each year he unfolds a Jewish comedy that grosses between eight and nine million dollars—and it always winds up on the screen with Rosalind Russell playing both parts.

I am flattered that you ask to become a more or less permanent guest at my little hovel in the Springs. As you know, it is a very modest little hovel and there's hardly room in it for my three children and three grandchildren. However, if you are willing to sleep in the kitchen with your head in the oven, I think we can work out something, even if it means my moving to another town.

Fondly,
Groucho

Paris—October 14, 1964

Dearest Hackenbush:

I am going to a wedding in Westminster Abbey (orthodox) next week and yesterday while my morning coat was being fitted I caught a glimpse of myself in the tailor's triple mirror and my mind went loping back across the years to your entrance in "I'll Say She Is" at the Walnut Street Theater, the jaunty insouciance with which you flicked the tails of your coat, and a plastic tear which I carry for just such occasions welled up in my eye. Hackenbush, I murmured, if I forget thee, Hackenbush, may my right hand lose its cunning. I clearly remember my arrival in Hollywood in 1938 and the slice of pot roast you handed me (by the way, now that 26 years have elapsed, the potato pancakes were soggy), and how that dreary hunk of meat sustained me through the long lean years.

I am gainfully employed (sandblasting some jokes for Freddy Kohlmar) and I am the author of a new play which is likely to turn W. 46th St. into a disaster area early next fall. I am quite active in a subversive group called Americans Abroad for Johnson and we had a rally last Sat. night featuring a live donkey but unfortunately the donkey had to leave at 8 P.M. because he was also appearing in "Carmen" at the Opera that night. And you, my beloved schlepper friend, are you still getting fat on re-runs or re-winds or whatever they call them in your quaint new world?

Affectionately,

H. K.

October 27, 1964

Dear Harry:

It will be nice to have you back in our little village, even though I only see you semi-annually. I think the last time was at Ardie Deutsch's. It was a nice party, but far too good for you. I would have enjoyed it more if that actor hadn't insisted on kissing me every time I entered the living room. At least Eden was safe.

The political campaign has dragged along for so many months that I doubt if anyone cares who wins. However, stealing a line from Criswell, I predict it will be the biggest landslide since Roosevelt took on Alf Landon.

Unless there is a big change in my plans, I will be in London in April, doing a repaint job on my old quiz show. Eden and I are looking forward to it for different reasons. You see, one of the elevator boys at Fortnum and Mason's is madly in love with me. It's a little scary, but whenever he takes me up or down (in the elevator, I mean) he quickly closes the door. This is because he wants me all to himself.

Eden wants to go to London because it's near France. She has
spent $4,000 with Berlitz for private lessons and now she tells
me she can't make any progress until she finds someone to
talk to in French.

As for your welcome home party, I will gladly pay for
the food and booze, but I would expect you to pay a cleaner
to remove the dog stains from the furniture and also have the
piano tuned. We can discuss the details after you arrive.
Until then,

Beaujolais,
Groucho

TO ARTHUR SHEEKMAN

December 16, 1954

Dear Sheek:

Recently I have been corresponding with your daughter.
She wrote me a long exuberant letter. In reply I wrote her a
short curt note. She then wrote me a letter twice as long as
the original one so I gave up and sent her a copy of "War and
Peace." This, I hope, will keep her quiet until after the holidays.

I just read in the Reporter that Irving Berlin's bite out of
his last two pictures was $1,300,000. Is it any wonder he keeps
singing, "There's no business like Show Business"? There is
also no businessman like Irving Berlin. Not that I begrudge
him this. He is a giant talent worth every nickel he gets.
Single-handed, if he were interested, I believe he could pay
off the British debt.

I could write you many more items but we're both busy,
have very little interest in each other and as I always say, why

try to keep a friendship alive that has been dying on the vine for twenty-five years.

My love to your beautiful Gloria even though she is hitting 35—and do try to come home one of these days.

Your loving friend,
Groucho

P.S. I just received the Look Award—which translated means their magazine gets a free plug on my show. . . .

London, 1955

Dear Grouch:

Aside from the fact that the Pinewood Studio still uses dirty roller towels in the men's room, I very much like working for the J. Arthur Rank company.

The executives I have met are courteous and considerate. They seem eager to avoid story conferences—on the theory, perhaps, that anybody from Hollywood knows more about pictures than they do.

People ask if you are as amusing off-screen as on and I—please forgive me—tell them the truth.

Our apartment is a few blocks from the Selfridge store, and we run over there as often as though it were Schwab's. The difference is that the people we meet here are bigger than Skolsky; but maybe that's because it's a bigger store.

Our love to both of you,
Arthur

P.S. How is your insomnia? In Paris I came across a new kind of soporific. It isn't a pill; it's a suppository. The other day I stepped on one and my foot fell asleep.

P.P.S. Parliament opens tomorrow and the studio got us passes to see the royal procession, which will of course include the Queen and her Duke. You aren't going to believe this but the passes will permit Gloria and me to stand in a preferred place on the sidewalk and watch. That should put an end to the absurd notion that it was you who lifted me from local to world-wide obscurity.

February 15, 1955

Dear Sheek:

My first impulse was to answer your first letter written January 28 and ignore the second one written February 2nd.

You probably are not aware of it but you and I have a completely different conception of me. You regard me as a kind of ancient crone—a talkative old chatterbox who upon the receipt of any kind of news—no matter how trivial—breathlessly rushes out to broadcast it to the world at large. I, on the other hand, regard myself as a mute stoic, silent as the Sphinx—a graven image, who, even if burning fagots were applied to his bare feet, would never reveal the slightest information to anyone. Perhaps I fit somewhere between these two poles. At any rate, your secret is as safe with me as though it were planted in a concrete tomb a thousand miles south of Cape Horn.

My son, Arthur, is blossoming out. This week he had a very good appraisal of Jack Benny in the Sunday New York Times. I guess it comes as a double surprise to me—first that he can write at all, being my son, and second that it is possible for a man to drop a tennis racket and take up the pen or the typewriter or the quill or whatever sons write with. He's a nice guy, and I'm very happy for him—so much so that I'm going to his home tonight for a free meal. The cooking isn't much but the conversation is wretched. I always enjoy going there because my grandchildren—neither of whom, thank God, resembles me—worship me. They have never seen me on TV and I've advised them not to. They are adorable children and resemble two elevator starters I used to know in Lima, Ohio, some years ago.

Regards,
Groucho

P.S. If you ever get back, and would like to have dinner sometime, just say the word and I'll be at your house before you can say Marvin Meyer (which isn't a particularly long name).

My best to you and your very sexy wife, and if she ever leaves you—I'm in the book.

FROM NORMAN KRASNA

Paris, February 1, 1955

Dear Hackenbush,

... Harpo wrote me to investigate his playing the Olympia with Marceau, the French pantomimist, and I did, and wrote him yesterday. They were pleased and flattered enough, but the business deal got down to no fares, and about three hundred dollars a day to cover everything. This seems to break down in working for fares and living expenses. I can't make up my mind whether Susan and Harpo would have a great time anyway, or whether it would be a lesser Las Vegas engagement. There are two ways to look at living and working here. You can emphasize the lack of toilet paper, or you can keep aware of the sauces, but it's really up to the individual and his genes to have a good time. And that's probably true everywhere. Erle and I quote a story we read someplace: A man was walking from one city to another, and he met a wise man. "How are the people in this city?" he asked the wise man, "I mean to live there." "And how did you find the people in the city you left?" asked the wise man. "They were mean, and jealous, and unfriendly," said the traveler. "In this city you will also find the people mean and jealous, etc." Good point, I think. Still, Harpo and Susan are probably the happiest people we know, and they'd have a great time in Russia.

This leaves me a comment on your own dazzling career, which I follow in the trades. To really confess something to you, your success is so enormous, and rockbound, and simple, for you, that you've taken all the suspense out of a theatrical career, and you're the only example I know. Maybe it's not that way to you, close up, but to your friends, a generation whose humor you single-handedly influenced more than any other single person, your fabulous popularity is an anti-climax to being Groucho Marx, and during your ebb, while it may have seemed a dip to you, it didn't to us, and all the Trendex-Nielsens can't influence us one bit.

So, kiss Melinda, shake hands with Arthur, Miriam, pretty Mrs. Marx, love to you from all of us and

Fondly,
Norman

Paris, June 4th, 1955

Dear Hackenbush:

You don't remember me *—but I'm an ex-contestant on your program. I'm a Congressional Medal of Honor winner; I saved four lives, two of them children, diving off the Golden Gate Bridge through the ice (it froze that August) to get to

* Mr. Krasna is, of course, chiding the old quizmaster for not having awarded any considerable sum of money to a Congressional Medal of Honor winner who had appeared on his program. Groucho's reply was that —unlike some of the other shows—his was not rigged; therefore the prize money could go only to the contestants who gave the right answers.

them; and I would have been the Unknown Soldier but I was passed over due to dirty politics. For being all this I was picked to go on your program and I won twelve dollars. I would have had much more but I thought you were whispering the answer to me, and while I thought you were wrong, I repeated what you said, and *I* was wrong.

I have heard from other Congressional Medal of Honor winners that they have had the same experience, which is rather discouraging, because if there is another war I doubt if I'll be tempted to charge a machine gun with my bare hands again. . . .

However, to get back to the point, I want you to know that I took your twelve dollars and went to France and went into the cinema business, as a backer. I backed two musicals and a satire about religion, and have cleaned up. So, in gratitude to you I am returning the twelve dollars, which you will find in this envelope, I am quite sure, and you may want to pass it on to another Congressional etc.

This is about all the news I have to write you, since I tell the same things to Harpo, Tugend and Buzzell and if it's pretty dull to them, reading it the first time, how do you think it is to me, who knew all about it even before I wrote it? I had a great idea in that sentence but I lost it. . . .

Love,
Norman

Blonay, Switzerland
August 3rd, 1955

Dear Hack: Or Groucho:

That was a very nice letter you wrote me: just the proper amount of sentiment offset by witty sayings and literary allusions, and A-number-one spelling. A little of that in "Time for

Elizabeth" * would have made all the difference in the world; all the difference being whether I'd still be living on my royalties or my having to work here for a deferred salary.

I have some bulletins on you through Nunnally. We had a hot time in the old town; dinner at the Pre Catalan in the bois, which is "park," and then naked women on the Left Bank. Erle and Dorris kept watch, and their clothes on . . .

I heard you have an expensive lot and are building a house to match. For ten minutes we toyed with the idea of my writing you a letter during which I casually mention an acquaintance of mine who got rooked by some architect called Neff, but we decided the joke was a little too horrifying. Put in brass plumbing, but watch the expense. For Christ's sake figure everything out in advance, changing is what costs. Do we need another pool table? On the other hand, the pool table is what will probably pay for the house.

(I have to leave suddenly, will finish letter later. Letter later? Further father? "Animal Crackers," circa '28.)

I have now come back to the typewriter, the following day, two-thirty in the afternoon, and I haven't had lunch yet. You might say a lot of people miss lunch in America, but missing lunch in America is not like missing lunch in France. What the hell do you miss not eating in America, ha? Am sending out for a snail sandwich.

I am working very, very hard, but I'm not complaining, and I think my picture will be very, very good. I think millions can be made in the independent field, and if done abroad, millions can be kept. Half the trick is to have a wife like Erle, who will not come home unless drugged, and the other half is find a script and star who will carry the picture.

Last week, if you please, I had supper with the Oliviers, having seen them do "Macbeth" at Stratford. They were just great, I need not emphasize, and the evening was what I call

* The play he and Groucho wrote together.

"memorable," or to "conjure with," as our friend Jessel would say.

I'm hoping the Sheekmans come back soon; we spend a fine time going over you, and if I could get the Johnsons in the same living room at the same time, our lives would be complete. I know we discuss you at home, too, but with the ocean between us it's better, and safer.

I find I quote you more when I'm away from you although this isn't the condition I'd like to see made permanent. Thank you for your warm and touching letter; I hope Eden is well; that your children are safe and happy; and that you, yourself, old gray master, are reasonably content, and sparing of your time and energy and emotion.

Love to all,
Norman

January 23, 1956

Dear Mr. Krasna:

A lot of water has gone over the dam since last I wrote you. And, if this were "Animal Crackers," I would then say, "A lot of dam has gone over the water." But times and humor change, and what was gold in 1930, turns out to be nothing but dross in '56.

Various friends of yours have filtered back from France, telling me of your exploits, achievements and conquests. In sifting all these tales, my guess is that you have a pretty good picture in the can. ["The Ambassador's Daughter"] This is not quite the same as having it in the theater, but at least it's a step in the right direction. I hear reports that you are returning in May for only a brief moment; that you are going to remain away two years; that you are going to remain away forever—and that you even bought five acres right across the street from Napoleon's Tomb and contemplate building. Personally, I hope that this early enthusiasm for "La Belle France" wanes in time, and that you will eventually return to the land of free enterprise and confiscatory taxes.

There is a slight possibility that I will come over for a few weeks in June. Last time, I played Europe in a series of one-night stands. I will not make that mistake again. If I go, I will rely on the airlines and the local cabs. Bouncing and lurching along those narrow roads in Europe is a little too much for my fragile frame.

The hegira to Palm Springs is in full swing. Harpo is selling his house, and building here. Zeppo is building. Chico is looking for a card game anywhere between Indio and Twenty Nine Palms. And I, the last of the stalwarts, disregarding the blandishments of my brothers, intend to remain a citizen of Beverly Hills. What keeps me here is my daughter. The day I don't see Melinda is a day lost. I suppose I'm an unusually foolish father, but I know that she'll be married when she's sixteen—and until then I want to see as much of her as I can.

Love from all,
Groucho

December 7, 1959

Dear Kras:

"I wonder often what the vintner buys one half so precious as the stuff he sells."

In the Sunday Times magazine section they have a long piece on Edward Fitzgerald who, as you damned well know, translated the musings of Omar from the eleventh century to the 19th. I thought this quotation would bring back some tender memories of the days when we were life-long friends, sitting on the beach at Ensenada, trying to pick up a tennis player's girl on a trolley car in Frisco, and so on, and so on.

Bob Dwan has done a masterly job in reducing our little play (mostly clipping the first act) so that it could possibly be done as a TV spec. I'm not sure that I want to do the straw hat bit again. I love playing it and hearing the boffs, but senility (like Hoover) is just around the corner, and when I think of those hot closets which the various innkeepers blandly assure you are bedrooms, and those open toilets deep in the woods which are all right except when it rains, and the Tax Dept. which does the rest . . . well, the hell with it. I think by this time you get the idea.

I remember two distinct times when you were terribly angry with me. This was when we had the two Congressional Medal of Honor winners on our show and neither of them won as much as a Swiss franc. It's a good thing I didn't yield to your blandishments or I would now be in some Federal court, perjuring myself under oath. I don't quite know why I remained honest for I spring from a long line of thieves. I guess I was just lucky.

Curiously enough, the disappearance of all the big money quiz shows has boosted my stock considerably. The last Nielsen rating had me top man on a totem pole which included "Playhouse 90," Goody Ace's "Big Party" and "The Untouchables." Bob Hope remarked, "I never thought the day would come when the only honest thing on TV would be the wrestling matches." The whole quiz investigation (and it's gone much further than that) is going to be opened again some time in December. Many of the disc jockeys have resigned under fire. I think, all in all, it's a very healthy situation for they're not going to stop with the quizzes or the payolas; the FCC is now charging down on the crooked commercials. To show you how scared the whole gang is, last week at the Ritz Hotel all the TV tycoons met in a sealed room for four and a half hours. As they left, with thin and bloodless lips all they could say to the twenty or so reporters outside was "No comment."

Needless to say, we miss you. Give the two little ones a big hug from me. If I were forty years younger I would wait and marry both of them.

Fondly,
Groucho

March 21, 1960

Dear Kras:

St. Patrick's Day has come and gone and I am still alive. I remember when I was ten years old, standing on the corner of Fifth Avenue and 93rd Street. In the parade, sitting in a luxurious barouche, was Tom Sharkey. He had just had his first fight with Jim Jeffries and most of his ribs had been caved in. As the carriage arrived at our corner, the parade stopped momentarily. With my customary wit I piped up, "Hey, Sharkey, what did Jeffries do to ya?" He leaned halfway out of the carriage toward me and yelled, "Come over here, ya little bastard, and I'll kill ya!"

In his condition (drunk and with his entire torso cracked like shredded wheat) I think I could have knocked him out, but as always in a crisis, I was yellow. So, I turned tail and ran as fast as I could toward the slum we lived in near Third Avenue.

The parades are less boisterous these days, and so are the Irish. In sports, the Irish have lost leadership. All the good fighters are Negroes. Most of the top baseball and basketball heroes are either Negroes, Cubans, Mexicans or Italians.

Like the Irish, the Jew, too, is being assimilated. I certainly did my share. I married a Mormon, a Swede and an Irish lass, all paupers.

I don't suppose there is anything about the current movie strike that you are not aware of. I assume the trades are shoved under your door each morning by a Swiss Jeeves, along with your brioche, croissant and second-rate coffee. I am in the fortunate position of being a neutral. None of the labor factions bother me. I think this is because I've been on TV so long that nobody knows I'm still there.

You won't receive any author's royalties this year from our mutual girl friend, "Elizabeth." In a way I regret not doing it again this summer. The audiences love the play and the laughs are loud and continuous, but the shabby accommodations were what did me in. I remember last year up in Sacandaga, it was 120 degrees during the day and 119 at night. I had a room about the size of an office desk with a window not much larger than the periscope lens of a submarine. One night I was desperate and tried sleeping with my head partly out of the window, but I withdrew it quickly: it was the height of the mosquito season. Besides, I was afraid some hunter would mistake me for an owl, shoot me and have my head stuffed for his living room. This is hardly the way a rich man, or even a poor man, should spend his declining years.

Literature: I don't know whether you get The New Yorker in the Alps, or if you do, whether you are reading Sam Behrman's seven pieces on Max Beerbohm. They are utterly delightful and I have now decided to hate Sheekman, because he met Beerbohm in Rapallo, and I didn't.

I don't think I've told you that I'm screwing up "The Mikado" April 29th for the Bell Telephone Company. This is my revenge for the lousy phone service they've given me over the years.

My daughter Melinda is playing one of the Three Little Maids from School. At a moment's notice she will sing you all the parts—Poo-bah's, Yum-yum's, Nanki-Poo's and Ko-ko's. I only wish I knew my part as well as she does. Last night she was on my show. She did a challenge dance with Gene Nelson and I would say that, for the first time, she didn't look like Groucho's daughter but like a real pro. She's been offered a job this summer singing in a nightclub, but since she's only thirteen and a half, I told her she could have my permission in about ten years. History is repeating itself.

Melinda's mother once told me that when she was 13, she applied for a job in a flashy nightclub in Culver City. Dressed in her mother's clothes, she said she was eighteen, and much to her surprise they engaged her for the lead.

She sang "Sophisticated Lady" and then danced in what was in those days a fairly skimpy outfit. They did three shows a night. She was excited at first, but after a few nights, the long wait between performances bored her, so she bought roller skates, and between shows she skated in the neighborhood.

One night, the manager, a well known hood, spied her skating. She looked familiar, so he said, "Ain't you the girl that does that 'Sophisticated Lady' in the show? How old are you?"

She answered, "I'm almost 14."

"You want the cops to take my license away?" he said. "You have to be 18 to work in these joints. You're fired—take your old lady's clothes and go home."

Speaking of little ones, be sure to give those two little females a big kiss from me. Since you make your living as a writer, I deliberately have waited two months before answering you. I don't want to burden you with the Damocles' sword of a steady correspondence. The next letter you get from me will be three years from now.

Fondly,
Groucho

P.S. I am starting my 14th season next Wednesday and this may be my swan song. This year my sponsors are Toni, who also make Paper Mate pens (how they do it I don't know, but

I believe they take bobby pins and pour ink over them. Then they test it. If it writes on margarine, it means it will curl your hair in 20 minutes). The other sponsor is Old Gold cigarettes. I should be a big help to them, sitting on a stool, puffing away at a very large, expensive cigar.

I am going to New York in October to see what's left of the American Theater and to listen to a lady friend of mine whine about the bad bleach job she gets at her favorite beauty parlor.

Lausanne, May 24, 1960

Dear Hackenbush,

. . . The further reviews of your performance (in "The Mikado") are quite good, and indicate that you could easily have been more Groucho without being sacrilegious. I consider myself a genuine Savoyard and am one of the original booers when the Aborn company interpolated up-to-date lyrics for "I've Got Them on My List," however, I would think your own patented leer was made to order for Ko-ko, and the lines and stage directions allow for it. This reminds me vaguely of your original interpretation of our play, in La Jolla, where you were so loyal to yourself as the author that you straitjacketed yourself as the actor, and while you succeeded in not being Groucho you left out any attractive identifiable personality. Even worse, it occurs to me, you have to erase what they expect of Groucho and ask them to accept a stranger. From a stranger they will take a stranger but from a known personality they must have some sort of bridge. I conclude, Ko-ko could have had more Groucho without violation of Gilbert's memory.

That is all, dear friend, for the moment.

Love and kisses,
Norman

December 13, 1960

Dear Krasola:

I understand Doctor Johnson never took more than thirty minutes to answer any letter. Times have indeed changed. Your letter before me is dated November 7th and this is now the 13th of December.

Christmas is rushing upon us. I have already received greetings from the milkman, the man who repairs the TV sets (which is almost daily), the letter carrier, the gardener, the makeup man, the publicity man, and a few dozen raggedy relatives. I also received the gas bill for the month of November for $48.50. You can't even afford to kill yourself in the Truesdale Estates.

I am sending you, under separate cover (that's the way they talk in literary circles), a tome called "The Politics of Upheaval," by Arthur M. Schlesinger, Jr. I realize you are a busy man but don't let the length of this book keep you from reading it. It could have been titled "The Fascist Era in America." There are a number of pages devoted to Father Coughlin, Gerald K. Smith, Townsend, and Huey Long, among others. Here is the whole lunatic fringe in full cry. It sounds terrifying but don't let it scare you away. I was going to send it to you via airmail, however my secretary investigated the cost and found it came to $5.30. Since the book only cost $6 we decided to send it by ship. That, too, proved prohibitive. What we finally did was engage a sailor who had been a frog man in the British Navy. He said that for eighty-five cents and keep he would be delighted to carry it in his teeth across the Atlantic and deliver it to you personally in Switzerland.

Plus this, I am sending you a record which I regard as one of the funniest I've ever heard. It was written and performed by Carl Reiner and Mel Brooks. Reiner is a magnificent straight man and Brooks used to write for Sid Caesar. They are a most effective combination.

About Hillcrest, there is nothing new to relate. [Eddie] Buzzell is back and says that as far as jolly England is concerned, he's had it. [George] Burns is still reminiscing about the Palace, Jessel is either in the card room or on his way (I presume) to some dame in Israel. Harpo is back playing golf and despite his recent illness, he outdrives me by fifty yards, even on the putting green.

Some weeks ago Harpo drove over to Indio to collect his first unemployment insurance check. I don't quite understand how it works, but from what he told me, he is entitled to $50 a week for 26 weeks. When he got to this office, the clerk asked his name. "Arthur Marx," replied Harpo. "And did you earn any money this year?" "Yes," said Harpo, "last week I worked for one day." "That's nice," nodded the clerk. "How much did they pay you for the day?" "Eleven thousand five hundred," said Harpo.

There was a conspicuous silence on the other side of the window. The man regarded him stonily for a few minutes, then turned and went to the back of the office, apparently to discuss this oaf with his superior. After deciding they had just inherited some unusual nut, back came the two of them together. The clerk, whose salary is $6,500 a year, and the head of the office who collects $9,500 a year, stared suspiciously at Harpo. "Now let's start all over again," said the head of the office. "You say you worked one day last week and your salary was $11,500?" Being basically a pantomimist, Harpo nodded. "And what did you say your name is?" prodded the man. "Harpo Marx," said Harpo. A light began to dawn. "I see," said the chief, "but how did you make $11,500 in just one day?" "Easy," replied Harpo. "I did a commercial for Proctor and Gamble."

I trust you and Erle will enjoy an enchanting Christmas, surrounded by your four little ones and a dog or two. Love from all, and if you ever get near the U. S. again, try to spend an hour or two in California.

Fondly,
Groucho

Lausanne, 31st January, 1961

Dear Hack,

This time I held back on writing, since I wanted to space out our letters and not make them a chore for you. However, having just finished listening to the record by Reiner and Brooks I felt like writing immediately. In this direction, I have a hunch, is the new wave. While I know it isn't exactly ad lib, it's also not a word for word delivery of six writers' collaboration. It's an off-shoot of the Sahls and Bermans, etc., but also is derived—I am sure of this—from the Marx Brothers' original departure from rigid book shows. To this day, in my opinion, your television success is based on the challenge of having to rise to exciting conversation extemporaneously. Of course Brooks and Sid Caesar are interchangeable in some of those characters. I think it was Caesar's invention but Brooks does it superbly and I don't belittle the fine art of straight man Reiner. I have heard Danny Kaye and Dore Schary do this type of feeding and answering, about a union man called Kaplan, and it's not below this standard. I am much obliged for the record. I have Newhart's and I think he's as good as any of the new ones, if not a shade better.

Now another expression of gratitude for the Schlesinger book. I was popeyed reading it. My God, they were only people, plain, ordinary people, behind all those earthshaking events. It may be something you know, but when you read it in all its authenticity you never fail to be surprised. Two similar appropriate pictures come to mind; the New Yorker cartoon showing the king, looking like little George V, on a balcony whispering to his Prime Minister, with the crowd below staring at the royal figure who is completely covered in ermine. "You know, all I wear under this is my underwear." And the other one is your announcing to the audience that you're not certain you remembered to empty the pan under the icebox. Earthy, human identification among the Olympians.

I haven't seen Nunnally for a while so I have nothing to mention about him except I know he's doing the script on "Cleopatra." Now! After all that time, and all those sets, they need a script! My idea of irony, and Nunnally's capable of it, is for the script to be very intimate, with no need for the eight acres of Old Egypte.

Love and kisses,
Norman

May 16, 1961

Dear Kras:

Thanks for the poems by François Villon, particularly the one you marked about the disintegration of a beautiful woman. I decided this was just a little too frightening to show to Eden but she discovered it and much to my surprise was less depressed by it than I was. Perhaps women enjoy watching other women aging. It's certainly much tougher on a woman to wrinkle and crumble. A man, no matter how old he gets, can always wear an ascot tie and toupee and pretend he's Fred Astaire. On the other hand, Sarah Bernhardt was making a pretty good living in her late seventies when she hardly had a leg left to stand on.

Wednesday night, the 17th of May I will wind up a 14-year career as the world's most prominent quiz master. No tears will be shed by yours truly. It's done wonders for me, psychologically and financially. Physically and mentally the show has always been a romp. It's rather odd not having anything facing me after this last show. I've had a number of offers to do different TV shows and also received a play from George Axelrod which I immediately returned. I am too old to be holed up in a second-rate hotel in New Haven, and at three in the morning, loaded with Seconal and Dexamil to be contributing my feeble best to rewriting the second act curtain and the entire third act.

There are two or three people around town who want to do "Time for Elizabeth" as a movie, but for the present at least, I don't want to do anything. As soon as the sun sets I grab my trusty guitar, gulp down two big shots of Tequila and start shouting "Gringo, go home!" It's strange how one goes through various phases of booze imbibing. I started many years ago on grape juice and when Prohibition came in I successfully guzzled my way through bathtub gin, Bourbon scraped off of Governor Faubus, and then on through Vodka. I had one siege with Irish whiskey. I didn't care for it much but the girl I was going with had read a lot of James Joyce. Since I've never understood Joyce, I decided the only way I could get into her good graces was to drink the whiskey. After she threw me out I wasn't sure what I wanted to drink. For a while I was toying with prussic acid. How I got to Tequila is a long story and one that will have to wait.

Love to all, and especially the two little girls.

Fondly,
Groucho

July 5, 1961

Dear Kras:

I am sending you the yearly edition of the Bawl Street Journal. It's not nearly as funny as last year's edition because last year the Dow Jones Averages were 50 points lower and, as we all know, the only real laughter comes from despair.

Speaking of despair, George Abbott has a play called "A Funny Thing Happened on the Way to the Forum," and I was sent another play called "Young Enough to Know Better!" If I were ten years younger I might have tackled one of these assignments, but I am old enough to know better. If it's a hit, you're trapped in what is probably one of the world's worst climates. If it flops, suicide seems like a very pleasant solution.

I am doing the narration for a DuPont spec this August. It's the history of the automobile and the title is pure genius. It's to be called "Merrily We Roll Along," and I'm sure some Vice President of the network got a raise for that one.

If it wasn't for the maritime unions I would now be on the high seas, throwing up all the way to Pearl Harbor. The unions are having what is known as a jurisdictional fight and it's all very complicated. The end result is that I'm sitting here until they condescend to let the boats sail.

Melinda, who is almost fifteen and as pretty as the day is long, thinks I am in league with the strikers. Every night around six she sits cross-legged on her bed and weeps bitterly. Her cry is, "The summer will soon be over and I'll be back in High School, and why aren't we going to Honolulu?" I show her the front pages each morning and she listens to all the accounts on radio and TV, but nothing has happened yet to convince her that I am not solely responsible for the stoppage of these vessels. As some woman in the Bronx once said, and I quote, "Go raise a family and see what it'll get you."

Now that I think of it, I wish I had been a hell-raiser when I was thirty years old. I tried when I was 50 but I always got sleepy.

Hoping this finds you, I beg to remain

Yours sincerely,
Old Doctor Hackenbush
and his magic bullet

Lausanne, April 26, 1962

Dear Hacklebush,

... We have bought the land for our home here, and the architect will shortly show up with preliminary designs. Somebody had better show up with preliminary money, since the whole venture will cost double what I got for the house in California. It turns out that land and building are the only two items that are higher than in America. Divorces, for instance, are very cheap, and women aren't even allowed to vote in my canton, which is why it is my canton. A man would be a fool not to snap up a bargain divorce in this country. I have discussed this with Erle who has a great nose for a bargain, but she does not see her way clear to dividing her mony with me . . .

Love,
Norman

P.S. Dictated to a beautiful Egyptian secretary and sent before correcting since I won't be back for five days. When you realize how many mistakes there are in this letter, you will know how beautiful this girl is.

P.P.S. This girl is now in dilemma. If she writes a perfect letter, you will deduce she is homely. If she is vain enough to make thirty mistakes, you will be certain she is beautiful, but a lousy secretary.

P.P.P.S. She has decided to make a small number of mistakes.

March 31, 1964

Dear Kras:

The die is cast and the deed is done. I just staggered out of Revue Studios which, in case you've forgotten, is at Universal.

The script "Time for Elizabeth" was truncated to a rich

46 minutes, leaving 14 minutes for commercials. I think it's going to be good. We'll see.

Last year, in a wild fit of abandon, you said, "Do what you want with 'Time for Elizabeth.'" As you know, I have tried for years to interest a studio into converting this into a movie. The reactions were always the same, "Yes, it's funny, but with the advent of TV, the teenagers are the ones who keep the picture houses open and they just won't go for this kind of a story."

I remember last year Ed Streeter, who wrote "Father of the Bride," wrote a book called "Chairman of the Bored." Despite the bad pun, it was a very interesting story, but he was not able to sell it. It was about an elderly man who retires.

If the TV episode is very good, we may still be able to unload it on some gullible producer. Naturally, we had to lose a lot in the shorter version, but I think a lot of it will play.

I never worked so hard in my life. We shot 62 pages in five and a half days. I remember the lush days at MGM and Paramount when we all considered the day a triumph if we had one shot in the can by noon. Revue operates a good deal like a department store on 14th Street.

I would write more, but I am so exhausted from the five and a half days in the meat grinder that I'll close this until I recover.

Kiss all your girls for me.

Fondly,
Groucho

March 15, 1965

Dear Kras:

Your letter to hand (whatever the hell that means—it seems to me hand to letter would make more sense).

Melinda has retired permanently from the halls of ivy.

When she went on the "Tonight" show with Johnny Carson, Ed Sullivan saw her and signed her for his show on the 21st of March. On April 17th she's on the Hollywood Palace with me. She has signed with a record company; is taking dramatic lessons from Jeff Cory and dancing lessons from a man who needs a haircut; and so far she owes me $1,200. All this will be fun for her for a couple of years and if she hits, fine. If not, there's always some ardent young man around who is looking for a young, pretty girl who will eventually inherit $3,000 in cash.

Incidentally, on the Hollywood Palace I sang "Hooray for Captain Spaulding" and did a scene from "Animal Crackers" with Margaret Dumont. She was terribly nervous, but good. Two days later she died. It's kind of ironical that she should have done her last show with me.

Tomorrow night, at U.C.L.A.'s Royce Hall, they are running "Night at the Opera," and I promised that both before and after the screening I would say a few words.

I keep getting offers for big parts in poor pictures and what are humorously referred to as cameo parts in important pictures. Last week some agent called me (I forgot to ask him the name of his agency) and offered me $20,000 to do a brief selling job on TV for a new cigar lighter. I told him proudly that $20,000 was just pin money, thinking he would call back the next day with a bigger offer. Well, he never phoned again. That taught me a lesson. Always write down the name of the agency and throw yourself on their mercy. If necessary, even cry a little.

Talk about offers! A producer called to ask if I would tour North Africa and the Middle East in "Time for Elizabeth," the proceeds to go to a lodge! That offer is funnier than anything we ever wrote. If I accept the deal, do you think Emily would be too young to play the daughter?

Since I plan on seeing you in the not too distant future,

I'll knock this off with a hey nonny nonny and a hotcha-cha.
That's what people were saying around Paramount in 1930—
and we sneer at the Beatles!

Kiss all the girls for me, and my best to you.

Fondly,
Groucho

TO NUNNALLY JOHNSON*

November 23, 1959

Dear Lonely,

My secretary has just informed me that you are now in
Sicily. Lonely, I beg of you, watch yourself carefully in that
Mafia-ridden country. It may interest you to know that this is
where "Mack the Knife" served his apprenticeship, so be careful. Don't turn your back on anyone.

You are an important asset to middle-class American society and we don't want anything to happen to you. When I
say "we" you realize, of course, that I am referring only to
myself. I cannot assume responsibility for anyone else.

Arrivederci Roma to you-all from we-uns.

Fondly,
Groucho

P.S. I won't write about the quiz scandals because I'm sure you
get the Paris Herald or the Roman Candle or the Florence
Nightingale or whatever paper you subscribe to.

London, August 17, 1960

Dear Groucho,

I've been meaning to tell you about the damndest critic
you ever heard of in your whole life. His name is Darlington

* The film writer and producer.

and he has been covering the theater for the Daily Telegraph here for about thirty years. What makes him so remarkable is that he is probably the only honest critic in history. He simply said frankly the other day that he didn't know what the hell those people up there on the stage were talking about.

Among these avant-garde writers, here and everywhere else, great store is laid on noncommunication. "Mr. Pinter's work is a brilliant symbolistic dramatization of mankind's inability to communicate." This means it doesn't make any sense. Mr. Pinter is the author of a big hit here named "The Caretaker." I went to it with Christie, who is avant-garde and herself the author of a thesis entitled "The Symbolism of the Umbilical Cord in Hamlet," and at the end of the second act we disappeared into the fog outside.

The way these fellows write a play, Mr. Pinter says to his wife, "I've got some scenes here, pretty good but no connection, and I don't know what to do with them." His wife says, "Are you out of your mind? You stick these scenes together and make everybody bums and the critics will tell you what you had in mind." This has worked magnificently. Mr. Pinter is unable to write a word that the critics don't understand perfectly. That is, until Mr. Darlington came along. He covered a new one by Mr. Pinter the other night and the next morning he said, and I quote: "I do not know what this audience was applauding, I do not know what the people on the stage were up to, I do not know why they took the old match seller into their home or why they finally let him leave. I suppose that if I put myself to it I could work out a symbolic explanation for the events of the evening, but I was, alas, too bored to bother with it."

We must remember Mr. Darlington. We will not know his like again.

Love from our house to yours,

Nunnally

Rome, February 7, 1961

Dear Groucho:

You would have heard from me before now if I hadn't been making monkeys out of Shakespeare and Shaw by writing dialogue for Twentieth Century-Fox's "Cleopatra," which Reuben Mamoulian has been signed to direct. But now that I'm benched I can write and thank you for the Carl Reiner record, which is wonderful, and "The Age of Roosevelt," which will take me a little longer.

Did you ever have anything to do with Mr. Mamoulian? Well, sir, he is quite a character. After a couple of meetings with him I managed the first successful prediction I have made in my whole life. I bet Walter Wanger that he would never go to bat. All he wants to do is "prepare." A hell of a pre-parer. Tests, wardrobe, hair, toenails. You give Reuben something to prepare and he's dynamite.

But I bet Wanger two pounds (32 ounces) that he would never step into the batter's box. If you make him start this picture, I said, he will never forgive you to his dying day. This chap is a natural born martyr. If you don't martyrize him he is going to be as sore as hell. The rest is history. But by then I was in the showers. It turned out that he wouldn't even read what I was writing, which created something of a bottle-neck. The writer he wanted, next to himself, was Paddy Cha-yefsky. (It's all right, I don't expect you to believe one word of this, though it's God's truth.) It seems that Elizabeth Tay-lor told him that Chayefsky was just the man to pick up where Shakespeare, Shaw and I had left off and old Reuben didn't want any better recommendation than that.

Myself, I don't see it. I don't think there's that much dif-ference between Chayefsky and me, especially when it comes to writing dialogue for an Egyptian goddess and a Roman god. We're both right for it, nobody denies that, we just approach it a little differently. Chayefsky writes about "little people" while my folks are about medium height and a little round-shouldered. Chayefsky's little people keep saying the same thing over and over again (he gets paid by the word) while my medium folks sometimes can't remember to say it even once. Otherwise there is not much to choose between us. It just depends on how little or medium you want Julius (Groucho) Caesar to be. Hell, I'll make him any size they want. Just tell me what size and I'll take a hack at it. (That's why they call me "a hack's hack.")

I've got to go now. They're waiting for me.

Godot

London, November 1, 1961

Dear Groucho:

I'd heard from two people that yours was the best of the successors to Paar, but then I never heard of anybody that I didn't think was better than Paar.

As you can imagine, the last week or so has been as terrifying here as it must have been there. There were several demonstrations in front of the U.S. Embassy (we live next door to it) demanding that Kennedy keep his hands off plucky little Cuba and stop bullying plucky little Russia and all that, but not nearly as much disorder or hard feelings as the papers indicate. Roxie and I joined the crowd one night. I stood on the grass across the street, which was just about what the young lions and lionesses were doing, standing and watching, and once I heard a fellow cry out, "Here come the Cossacks!" Well, now, I dearly love to see those fellows in fur hats riding standing up on their fiery steeds, so I turned to look. Two bobbies were strolling toward us with their hands behind their backs. Not even on horses.

(285)

As for Roxie, she said, "Can I mingle with 'em?" I said, okay. So she emerged from the crowd a few minutes later with three boys who assured me they were going to protect her. Which they did when there was some pushing and shoving, and presently delivered her back to me safe and sound and happy. There is no international crisis known to man that Roxie can't get a cute boy out of.

Dorris is down in the Confederacy visiting her family. In Dallas the other morning she was having breakfast in the hotel coffee shop and there were three colored people at the next table. As they were leaving, a fat tub-of-guts, as Dorris described him, white, said to her loudly, "Looks like the niggers are taking over." In just as loud a voice, Dorris replied that if people had the money and the manners she saw no reason why anybody shouldn't eat anywhere they wished. She said he brooded over this incomprehensible view for some time and then he finally hit on the explanation. "Where you from, lady?" he asked. "Mississippi," Dorris said. First time in her life, she said, that she had been happy to give that truthful answer. She didn't care that she had shaken that poor fellow's entire concept of human society.

I've just finished reading this week's Time and I'm still wondering how long it's going to take the American people to come to their senses and make Time President. Week after week, with the greatest patience, they explain how Kennedy was wrong, how the Army was late or slow or misguided, how the Navy should have handled the situation, with now and then a kindly pat on the head for this government or that—"Well done that time, United Kingdom!" How long are we going to ignore this infallible intelligence? All I can say is that I'll never feel really secure until Time is in the White House with its hand on the throttle. Shouldn't we speak to somebody about this?

Always my best to you,
Nunnally Johnson

P.S. Interpretation of the attached:* "I do not know what the hell went on up there on that stage last night but I'll be a son of a bitch if I'm going to admit it."

December 17, 1961

Dear Grouch:

I enjoyed your letter but it came about the time that Thurber was sliding down the chute and I felt nothing but gloom. Not that I expect things to get any better. I used to be able to clear my throat by noon; these days I'm doing good to breathe without sounding like a death rattle by 3 P.M.

. . . Meanwhile, all my friends are turning out hit after hit (former friends, let's say, when the hit is unquestionable) while I continue to put my faith in actors who turn me down at the last moment. I can't see that there's anything to be done but sneer at popular, commercial success. Who would want to write a cheap, vulgar trashy thing like (supply your own title), no matter how much it makes! (I would.) I write for a very small public (Dorris, Scotty, Roxie, and my secretary. I started to include Chris, but I remembered that she is even more scornful of what I do than ever, since she started going around with a local poet who wears one earring and writes poems like:

> the sigh
>
> > remains
> nor did it ever
> man
> Close parenthesis.)

---

* Attached was the following paragraph of Howard Taubman's N. Y. Times review of the Samuel Beckett play, "Happy Days":

"Mr. Beckett's threnody is grim, but in its muted, tremulous way it shimmers with beauty. For he has refined his theater into something that parallels the elusiveness and overtones of music. His writing is spare and allusive, wry and grave, direct and poetic. He dispenses with the commonplaces of plot and action; nevertheless, he arrives at an emotional essence."

Chris lives in a grotto in Kensington with two girls from Sarah Lawrence who are spending a sabbatical year here, and when the three of them come to call on us, which they do just before mealtime, there is a constant struggle in the lobby of this apartment house. The porters refuse to believe that these three young hobgoblins haven't got the wrong address. People comfort us with the reminder that "it's just a phase" but I'm getting a little old for phases. They had a party in their cave last week and about forty beards showed up. Where she gets them God only knows. Before the evening was over they had gone through the place like ants, even eating the raw stuff in the icebox, and one, more enterprising than his colleagues, had nipped out early after having gone through their pockets making a haul of about twopence ha'penny, is my guess.

As you can judge for yourself, this doesn't leave me in the cheerfullest of moods. All I know in a lighter vein is a sign reported on a local church: ARE YE WEARY OF SIN? COME IN AND REST. Below it was written in pencil: If not, call Bayswater 12345.

I hope you and yours are well at this Yuletide season. I send you, as always, my very best.

Nunnally Johnson

December 29, 1961

Dear Grouch:

There was really a touch of Dickens about our Christmas —three kids and Dorris doing The Twist around our tree. Roxie is the expert. Scotty does it well enough but is handicapped by the lights; it seems that he learned it in the dark at parties. (Yeah, he's reached that age!) Christie, who dresses like an old clothes tree, does it disdainfully; she tells me that in her set it was obsolete even before Elsa Maxwell and Chubby

Checkers ever heard of it. As a matter of fact, its successor, The Pony, is already on the way out. And to think that I only mastered the schottische last week! Dorris manages to swing it very skillfully but so far as I'm concerned it's a spectator sport.

New Year's Eve doesn't promise to be much better. The Panamas went to Spain to get out of the whole business, while the Franks are going to Paris for that night. They can have it. I've seen Notre Dame and the Folies-Bergère, and I can't read the menus, so the hell with it. I'll just lean out of the window here in Grosvenor Sq., and yell, God rest ye merry, gentlemen! and get back into bed. Roxie's crowd is all set for a do, while Scotty has been invited to another lightless gathering, so they're all fixed. Christie has a date with her young man, the one who wears one earring, so in the immortal words of Tiny Tim: God help us all!

We send our love to you and Eden and Melinda, and a better year beginning Monday.

Lonely

July 31, 1963

Dear Grouch:

At lunch with our old friend Doug Fairbanks yesterday, I explored the possibilities of getting you and me mentioned by one of his tart friends in this trial of that celebrated Man in White, Dr. Stephen Ward. I made it quite clear that money was no object; we simply wanted to be charged publicly with an association with one of the young ladies. At this stage of the game an ugly rumor is better than nothing. Doug promised to do what he could about it.

My life gets no more uncomplicated. The latest crisis is that Christie has fled to Sweden leaving a note that she is going to marry a fellow whose name I haven't been able to make out yet. She met him last year when she and other local Ban-the-Bombers went to Stockholm to protest the Swedish H-bomb. I know, I know! But that's immaterial to a Ban-the-Bomber. Once a true Ban-the-Bomber gets her heart set on protesting nuclear tests it doesn't matter whether that country has any nuclear power or not. Resign! Resign!

But if she marries the fellow he's going to have to face something a good deal nearer home than nuclear tests—clothes on the floor. Christie hasn't picked up a garment off the floor since she was old enough to realize that the floor is where discarded garments belong. Any time he is called on to respond to an emergency demonstration in the middle of the night it will take him an easy 25 minutes to wade through the laundry on the floor. But maybe Swedes like that.

Scotty, who is now 6 ft. tall, and I follow baseball closely and to hell with the Yankees. Also with the SF Giants. I may turn to cricket.

If you go to Israel I have a young woman friend there who is an adorer of yours and has adopted Israel, she being Jewish AND South African, as well as smart and pretty and you could do far worse than let her be a guide for you and Eden. (I have contacts everywhere.) But I doubt if you should cut me in on T. S. Eliot, because if I haven't read any of his stuff by now it's not likely that I'm going to be any better off by fall. You can make a lot of money by betting people that if it's really great writing, Johnson hasn't been able to get through it.

I suppose this will eventually reach you in a New England village where you are playing "Time for Elizabeth." In spite of which, Dorris and I send our best to you both.

Nunnally Johnson

P.S. I was reading a book about Rudolph Hess's parachuting into England during the war the other night. It told how the

Duke of Hamilton brought the news to Churchill, who was just finishing dinner. He listened for a moment and then said, "I'm sure this is all very interesting but would you mind seeing me later in the evening? We're running a Marx Brothers picture here now." History.

August 12, 1963

Dear Nun:

I felt sorry for the late Dr. Ward. At least the poor bastard gave England some class. Until he came around, nobody suspected that there was that much hanky panky going on in among the British nobility. I predict that someday London will be the next Paris.

Then came the great train robbery. I had no idea England had that much money left. Luckily, the pound isn't what it used to be. You certainly live in an exciting country.

This town, by contrast, is nothing. There are 400 reporters here from all over the world and they have nothing to do but rehash that tired stuff about Liz and Burton. The only important piece of news that came out last week was in Hedda's column. It said that Ginger Rogers is now considered to be one of the best tennis players in the movie industry. Oh yes: she also said that Liz was getting fat. And some male columnist, a gentleman of the old school, said she had hairy legs.

I'm sorry your daughter, Christie, contemplates marrying a Swedish sailor. I didn't even knew they had a navy. You might point out to her that women are not allowed aboard battleships. This may not be true in Sweden, but it certainly is in the United States Navy. The only time I saw this rule violated was in a picture that MGM made a few years back. Zsa— or wasn't it Eva Gabor?—managed to sneak on board in a male sailor suit. I don't remember all of the story except that, until she sneaked into the john and they caught her applying lipstick, they never suspected that she was a woman! The rest of the picture, I don't remember. Only the finale. While the band played "Anchors Aweigh" Miss Gabor's lace panties were flying gaily from the masthead. The picture was a sensational success. Someone told me later that it was a musical version of "Outward Bound."

Best to you all,
Groucho

P.S. Last night we caught a rat in the back of the icebox.

The
Faintly
Political
Scene

FROM BOOTH TARKINGTON

June 30, 1943

Dear Mr. Marx:

I don't know whether you remember me; but you, your brothers and wives and a child once called on me *without* Alexander Woollcott and talked about Spinoza a little while, then hurried out partly because you had that morning severally purchased new brightly painted automobiles manufactured in Connersville, Indiana, and desired to be seen all over Indianapolis in them.

I should like to reply in detail to your criticism in order to lead up to something I hope you can change for the better in your Saturday night broadcasts. You inform me that you have received a letter from the Republican Postwar Policy Association and you announce that it discusses the Republican Party and its Postwar Policy. I don't see how or where you got the idea that it discusses the Republican Party and its Postwar Policy because it is inevitably evident that after reading what was printed on the envelope, "A Message from Booth Tarkington," you quit like a dog and didn't even look at what was inside.

Then you go on to say that you're not a New Dealer, a Republican, a Communist or a Socialist, because you want me to guess what you *are*. All right: What could be easier? There's only one thing left: you're a Prohibitionist, and naturally pretty cross these days. You needn't be cross with *me*, though, as I have contained nothing with a drop of alcohol in it since 10:23 A.M., January 16, 1912.

Then you go *on* to say that you have "always voted for the man and never for the Party," which means that if you like anybody you don't care what kind of crowd he runs with and's going to put over you. I think this is praiseworthy but reckless, like your saying that if the Republicans nominate a person you don't approve of, you'll vote against him no matter if the Democrats put up Mussolini.

After that you sort of quiet down and merely holler at me that Gov. Bricker is nothing but a "repainted Warren Harding," evidently because you're shrewdly pretty certain that an envelope with "A Message from Booth Tarkington" printed on it is for Gov. Bricker.

As I have now logically led up to my criticism of your Saturday evening broadcasts, I will proceed to perform that function and I hope that my so doing will not interfere with your amour propre or feelings.

Since you began these exhibitions we have missed only one, which took place while we were on the train for Kennebunkport, Maine. We have never once switched the program off immediately upon hearing from the announcer that it contained a Message from Groucho Marx, and so I believe we're entitled to offer this criticism.

For about five weeks past the country lying between Maine and California has been constantly ravaged by thunderstorms, especially on Saturday nights. Either with or without your connivance this introduces into your program an element that many of the more fastidious of your Eastern seaboard audiences could well do without. The remedy is of course what is called obvious. You persist in broadcasting from California, whereas within a few hundred rods of Kennebunkport there are delightful spots where a station could be set up—the Wildes District, Munion-town, Alewives, Prouts Neck or even the Coast Guard post at Turbat's Creek, all in this county.

If you'd merely take the step hereby indicated we should be a less profane family because every Saturday night at 10:15 we shouldn't be missing four or five words out of anything you say.

In brief, my criticism is that if you've lifted a single finger toward the elimination of all these thunderstorms I haven't heard of it, and that I don't believe you've taken the first step toward moving to Maine.

In conclusion, I shall ask my secretary to be careful not to put my name on the outside of the envelope containing this response.

With best wishes, believe me,

Faithfully yours,
Booth Tarkington

TO THE HON. C. A. ROBINS
GOVERNOR OF IDAHO

November 28, 1947

Dear Guv:

Thanks for the potatoes. Would have thought you'd have stuck a piece of butter in each one. They were very nice potatoes. I wish all governors would acquire the habit of sending me their state's best known product. In that way I might get a De Soto from Michigan and a quart of Old Taylor from Kentucky.

Thanks again.

Cordially yours,
Groucho Marx

TO GOODMAN ACE

November 25, 1953

Dear Goodman:

I have always heard that if one stayed long enough in Port Said the whole world would pass before him. This is a God damned lie. The whole world passes before you if you have a room on the 5th floor of the Muehlebach Hotel, facing one of Katz's numerous drugstores.

The din that a small, corrupt city can raise between the hours of 1 P.M. and 10 A.M. is indescribable, certainly by me. Rudyard Kipling could probably do it, or James T. Farrell. Every bus, streetcar, vendor, hawker, factory whistle, blows and clangs at full blast. Every streetcar has at least one flat wheel, and every bus one flat tire. It was as close to a madhouse as I ever expect to get, present company excepted. The concerted din that rolls past Katz's drugstore can make a 5-grain Seconal hang its head in shame. Having tried everything else, I finally crawled under the bed and rooted for the atomic bomb.

Well, I learned one thing. For years I had accused you of leaving Kansas City because of the Pendergast machine. I know better now.

I had lunch with Truman in Kansas City and we had a lot of fun. He was very cute. Referring to his television speech of the previous night he said, "Groucho, every word I said was the God's honest truth." This, of course, was a lie, but since I was getting a free lunch I was disinclined to argue with him. He was surrounded by five henchmen who looked exactly like what they were—Kansas City politicians. He started to tell me a funny story and before he was halfway through, one of these characters picked up a telephone and started talking.

Talking? He was shouting into the mouthpiece. I couldn't hear what Truman was saying and I finally said, "Harry, remember you used to be President. Why don't you throw that guy out?" I added, "If I were telling a story and someone kept shouting through it, I would certainly ask him to stop."

He leaned over to me and said, "Groucho, I don't like it any better than you do, but we are having a Democratic rally here next week and the man on the phone is trying to raise money for it."

I am completely exhausted and hope this finds you the same.

My best to your blond wife.

Groucho

TO PRESIDENT TRUMAN

August 15, 1954

Dear Harry:

I don't know if you will remember me, but I am the chap with the black mustache, glasses, and increasing baldness who, I hope, convulses you every Thursday night on television.

I just want to join with the thousands who have written you wishing you a speedy recovery and many happy years as our living former President. Oh, I forgot Hoover is still around.

I know you are busy writing your memoirs and dozens of other assorted jobs, but I think that one of these days you ought to pay a visit to the Coast as a private citizen. If you want to come I can put you up. I have a swimming pool and a pool table. I shoot very badly and if you are any good with the cue, you could possibly win enough to pay your expenses.

At any rate, I am glad you are up and around and I certainly enjoyed that lunch we had together in Kansas City although I could have stood less of those henchmen chattering in back of you.

Cordially,
Groucho

TO EDWARD R. MURROW

November 21, 1955

Dear Ed:

Thanks for the Churchill recording. They are not merely speeches, they are history—and it's thrilling to hear his voice.

The day the record arrived, I was saddened by the death of two friends, both of whom have contributed substantially to American liberalism, Sherwood and De Voto. It seems that the Father Coughlins and the McCarthy's never die. Maybe it's true that the good die young.

I listen to you every day at five and, though I didn't think it possible, you are better than ever.

Regards, affection, admiration and, if you want to toss in a few superlatives of your own, I have no objection.

Yours,
Groucho

FROM JOSEPH N. WELCH

May 8, 1957

Dear Mr. Marx:

It was gracious of you to say what you are quoted as saying about me in the April TV Guide. It could be that you didn't actually say it, and that Dan Jenkins thought it up all by himself. In any event, it is nice to read.

Actually, it has not been necessary to engage extra help in the office to hold at bay swarms of people anxious to get me to appear on television or in the movies.

Now that I am writing, may I say that I have long admired your work, and the high degree of intelligence displayed by you and others in your family as you have produced what I have laughed at so heartily through the years. It must be wonderful to be

        (a) Rich
        (b) Intelligent, and
        (c) Funny

I trust I list them in their correct order.

                     Sincerely,
                     Joe Welch

                     May 31, 1957

Dear Mr. Welch:

Those immortal words in the April TV Guide were said by your correspondent who, incidentally, has been an ardent fan of yours ever since watching you permit Senator McCarthy to hang himself.

I was a little frightened when I read the imposing list of lawyers on your letterhead. There are at least forty. Over the years I have been sued by groups of attorneys on most of the minor charges—rape, larceny, embezzlement and parking in front of a fire plug—but none of the legal documents received at my residence ever had more than four names on it.

How do you all get along in the office? Do you trust each other? Or does each one have a separate safe for his money? Isn't there some danger that you and one of your many partners could both be in a courtroom representing opposing clients, and not be aware of it until you faced each other before the judge? Do you have one community storage room for your briefcases—or does each one sit on his own case?

Some day, if I ever get to Boston, I would like to come in and gaze upon this vast array of legal talent at work—or even at play.

No, I'm not rich. I'm rich enough, however, to know that inflation is knocking hell out of what I have.

I hope that you are well and enjoying the Harvard football team.

Cordially yours,
Groucho Marx

P.S. On your letterhead, I note the name JAMES A. BRINK. Well, at least I know who HE is.

June 13, 1957

Dear Mr. Marx:

You quite misunderstood this firm's letterhead. All the names below the first line are the names of our professional witnesses. They hang around street corners and turn up unexpectedly as witnesses in all of the automobile cases we try.

As to the questions you ask, I am sure they were mostly rhetorical but I list them with appropriate answers:

Q. How do you all get along in the office?

A. By leaning on each other heavily and on our secretaries.

Q. Do you trust each other?

A. In every area except money, property and women.

Q. Does each one have a separate safe for his money?

A. Yes, except I have so much money I have two safes.

Q. Isn't there some danger that you and one of your partners could both be in a courtroom, representing ing opposing clients?

A. Damned if there isn't and every now and then somebody takes in a case where the client is against the
client of another guy in this office and there is hell to
pay and no foolin'.

Q. Do you have one community storage room for your
briefcases? Or does each one sit on his own case?

A. I do not understand this question. I sit on what you
sit on only I do more of it than you do.

If you ever do come to Boston and do not come to see
me now that you have gone to such length in writing me, I
will do all that I can to harm you. Come to think of it, perhaps the most harmful thing that could happen to you in
Boston would be for you to call on me and have that fact
become public. While a very choice collection of people
across the country seem to think favorably of me, a highly
numerous and vocal collection of people in Boston thought
and still think that hanging is too good for me.

Sincerely,
Joe Welch

TO GOODMAN ACE

July 19, 1960

Dear Goodman:

I'm goggle-eyed from watching the convention. Until
TV, nobody knew the caliber of the clowns governing the
country. It's impossible to observe these chowder heads in
action with their funny hats and balloons, without feeling sure
we're destined to go the way of Rome, Greece and big-time
vaudeville . . .

I read a very interesting quote by Senator Kerr of Okla-
homa. In summing up Ike, he said, "Eisenhower is the only

(303)

living unknown soldier." Even this is giving him all the best of it.

Melinda [Groucho's youngest child] is at summer camp and our house is now as quiet as the balcony of the Fulton Theater when "Time for Elizabeth" was playing there.

My best to you, Jane and the entire Anacin family.

Fondly,
Groucho

TO JAMES RESTON OF THE
NEW YORK TIMES

September 16, 1960

Dear James:

Ordinarily I don't get this familiar with a political pundit, but since I read you religiously (that means I wear a hat when perusing your column), I feel I ought to thank you for showing up these two pretenders to the throne. So far, in my travels, I haven't met anybody who wants to vote for either of them.

I think it would be a great thing for the country if both of them were defeated and Coolidge was re-elected. One way or another, I'm sure the world will still go on.

My best to you and your columns.

Sincerely,
Groucho Marx

TO SIDNEY SHELDON

July 17, 1964

Dear Sidney:

I won't have much free time during the five days of the "Tonight" show but we can certainly plan to have a meal or two together.

As for the convention, Eisenhower knows that he was once a poor farm boy, and Goldwater confesses that his grandfather was a Polish peddler. I hope he wasn't peddling the same stuff that his grandson is now. My eyes are bloodshot from watching that harlequinade up north. Whoever named it the Cow Palace certainly had a flair for descriptive titles. The amount of manure that was spread over that auditorium would solve Khrushchev's fertilizer problem for the next ten years.

Love to all, and I'll see you next week.

Regards,
Groucho Marx

TO THE HON. WILLIAM R. SCRANTON GOVERNOR OF PENNSYLVANIA

February 24, 1964

Dear Sir:

If you contemplate campaigning in any more Jewish neighborhoods, I suggest you learn how to pronounce "mishmash."

It is not pronounced "mash," as you said on "Meet the Press," but rather as though it were spelled MOSH.

Sincerely yours,
Groucho Marx

*Short
Shrift*

TO TIME MAGAZINE

April 11, 1946

Gentlemen:

I see where numerous relatives of mine have written Time, frantically yelping that they are cousins of Sam Marx of MGM. The Marx fortunes have certainly sunk to a low ebb when members of the family find it necessary to rush into print to claim relationship to anyone.

I don't know about the rest of them, but I was born during a volcanic eruption in one of the banana countries in Central America. I don't remember which one—I don't even remember the bananas, I hardly remember the stalk.

At the age of three, an utter stranger apprenticed me to a basket weaver in Guatemala. I soon learned to weave with such dexterity that, by the time my second teeth arrived, I was known throughout the village as the basket child of Guatemala.

After I was run out of Guatemala, I met two other fellows named, I believe, Harpo and Chico. After considerable bickering, they convinced me that America, softened up by an excess of rationing, could be persuaded to swallow another dose of Casablanca—this one to be called "A Night in Casa-blanca."

Well, we made the picture and that's that. The point is that Harpo and Chico are brothers but they are both strangers to me. And, as for Sam Marx of MGM who reluctantly confesses to being their cousin—well, he's slightly mistaken. The fact of the matter is, he happens to be their joint child by a former marriage.

Sincerely,
Groucho Marx

TO SIMON AND SCHUSTER

March 24, 1950

Dear Boys:

I received a wire recently congratulating me on the merits of my radio show. I must say I was flattered by its enthusiastic tone, but without inquiring too deeply into your affairs, it would be helpful if I knew whether the wire was Simon's idea or Schuster's.

It is difficult to thank partners, for in a partnership there is always the likelihood that one of them is a mastermind and the other a stooge, and in spreading thanks equally I could conceivably be offending the brains of the organization. Eventually this could create a serious schism in your young publishing company. Frankly I don't know why they still refer to your outfit as a young concern. I realize that you weren't around during the days when Carrie Nation was demolishing saloons and somebody was laying a cable under the Atlantic (a hell of a place, by the way, to be laying a cable when it's a known fact that there are motels strung strategically all the way from Salt Lake to Bangor).

But, gentlemen, let's face it. You're not callow kids any more. Today you must be regarded as a fairly elderly and crusty publishing company with a long history of gimcrack literature as your sole claim to existence and I must say I think it's about time you grew up and stopped sending bootlicking wires to your betters. A Bulova watch, perhaps, a crate of tinker toys, a side of beef, but not just words. Send me something I can get my teeth into and, for that, gentlemen, remember there's nothing like a dame.

My love to you both and I will be at the Waldorf the middle of April, for what it is worth.

Regards,
Groucho Marx

TO MR. GELLMAN OF ELGIN AMERICAN COMPACTS

1951

Dear Mr. G:

You could have knocked me over with a compact when one of your hirelings arrived here last week with a solid gold watch in his hands. My previous sponsors sold gasoline, corn flakes and beer. These, needless to say, have their value, but how would a man look walking around with a bottle of beer tied to his wrist?

The watch is a thing of beauty and will be a joy forever, and I would have thanked you sooner, but I purposely waited a week, for I wanted to be sure that the lousy thing would run.

Sincerely,
Groucho Marx

TO JAMES A. LINEN,
PUBLISHER OF TIME MAGAZINE

January 4, 1952

Dear Mr. Linen:

The picture of me on the cover of Time has changed my entire life. Where formerly my hours were spent playing golf and chasing girls, I now while away the days loitering around Beverly Hill's largest newsstand, selling copies of the December 31st issue of Time at premium prices.

Admittedly the picture on the cover didn't do me justice (I doubt if any camera could capture my inner beauty), but nevertheless my following is so fanatical that they buy anything that even remotely resembles me. Yesterday, despite the fact that it was raining, I made $13. This is all tax free, for I steal the copies of Time while the owner of the newsstand is out eating lunch.

Please use my picture again soon and next time I promise to give you half of everything I get away with.

Cordially,
Groucho Marx

P.S. In addition to Henry James, I also read the St. Louis Sporting News.

TO DONALD BUDGE

January 28, 1952

Dear Donald:

As you pointed out, my game is so close to perfection that it would be sheer waste of money for me to take any additional lessons.

(312)

I must say that I envy you your vacation. It is not every man who can make a living merely by having an 18-year-old girl on the other side of a tennis net with all of her equipment bouncing up and down. Since you are still young enough to jump over the net I predict you will spend many a happy afternoon, particularly if your wife is out of town.

I hope you prosper in your new venture.

Regards,
Groucho

TO ALISTAIR COOKE

July 8, 1957

Dear Mr. Cooke:

I was a little disappointed on receiving your rather lengthy letter, to find no mention of money. I am of course, an artist, with my head in the clouds. And I was very happy to be invited to appear, gratis or thereabouts, on "Meet the Press," "The Last Word," the City Center Theatre in New York, two all-night telethons, etc. But my business manager, Mr. Gummo Marx, has a passion for money that is virtually a sickness. I am constantly being embarrassed by it. Still, he is my brother, and rather than upset him, I have to bow to his wishes.

I hope you and your charming wife are happy and as gay as the weather permits; and that this note will not end our fragile friendship.

Regards,
Groucho

TO MR. HERMAN E. GOODMAN
OF THE FRANKLIN CORPORATION

March 15, 1961

Dear Mr. Goodman:

I wrote to Mr. Salwyn Shufro, my financial adviser, who is responsible for my being hooked by the Franklin Corporation, and told him what a pleasure it was going to be to lose my life's savings in a company whose President is a humorist.

Eddie Cantor, a well known comedian (circa 1930-40) inveigled me into buying forty thousand dollars' worth of Goldman-Sachs which was worth, after the crash, somewhere in the vicinity of twelve dollars.

Stevenson was defeated twice when he ran for President because he persisted in telling jokes to his constituents.

While the Franklin Corporation is still in a formative stage, I suggest that all correspondence with your stockholders be as grave and humorless as the speeches of Herbert Hoover. However, if in time your outfit grows and blossoms into a holding company as successful as the Lehman Brothers Corporation, you can then be as funny as a combination of Mark Twain, S. J. Perelman, Robert Benchley and the last statements made by those General Electric executives just before they escaped the pokey by paying some very large fines.

I am sending a copy of your letter to Mr. Shufro and to my attorneys so, Herman, watch yourself.

Sincerely,
Groucho Marx

April 24, 1961

Dear Mr. Goodman:

I received the first annual report of the Franklin Corporation and though I am not an expert at reading balance sheets, my financial adviser, (who, I assure you, knows nothing) nodded his head in satisfaction.

You wrote that you hope I am not one of those borscht circuit stockholders who gets a few points' profit and hastily scrams for the hills. For your information, I bought Alleghany Preferred eleven years ago and am just now going through the process of disposing of it.

As a brand new member of your family, strategically you made a ghastly mistake in sending me individual pictures of the Board of Directors. Mr. Roth, Chairman of the Board, merely looks sinister. You, the President, look like a hard worker with not too much on the ball. No one named Prosswimmer can possibly be a success. As for Samuel A. Goldblith, Ph.D., head of Food Technology at M.I.T., he looks as though he had eaten too much of the wrong kind of fodder.

At this point I would like to stop and ask you a question about Marion Harper, Jr. To begin with, I immediately distrust any man who has the same name as his mother. But the thing that most disturbs me about Junior is that I don't know what the hell he's laughing at. Is it because he sucked me into this Corporation? This is not the kind of a face that inspires confidence in a nervous and jittery stockholder.

George S. Sperti, I dismiss instantly. Any man who is the President of an outfit called Institutum Divi Thomae will certainly bear watching. Is he trying to impress stockholders with his knowledge of Latin? If so, why doesn't he read, "Winnie ille Pu"? James J. Sullivan, I am convinced, is Paul E. Prosswimmer photographed from a different angle.

Offhand, I would say that I have summed up your group fairly accurately. I hope, for my sake, that I am mistaken.

In closing, I warn you, go easy with my money. I am in an extremely precarious profession whose livelihood depends upon a fickle public.

Sincerely yours,
Groucho Marx
(temporarily at liberty)

TO STANDARD OIL COMPANY OF CALIFORNIA

December 27, 1962

Gentlemen:

In mailing your statement to me this month, you neglected to put sufficient postage on the envelope. This meant that I had to scurry around to find four hard pennies to drop in the mailbox for the postman.

Inasmuch as I am a new customer, I believe that if there was a doubt in your collective minds regarding the amount of postage required, it would have been wiser to overstamp the envelope, rather than vice versa.

I realize that the running of your giant company involves many hazards. I, therefore, do not wish to be reimbursed the additional four cents. Instead, I suggest you take this money which, legally, you owe me, buy a four-cent CARE package and send it to the president of your company.

Sincerely yours,
Groucho Marx

FROM McCALL'S MAGAZINE

April 8, 1963

Dear Mr. Marx:

Could you send us a few quick quotes about cars in connection with an article we are planning for summer?

. . . If you drive, we would like to have a list of the items you keep in your glove compartment. What "extras" do you wish glove compartments had room to hold? . . . and many thanks.

Cordially,
Bernice Connor
Senior Editor, McCall's

April 15, 1963

Dear Miss Connor:

You ask what I keep in my glove compartment. The last time I looked I had a woman's bikini, one half a cheese sandwich without mustard and a letter from the finance company saying that if I don't pay the $5,000 I owe on the $5,000 car, they will take the matter into their own hands. If they do, they'll find it pretty messy in that glove compartment.

Any further information you may want will have to come from my attorneys, Schrecklichtheit, Schrecklichtheit and Meyer.

Sincerely yours,
Groucho Marx

TO MISS MARJORIE DOBKIN*

November 17, 1965

Dear Miss Dobkin:

I wish I could accept your kind offer to tea and cookies but the whole project isn't feasible, logical or sensible. To begin with I am approximately 3,000 miles away and I am tied up with my secretary. These ties are very strong. They are almost as sacred as the bonds of matrimony and because of this and many other reasons I am unable to accept your kind and generous offer. Besides, it is raining outside and I never go to New York when it is raining.

I remain insincerely yours,
Groucho Marx

TO THE NEW YORKER MAGAZINE

February 28, 1966

Sir:

Each week in the capsule review of the Broadway play "The Impossible Years" you refer to one of the authors, my son Arthur, as a TV veteran. You may not be aware of it, but this has had a catastrophic effect on my career. When my agent tries to hawk me to one of the producers for a TV show, as you so aptly phrase it, they say Groucho Marx? (As though they were saying Sonny Tufts?) Groucho Marx? they repeat. Is he the father of TV veteran, Arthur Marx? We thought he was dead.

Last week for example, I was up for the part of Noah in a revival of "Green Pastures," but when the producer discov-

* Lecturer in English, Barnard College.

ered that I was the father of TV veteran, Arthur Marx, he said forget it, he's entirely too old. We'll use the original Noah.

So, please see if you can't do something about this. My son actually is still a fairly young man. He plays tennis—just doubles of course—and twice a week he does setting-up exercises. As for me, except for an occasional heart attack, as Benchley once said while attending a Harvard football reunion, I feel as young as I ever did.

Groucho Marx

Printed in the United States
By Bookmasters